THE WORLD'S
RELIGIOUS TRADITIONS

THE WORLD'S RELIGIOUS TRADITIONS

CURRENT PERSPECTIVES IN RELIGIOUS STUDIES

Essays in honour of
WILFRED CANTWELL SMITH

Edited by
FRANK WHALING

Crossroad ● New York

1986

The Crossroad Publishing Company
370 Lexington Avenue, New York, N.Y. 10017

Printed and bound in Great Britain by
Billing & Sons Ltd., Worcester

Library of Congress Cataloging-in-Publication Data

The World's religious traditions.

　　Bibliography of the works of Wilfred Cantwell Smith: p.
　　Includes index.
　　1. Religions. 2. Smith, Wilfred Cantwell, 1916–
I. Whaling, Frank, 1934–　　. II. Smith, Wilfred
Cantwell, 1916–
BL87.W67　　1984　　　　291　　　　86-4149
ISBN 0-8245-0747-9

PREFACE

When a book in honour of Wilfred Cantwell Smith was first mooted, it was decided that it should be planned as a book in its own right. The aim was that it should attempt to make a major contribution to the field of Religious Studies at the same time as it paid tribute to the work of Wilfred Smith. In order to achieve this goal it was necessary that thirteen chapters should be written especially to fit into the pattern of this volume.

It is to the credit of Wilfred Smith that the contributors to this work agreed unanimously and enthusiastically to take up the challenge of working to a constructive plan instead of handing in the latest essay they happened to have written and instead of following their own whims. The result is that a number of world-class scholars who are busy people have worked as a team to attain a common goal. Five have written on faith and tradition in five of the world's religious traditions, and seven have written on current approaches to the study of religion. Although the jumping-off point for these chapters is provided by Smith's themes of faith and tradition and Smith's approach to the study of religion, this book does stand in its own right as a major contribution to both content and method in the global history of religions.

I am grateful to my colleagues for their promptness and for their fellowship. My thanks are due too to Dr. Geoffrey Green of T. & T. Clark for his constant helpfulness. Planned originally at Harvard, edited in Edinburgh, written in nine places around the world, this book is motivated by a desire to advance the work of Religious Studies. The time is ripe academically, culturally, religiously and globally. Insofar as we are successful in creatively recognising and harnessing this *kairos*, we stand on the shoulders of a number of post-war scholars not least of whom is Wilfred Cantwell Smith to whom we offer this volume.

Frank Whaling,
December, 1983

v

CONTENTS

Section A

INTRODUCTORY ESSAY

INTRODUCTORY ESSAY

Frank Whaling

Twenty-five years ago a book was published that had a subtle influence upon the development of reflection upon the theories, methods and content of the History of Religions. The name of that book was *History of Religions: Essays in Methodology*, edited by Eliade and Kitagawa. One of the essays in that collection was by a young scholar, Wilfred Cantwell Smith. It was clear already that here was a thinker of creative originality and, since the writing of that essay 'Comparative Religion: Whither and Why?', Smith has continued to innovate within the whole area of the study of religion.

Much has happened within Religious Studies since 1959 and in this introductory essay I shall refer to some of the trends and developments since that time. What is beyond doubt is that the work of Wilfred Cantwell Smith ranks as one of the major factors within the evolution of Religious Studies since the Second World War, and this book is offered as a tribute to Wilfred Smith as well as a contribution to scholarship in its own right.

This present work is divided into two sections. In the first part, five leading scholars write about living religious traditions: J. L. Mehta on the Hindu tradition, Wei-Ming Tu on the Confucian tradition, Louis Jacobs on the Jewish tradition, George Williams on the Christian tradition, and Annemarie Schimmel on the Muslim tradition. In the second part, seven other well-known scholars write about alternative contemporary approaches to the study of religion: Seyyed Hossein Nasr on *philosophia perennis*, Raimundo Panikkar on dialogue, John Hick on religious pluralism, Ninian Smart on scientific phenomenology, Geoffrey Parrinder on comparative religion, George Rupp on the relations between theology and history of religions, and John Carman on the tension between understanding and evaluating religions.

3

By contrast with the 1959 work *History of Religions: Essays in Methodology*, of which this book is in some ways a contemporary analogue, there is present here a common starting theme, and a common motivation. The motivation is simply to honour Wilfred Cantwell Smith for whom this is a richly deserved Festschrift. The starting theme is the work of Smith himself viewed in its widest perspective, namely his twin concepts of faith and tradition which represent the jumping-off points for the five chapters on the major religious traditions, and his general approach to the study of religion which provides the stimulation point for reflection on the variety of present-day approaches to the study of religion. In this way, unity and pattern is given to a series of chapters that range over most of the significant issues that are important in the field today.

It will be seen therefore that this is a somewhat unusual Festschrift in that it is not a random series of essays; it is not, in the main, written by former students; nor is it a mere eulogy of the work of Wilfred Cantwell Smith. We have attempted to steer a middle way between the Scylla of undue tribute and the Charybdis of excessive criticism. We have used the occasion of this Festschrift and the work of Smith himself to fashion what we trust is an original contribution to the ongoing task of scholarship within the History of Religions. It is our hope that the coming together of leading scholars in the field to speak to the present situation within Religious Studies on the unifying basis of themes arising out of Smith's own thought will be pleasing to Wilfred himself, will be of significant help to scholars in general, and will be an appropriate symbol of the seeking for creativity and excellence that has been the hallmark of Smith's own work.

It is not the intention of this introduction to give a long and detailed survey of Smith's life and thought. Willard Oxtoby has already begun this process in his introduction to *Religious Diversity*, a series of Smith's own essays.[1] Rather we will look briefly to begin with at the essay on 'Comparative Religion: Whither and Why?' in the book of 1959. This represents a kind of watershed between Smith's greater concentration upon Islam, during his work in Lahore in Muslim India from 1941–49 and his leadership of the McGill Institute of Islamic Studies which he founded in 1951, and his global concern for the total religious

4

situation of mankind which has become a feature of his later years.

In this essay, Smith traced the progress in the study of the History of Religions in various stages.[2] The first stage saw the accumulation and analysis of facts. At first there was the impersonal accumulation of facts about 'it', a religion so-called. Then it became the accumulation of facts about 'they', the people of a religion, by scholars still personally uninvolved. The next stage saw the personalisation of the work so that scholars as people, as 'we', were investigating 'they' who were also seen to be people. Not only was it the glory of the scholar to 'study not things but qualities of personal living',[3] the investigator's own personal qualities were also seen to be relevant. A further step came when it was seen that personal relationships with people of other traditions were important so that dialogue was no longer a merely conceptual matter conducted from a study at Oxford, Harvard or Edinburgh with 'they' but an actual discussing with other people who through this relationship became 'you'. A final stage involved not merely the inter-dialogue and study of two people or traditions on the basis of 'we-both' are doing this together, but that 'we-all' should do this together. It involved an international group of scholars writing for a world audience so that 'comparative religion may become the disciplined self-consciousness of man's variegated and developing religious life.'[4] The religious history of man would thus concern itself primarily with the development of *all* rather than *each*. For Smith the two matters of supreme importance had become 'the relations among persons within the total community, and the relations between man and God.'[5] The History of Religions had been lifted from the impersonal accumulation of facts to a matter of humane importance for the life of persons in community on earth.

This little cameo in effect set most of Smith's agenda for his future work. His account did not necessarily coincide with that of the other contributors to the 1959 volume. His analysis was, and remains, partly prophetic. However his aim was not to form a school of disciples who would follow his 'method' (his scepticism about methodology per se is well known) but to follow his academic and humane vision of the truth with the utmost scholarly rigour and personal integrity wherever his subject matter would lead him – and to encourage others to do the same.

Already in 1959 the seed of his underlying approach was there waiting to burst into fruit in his later books, and in his work at the Harvard Center for the Study of World Religions (1964–73), Dalhousie University (1973–78), and the Harvard Committee on the Study of Religion (1978 onwards). We see hinted at already eight potentially important concepts: his stress upon persons, his concern to understand the world-view of others, his notion that religious truth must encompass the data of faith as well as the data of ongoing tradition, his global awareness of the total human community, his perception that Transcendent Reality (however defined) is part of the subject matter of the study of religion, his emphasis upon dialogue and more importantly colloquium as involving corporate critical self-consciousness, his conviction that the study of religion although crucial is part of the greater whole of humane knowledge, and his insistence that the views of non-westerners and persons of other religious traditions must be given due seriousness within this greater whole. These important future themes were there in embryo in this early essay. After 1959, Smith's attention was increasingly given to these and allied themes. As far as writing was concerned, although in the area of Islamic Studies a volume of essays *On Understanding Islam* (1981) followed his earlier *Modern Islam in India* (1943) and *Islam in Modern History* (1957), greater priority was now given to the inter-religious and inter-cultural themes of his wider global academic vision. They were grappled and wrestled with, adjusted and enlarged, interpreted and refined, in *The Faith of Other Men* (1962), *The Meaning and End of Religion* (1963), *Modernization of a Traditional Society* (1965), *Questions of Religious Truth* (1967), *Belief and History* (1977), *Faith and Belief* (1979), and *Towards a World Theology* (1981), as well as in a series of articles, some of which were edited by Oxtoby in *Religious Diversity* (1976).

During the course of his work in the areas alluded to above, Smith also made contributions in more educational matters such as the relationships between scientific and humane knowledge (where he went in a different direction from European scholars such as Habermas, Rescher, and Hesse),[6] and the relationships between Christian theology and the study of religion (where his notion of universal theological categories that are Christian but more-than-Christian fed into what amounted to a new academic endeavour, namely the theology of religion).[7] In all of this work, Smith influenced others, sometimes in ways that neither he nor they anticipated, by the sheer fecundity and creativity of his thought. Meanwhile, backing up his originality, there was the apparatus of sound scholarship as evidenced, for example, by the extent of his footnotes which constituted 161 pages compared with 172 pages of text in *Faith and Belief* (1979).

As we intimated earlier, this is not the time nor the occasion for a long summary or critique of Smith's thought. Let us rather pause for a moment and examine how this present volume starts off from some of Smith's basic ideas and advances them in directions consonant with the expertise of the scholars concerned.

Prior to this it is worth stopping to comment upon the identity of the scholars, half of whom are non-western or at any rate non-Christian. This accords with Smith's own principle of verification whereby responsible writing on other religious traditions should not only conform to high academic standards of historical and linguistic accuracy but should also be verified by or written by acknowledged scholars of the tradition concerned. In partial fulfilment of this principle, the McGill Institute of Islamic Studies brought together equal numbers of western and Islamic students and faculty, and the Harvard Center for the Study of World Religions used examiners for its doctorates from the religious tradition being studied as well as from the student's own tradition and the academic tradition per se. This may seem reasonably commonplace now. However it is only so because of the work of insightful western scholars such as Kenneth Morgan of Colgate[8] and Wilfred Cantwell Smith and because of the work of pioneer thinkers from other cultures such as Radhakrishnan, Suzuki, Coomaraswamy, Buber, Nasr, Mbiti, and Wing-tsit Chan.[9] It is therefore appropriate that a Hindu J. L. Mehta should write in our volume on the Hindu tradition, a Confucian Wei-Ming Tu on the Confucian tradition, a Jew Louis Jacobs on the Jewish tradition, and indeed that a Christian George Williams should write on the Christian tradition. To make the point that western scholars can and should write on non-western traditions and that non-western scholars can and should write on theoretical matters not necessarily connected with their own traditions, an outstanding western scholar Annemarie Schimmel has written on Islam and a Muslim scholar S. H. Nasr and an Indian/western scholar Raimundo Panikkar have written on the theoretical issues of *philosophia perennis* and dialogue.

What then do they say? In what direction do they take the seminal dual notion of 'faith and tradition' derived from the thought of Wilfred Smith? It is fascinating to see what happens. It is clear that faith and tradition are two of the key concepts within the whole range of Smith's thought – that is why they are chosen as leitmotifs for the investigation of the main religious traditions of the world in this book – and he came to them partly as a result of his unease at the undifferentiated use of the word 'religion'. In *The Meaning and End of Religion* he wrote, 'by faith I mean personal faith ... an inner religious experience or involvement of a particular person; the impingement upon him of the transcendent, putative or real'.[10] By 'cumulative tradition', he wrote, 'I mean the entire mass of overt objective data that constitute the historical deposit, as it were, of the past religious life of the community in question: temples, scriptures, theological systems, dance patterns, legal and other social institutions, conventions, moral codes, myths, and so on; anything that can be and is transmitted from one person, one generation, to another, and that an historian can observe.'[11] For Smith these were all-embracing terms. 'It is my suggestion', he wrote, 'that by the use of these two notions it is possible to conceptualise and to describe anything that has ever happened in the religious life of mankind.'[12] This is a large claim. It has been implicitly adopted in works emanating out of Harvard and elsewhere. This present writer has spoken to leading scholars in places as far apart as Patiala and Peking who have been impressed by Smith's approach based upon faith and tradition. Curiously it has not been made the basis for a wide-ranging research programme, and this present book is one of the rare instances where faith and tradition have been applied more explicitly to the great religious traditions.

There is not the space in this introductory essay, nor would it be desirable, to summarise what Mehta, Wei-Ming Tu, Jacobs, Williams and Schimmel have to say in detail about the great religious traditions. Even if it were the case that they had not started out with Smith's ideas, their mature views on the traditions that have formed their lifetime's work would have been welcome and valuable. The reader of this work will be able to savour the summaries of the cumulative Jewish, Christian and Muslim traditions offered by Jacobs, Williams and Schimmel, and the analysis of more particular themes within the Hindu and Confucian traditions offered by Mehta and Wei-Ming Tu. Insofar as we *do* attempt to apply to Smith's concepts to five religious traditions, this section of our book is not merely a commentary upon the religious traditions concerned, it is also a commentary upon Smith's categories.

The first thing that emerges is the sheer complexity of these twin concepts of faith and tradition. In Smith's hands they appear to afford a straightforward heuristic tool for understanding mankind's global religious history. In general Smith's approach is vindicated, but in the process there is a complexification of the notions of faith and tradition. For example George Williams looks at the richness of the notion of cumulative tradition in the case of the Christian community by showing its extraordinary diversity throughout time and space to the extent that the Christian tradition, quite apart from the obvious differences between denominations, has really been a congeries of diverse traditions. Professor Mehta points out that in the Hindu case there was a history, there was a 'community of shared vision on the march', but the Hindu ethos makes it less easy to uncover and isolate the Hindu cumulative tradition. Moreover, there is an interplay between the overt objective data of a tradition and the interpretation of those data, between faith and tradition, which complicates the attempt of the believer and the historian to recapture any particular cumulative tradition as such. If the easier concept of tradition is seen to be complex, this is even more the case with the concept of faith. It is susceptible of various levels of analysis and interpretation. It would be counter-productive to summarise the minutiae of nuances of the interpretation of faith at this point. It is not just that Annemarie Schimmel is (like Smith) approaching Muslim faith from the viewpoint of a sympathetic non-Muslim whereas the other scholars belong to the tradition they are investigating, it is not just that some scholars are asking how believers themselves have viewed faith in the history of their tradition, it is not just that someone like Wei-Ming Tu is analysing

9

how the scholar's personal orientation may be used as an academic tool to reflect upon the faith made available within a tradition. Something deeper is happening. Within the welter of reflection there is emerging the realisation that faith and tradition can be viewed as symbols with various layers of meaning. They are twin symbols that need each other, but within Smith's basic structure of meaning – that tradition is the objective data, the texts, the religious observables, etc., that people inherit and faith is what the data suggest, what the texts mean, and what the religious observables imply for the people concerned – other levels are uncovered that are not necessarily indicated in Smith's work but which can be opened up when scholars of insight take faith and tradition with the utmost seriousness.

It may be objected, in the second place, that the procedure we have adopted in this book of applying faith and tradition to religious traditions is too narrow. After all, it may be argued, Smith's main emphasis is not upon religions but upon persons. Religious traditions although important are secondary. The two basic axes lying behind Smith's thought are those of 'God' and 'man', and they are joined by his personalism. Should we then not have concentrated upon persons and their faith and the transcendent reality that is apprehended by personal faith instead of focussing upon the religious traditions as such? By stressing religious traditions which never saved anybody but are merely the linking vehicles whereby men and women can be put in contact with ultimate reality have we not given them a primacy they do not deserve?

There is an element of truth in all this. In his emphasis upon the importance of an I-Thou relationship between persons and persons and persons and God Smith is in succession to the thought of Martin Buber.[13] It is instructive however to analyse how Smith is different from as well as similar to Buber. At first sight there is a resemblance between Buber's notion of I-It and Smith's notion of cumulative tradition, and between Buber's notion of I-Thou and Smith's notion of faith. For Buber all objective knowledge is I-It knowledge just as for Smith objective data belong to the realm of tradition which is seen as a sort of ongoing it. For Buber I-Thou knowledge is subjective knowledge of other subjects recognised to be Thous and known as real people rather than abstractions just as for Smith 'the two matters of supreme importance are the relations among persons within the total community, and the relations between men and God.'[14] Moreover their view of God is not dissimilar. For Buber God is the 'Thou who can, by its nature, never become an It' just as for Smith 'traditions evolve, man's faith varies, God endures.'[15] Buber and Smith are therefore fairly close in regard to three important issues, the I-It concept, the I-Thou concept, and the question of God. However it would be unwise to overstress the similarities. Buber is more inclined to philosophy whereas Smith is more inclined to history; Buber is more ready to stress the difference between the I-It and I-Thou relationships whereas Smith is more ready to stress the dialectical intertwining between tradition and faith; and Buber is the theologian concerned to give some theistic content to the notion of God whereas Smith does not theologise about the given but unobservable God who is 'the something, or Someone, behind or beyond Christianity, or Buddhism.'[16] In spite therefore of Smith's significant stress upon persons and their relationships with other persons and God, in which he rivals Buber, his deep concern for history, his greater interest in man's religiousness than in God's nature, his intuition that faith is personal *rather than* individualistic, and his awareness that faith and tradition are in practice intertwined lead him back to a sustained involvement in the study of religious traditions. It is by participation in particular traditions, in all their diversity, that persons achieve faith and apprehend or are apprehended by God. Particular religious traditions therefore matter and at the heart of them remain the concepts of faith and tradition.

The third thing that emerges, assuming as we have suggested that faith and tradition within the context of religious traditions remain important within Smith's thought, relates to the range of religious traditions that are open for consideration. Following Smith we have limited ourselves in the main to the living major traditions of the world. However, elsewhere in the volume, the suggestion is made that Marxism and the primal religions are relevant in contemporary discussions of the study of religion.[17] Equally it would be true to say that relatively little attention is given in this book and in Smith's work to the archaic religions of mankind which in their day and context were major realities but

11

which are no longer present on the face of the globe, or indeed to the minor religions which are present but not prominent. The case to be made for including Marxism, the primal religions, and the archaic and minor religions within the orbit of our analysis is a different one in each case. And, of course, underlying the whole discussion is the basic question as to whether religious traditions *themselves*, whether major or primal, living or archaic, sacred or secular, should be the primary talking-point rather than say phenomenological typologies (with Eliade), area studies (with some Indologists, Sinologists, Arabists, etc.), religious archetypes (with Jungian psychologists), binary structures (with Lévi-Strauss), and so on.[18] It is to the credit of scholars such as Smith, in spite of his own view that religious traditions are the vehicle for rather than the reality of man's religiousness, that greater attention has been placed upon them as providing the arena in which we can locate the premier issues in religious studies. However, in view of the potential fruitfulness for prolonged and deep research of the twin notions of faith and tradition, it would appear that there is a promising future in extending their application beyond the major religious traditions to the primal religions, the archaic and minor religions, and Marxism. This would be to go beyond Smith's own work and priorities in that the primal religions are not directly emanable to his historical categories, the archaic religions are not directly amenable to his contemporary interests, Marxism is not directly amenable to his transcendental emphases, and the minor religions have not been influential in great civilisations past or present. Nevertheless part of the burden of our concern has been to show that when the concepts of faith and tradition are applied to the major religious traditions they open up new complexities and layers for consideration. The concepts themselves are important and it would be valuable to test them in relation to other traditions. In short what is being suggested is that serious thought should be given to the setting up of a research programme by a group of scholars wherein the concepts of faith and tradition could be applied to a wide range of religious traditions. Wilfred Cantwell Smith has opened up the possibility of such a development by means of his creative suggestions. There is little danger that his own reservations about methodology might rebound disastrously upon this programme because, as we have shown, the notions of faith and tradition contain different levels of meaning within and between particular religious traditions that would defy any attempt to straightjacket them within the constraints of a narrow method. It is our hope that the work begun in this Festschrift of applying faith and tradition within specific religious contexts can be extended and expanded to the benefit of the field as a whole.

The second section of our volume passes beyond the notions of faith and tradition that have held our attention so far to the wider matter of Smith's total approach. Seven leading scholars react to Smith's approach and they offer a comment upon it or a variant from it. Again it is instructive to examine the width of their reactions. From a starting-point or suggestion in Smith, they develop their chapters in seven alternative directions, directions they themselves have popularised but which presume overlapping contacts with Smith's work. The catalyst is provided by Smith's approach but the section could stand on its own as providing a spectrum of some of the main recent thinking on theories in the study of religion. We will briefly analyse these seven viewpoints both for their own worth and for the light that they throw upon Smith's work.

John Hick takes up again the themes of faith and tradition but looks at them not from the standpoint of a particular religious tradition but from a wider perspective. He points out how, due mainly to Smith, we no longer view the religions of the world as separate rival entities or solid structures but as dynamic ongoing movements within human history wherein persons can move from self-centredness to Reality-centredness. Hick extends Smith in suggesting that ultimate Reality in itself is one but it can be experienced by persons in a multitude of different ways. In spite of the variety of these ways of religious experience one can see, across the religious spectrum, the dominance of two modes: experience of God, the Real, as personal, and experience of the Absolute, the Real, as non-personal. Hick goes beyond Smith in analysing in some detail the nature of the Real as personal and the nature of Real as non-personal. In other words he engages in theology. He points out how the Real as personal is experienced as different divine personae in different religious traditions, for example as God the Father, Adonai, Allah, Śiva, Kṛṣṇa, etc., whereas the

Real as non-personal is experienced in different religious traditions as Brahman, the Dharma, the Tao, Nirvāṇa, Śūnyatā, etc. Thus Hick conceptualises a religious pluralism whereby ultimate Reality is experienced in different ways within the religious traditions which therefore open up varied dimensions of the Real that is ultimately one. In *God and the Universe of Faiths* and other recent writings including the present chapter, Hick has given some theological content to Smith's notion of 'God'.[19] Smith, by contrast, has never formally done this. In *Towards a World Theology*, and in his other writings that impinge upon this theme, the emphasis is on universal theological categories (such as faith, tradition, participation, and religious truth) that are applicable to all religious traditions. However these could equally be labelled comparative religious categories or philosophical categories in that they focus more upon man's religiousness than on knowledge of God. For Smith there may be a 'historically persistent consciousness of a surpassingly great Other'[20] but content is not clearly given to this Other to which persons respond through the religious traditions of mankind. To that extent he is not so much a theologian as a historian of religion and a comparative religionist. Hick however is a theologian responding theologically to Smith's intimations concerning transcendence.

George Rupp responds theologically in another way. He sees a growing convergence between theology and the comparative history of religion. He asserts that Smith's work points to and in a sense characterises the growing relationships between these two areas of concern. Corporate critical self-consciousness rests upon the notion that 'the truth of all of us is part of the truth of each of us', and to this extent it is natural that theology and religious studies should stake out more common ground. Each religious tradition and its theology is therefore in the position of comparatively and critically appropriating other religious traditions. While the roots of religious participation may lie in one religious tradition, increasingly there is a growing awareness of the need to participate across religious boundaries and to see one's own tradition as part of a global whole. Rupp's approach is essentially that of an empathetic and enlightened theologian looking out from within a religious tradition in the direction of the comparative history of religion and saying we must universalise and globalise our theology in order to be theologically literate in our interdependent world, and we must do this with the help of and in collaboration with the history of religions. Smith, on the other hand, tends to look back from his global position and his universal 'theological' categories in the direction of particular religious traditions and specific theological systems – he is the historian of religion looking towards the theologian rather than the other way round. However, although he is not himself a systematic theologian or a philosopher of religion, Smith has exercised a powerful influence upon other people such as Rupp who are. Whether or not Smith's full-blown world theology of religion achieves persistent acclamation and articulation as a separate academic enterprise, it is clear that Christian theology is not unaffected by his work.

The third response is that of *philosophia perennis* and it is outlined by Seyyed Hossein Nasr in one of the few systematic formulations of this position.[21] This approach works back from a global presupposition – the perennial philosophy which lies at the heart of all religions – to the actualities of external religious traditions. To this extent it offers an analogue to Smith's notion of faith. It accepts that Ultimate Reality is given in a similar way to that in which Smith accepts that 'God' is given, but it would talk about a science of Ultimate Reality and give metaphysical content to that Reality. Nasr recognises what he calls the Absoluteness of the Absolute just as Smith recognises the ultimacy of the Truth that is 'God'; Nasr also recognises that the manifestations of the Absolute within each religious tradition are 'relatively absolute' just as Smith recognises that the manifestations of the Absolute Truth are received as personal truth by persons through the medium of the religious traditions. In short both approaches proceed from the global to the particular, and both contain a transcendental structure that is given. Nasr also departs from Smith in various ways. *Philosophia perennis* has a deeper metaphysical underpinning that Smith's notion of faith; it has a greater interest in traditional and ancient wisdom whereas Smith's concern is geared more to the present condition and future potentiality of tradition than to the past for its own sake; it has a greater emphasis upon hierarchy than Smith; and it has a deeper fascination for the content of its transcendent structure than

15

Smith whose academic absorpion is more with the faith of persons than with the structure of Reality. *Philosophia perennis* is an interesting variant to Smith's approach both in its similarities and in its differences.

Raimundo Panikkar takes up the theme of dialogue and opens up the question of what he calls dialogical dialogue, the in-depth encounter of persons in our cross-cultural and pluralistic world. He contrasts this with dialectical dialogue which is a dialogue about objects rather than a dialogue among persons. He plays numerous variations upon this theme of dialogical dialogue and in so doing illuminates the meaning of personhood, a theme of obvious importance in Smith's work. 'Persons', he writes, 'are fields of interaction where the real has been woven or striped by means of all the complexity of reality; they are knots in the continuous weaving of the net of reality.' Panikkar's position both agrees with and diverges from that of Smith. His stress is upon dialogue whereas Smith's greater concern is with colloquium and in this respect Smith has gone beyond his former emphasis upon dialogue to which others would seek to bind him.[22] This divergence between dialogue and colloquium, although arising out of a concern for persons that is common to Smith and Panikkar, has three implications. Dialogical dialogue in Panikkar's sense has a greater stress upon inwardness and spirituality whereas Smith's colloquium relates more to conceptual discourse; Panikkar's dialogue notion presupposes roots within a tradition out of which one can dialogue whereas Smith's colloquium view presupposes a corporate global religious situation which points back to roots in a tradition; and Panikkar's intensity of dialogue implies the need for an expenditure of time and concentration that would practically limit in-depth dialogue to individuals who would usually belong to two traditions whereas Smith's colloquium implies the possibility of multiple if less agonisingly existential interchanges at a more corporate level. However divergence pales before the striking stress upon personalism that is common to them both.

John Carman raises the question of the relationship between understanding and evaluation in the study of religion. He does this interestingly in the context of a re-evaluation of a consultation on 'The Study of Religion in Indian Universities'[23] held in 1967 at

Bangalore in which Wilfred Cantwell Smith played a prominent part. A number of important issues emerged at that consultation and are aired in this chapter. At Bangalore Smith pointed to some distinctions that could be made in studies of religion in the western academic world. They included the distinctions between religious studies in universities and those in theological seminaries, between normative and descriptive studies, between studies of past and present religions, between the study of religion and the study of religions, and between the incidental and deliberate study of religion. It is interesting to ponder on Smith's own balancing act in relation to these distinctions: his stress upon the givenness of transcendent Reality but outside the seminary setting, his passing beyond descriptive categories based upon objective knowledge while eschewing value judgments between religious traditions, his preference for the study of present religions without neglecting the past, his emphasis upon the historical development of separate religions but on the assumption that faith and tradition are universal and that man and God are one the world over, and his pursuance of the deliberate study of religion while admitting that it is part of a greater whole. In some ways even more interesting is the implied distinction at Bangalore and more recently between western and non-western approaches to the study of religion. As Carman points out, in some respects Smith's work is overtly and unashamedly western, for example his coveting of western categories of historical development. In other ways he is a standard bearer for the cause of allowing members of other religious traditons to conceptualise and verify their own faith and tradition, and he has indicated the problems associated with applying western disciplines and western scientific canons of objectivity to humane knowledge in general. If we are beginning to realise the veiled arrogance of those westerners who, in the name of objective scholarship, supposed that it was only they who had the requisite academic equipment to describe for others the data of their own traditions, the reason lies not only in the prophetic anger of statements such as Said's *Orientalism*[24] but also in the insight of scholars such as Smith that the global study of religion required statements *from* as well as statements *about* the non-western religious traditions of mankind. In Smith's words, 'One of the most exciting intellectual adventures of our day is the emergence of critical and disciplined participant observation, whereby man studies not other men, "objectively", but his own group – ideally mankind – in a critical, disciplined, intellectually rigorous, empirical, academic way.'[25]

Geoffrey Parrinder treats of the theme that he has uniquely made his own, namely that of thematic comparison. Quite apart from theological or other value judgmental forms of comparative religion that have no place in a book related to Smith's work, there are many ways of impartially comparing religions. They range from phenomenological typologies, Jungian archetypes, Lévi-Straussian structures, and Panikkarian spiritualities to more empirically oriented comparisons that are more anthropological, sociological, or historical. Within the more empirically related comparisons there are in turn a number of different modes of comparison ranging from cross-historical comparisons at particular periods to the cautious comparison of religious traditions as organisms found in Pettazzoni and Widengren and the more systematic comparative models of scholars such as Smart. Some anthropological comparison concentrates upon themes such as purity and pollution, right and left, various myths, rites, and symbols, and so on illustrated from field studies of various tribal groups. However it is in the work of Parrinder that thematic comparison has come into its own. He has tackled themes ranging from witchcraft, worship, religious teachings and scriptures to mysticism and sex by taking the theme in question and tracing it through each religious tradition in turn. The idea is to compare objectively but sympathetically by grouping together data from the histories of separate religious traditions and observing them 'across the board'.[26] Smith's stake in comparative religion has taken him in a slightly different direction. He has reminded us that comparative religion is the comparative study of man in his religious dimension rather than the study of typologies, structures, archetypes, themes, or religions in separation from man. This is a salutary word but perhaps we should add that it is not the whole story. It is helpful to take seriously the faith of persons, and to compare on the basis of the question 'what has this point of comparison meant to the people concerned?'. It is also helpful to remember that faith, although important, cannot be studied in principle in isolation from wider psychological, sociological and other factors of which the believer may not consciously be aware. Indeed, Smith's four universal comparative categories of faith, tradition, religious truth, and participation are arrived at by academic processes not limited to considerations relating solely to the faith of believers. Some types of comparison are more closely linked than others to the faith of persons, for example comparison of concepts; other types of comparison, for example anthropological and sociological comparisons of primal religion, religious communities, and social involvement, are less anchored in persons. I will submit in a moment that the seeming divide between Smith's work and the efforts of the social scientists of religion can be seen in complementary rather than antagonistic terms. His own assertion is insightful that meaningful comparison at an in-depth level may only be possible in regard of two traditions, and that this kind of comparison will often show that themes or typologies are not the correct norms of comparison in that the Qur'ān, the Muslim scripture, is equivalent in the Christian tradition to Christ, a person, at the deepest level. However it is also the case that it is possible to compare Christ and Muhammad as persons, and the Qur'ān and the Bible as scriptures, because the fact that they appear with different weights and are not equivalents is *itself* an important comparative point. Moreover although original comparative work may only arise out of studies wherein the scholar is expert in two traditions, this does not lessen the contribution to hermeneutics and understanding afforded by comparative studies of themes spanning many traditions that are based on secondary sources.[27]

This leads us to a consideration of our final chapter by Ninian Smart on scientific phenomenology. He follows Smith in suggesting that the scholar of religion needs above all right intentions. I mention in passing a thought there is no time to dwell upon, namely the similarity or otherwise between the phenomenological stresses on intentionality (from the beginnings of phenomenology of religion down to Smart and Jacques Waardenburg's new-style phenomenology)[28] and Smith's emphasis upon faith. Smart also follows Smith is stressing the human qualities needed in the study of religion, namely moderation, openness, warmth, imagination, concern with cultures other than one's own, learning, and the desire for descriptive and evocative success. However, in the course of his eirenical chapter, he implicitly departs from Smith in three ways. It is important to glance at these departures because they are echoed elsewhere and they help to put Smith's work and impact within a wider context. Firstly Smart addresses Smith's misgivings about methodology as such. The latter scholar has always stressed the content and substance of religion and the creativity of the scholar over against the need for the scholar and his data to be straightjacketed within a rigid methodology. Much depends, of course, upon what is meant by methodology. No worthy scholar, least of all Smith, would be content with merely multiplying the content and substance of religious data without any relation to 'method'. As Jordan put it in 1905, 'The accumulation of information, indeed, has never slackened for a moment; and the special embarrassment of today is the overwhelming mass of detail, still rapidly increasing, which confronts every earnest investigator.'[29] For 1905 read 1984! In some ways what is needed is more 'method' in the sense of ordering criteria and hermeneutical procedures. Indeed we have suggested earlier that Wilfred Cantwell Smith's twin concepts of faith and tradition constitute a pair of ordering criteria and a hermeneutical principle that could with profit be applied on a wider scale and, as we have seen, they are part of a larger approach that contains its own implicit presuppositions. Secondly it appears therefore that Smith's deeper misgiving is about the 'harder' methods, notably those applying in the social scientific disciplines. His concern is that these disciplines have erected their own specialised disciplinary boundaries centred upon their internal methodological norms within which knowledge and truth become structured with the result that truth comes to be found within the discipline rather than in religiousness itself, it comes to be found in the academic specialisation rather than in man. This is compounded by the fact that these disciplines emerged after the Enlightenment which gave to religion a more abstract and eventually a more historico-sociological (rather than personal) meaning, and which saw the religious aspects of culture as distinguishable from other aspects viewed as aesthetics, politics, art, science, and so forth. This appears to be a formidable misgiving but I wish to suggest shortly that it is perhaps not as serious as appears to be the case at first sight. Smart's third departure relates to the notion of transcendent reality. For Smith, as we have seen, the Real is given even though he gives little or no content to it. It is that to which persons within religious traditions respond, it is that which they apprehend or by which they are apprehended. Smart however, while eschewing the methodological atheism of a sociologist such as Peter Berger, adopts the stance of methodological agnosticism. From his viewpoint it is not the task of the scholar of religion to either affirm or deny the various foci of faith, such as Christ, Kṛṣṇa, the goal of liberation, and so on. What matters and what is relevant is not the reality or existence of transcendent foci which are not a valid subject of enquiry but the fact that transcendent foci exist for and are real to believers.

At this point the temptation is to close this essay with the assertion that there is an impasse between these viewpoints. Why not just admit, it may be asserted, that Wilfred Cantwell Smith's contribution has been to reintroduce transcendence on to the agenda of the secular university, to reconnect religion with people as opposed to impersonal concepts or reified entities, and to reassert the relevance of man's religiousness in the development of global history? In fact these contributions are gladly admitted. The seven chapters of part two of this volume bear witness to this in the way that they both follow and depart from Smith. What does it matter, it may be said, that others have disagreed with Smith and charted different journeys of exploration within the waters of religious studies? Does not this highlight the distinctiveness of his contribution and validate his notion that great scholars should be creative in *their* way rather than toe the line of disciplinary boundaries?

In many ways it would be easier to close at this point. However, insofar as we have already suggested that Smith's concepts of faith and tradition are susceptible of wider application and further explication at the hands of others, let us also explore the implications of his approach when it is linked to other developments in the study of religion as a whole. As space is short, and as the chapters of this volume cry out to be read, I will indicate in shorthand some of the guidelines of what promises to be a major ongoing discussion in our field.

Two points have been made already: the study of religion

cannot be confined in principle to the major religious traditions and a case can be made for including primal religions, archaic religions, minor religions, and world-views such as Marxism within the legitimate orbit of the study of religion; and the faith of persons, although important, is influenced sociologically by human collectivities and psychologically by unconscious factors that complicate the concepts of 'faith' and 'person'. Moreover, as I have pointed out in another context, in recent years there has been an increasingly complex involvement of the humane and social sciences in the study of religion to the extent that virtually any theory or method of investigation in any of the humane and social sciences can be and often is applied to specific sets of religious data. In any impartial survey of the contemporary giants in the field of Religious Studies room would have to be made not only for scholars such as Smith but also for Lévi-Strauss, Berger, Bellah and other social scientists.[30] The growing importance of the computer and the increasing ease of travel enhance the possibility and the actuality of further social scientific studies not only in the quantitative sense but also in the sense that new 'shoots' such as the ecology of religion can and do arise. To add to the complexity, it is also true to say that the other stream of thought within Religious Studies that has taken seriously the notion of transcendent structures (namely the succession of thinkers ranging from Rudolph Otto to Mircea Eliade who have emphasised the 'holy' or the 'sacred') has given an alternate account of 'transcendence' from that given by Smith. How quaintly echo the words written by Burnouf over a hundred years ago:

> This present century will not come to an end without having seen the establishment of a unified science whose elements are still dispersed, a science which the preceding centuries did not have, which is not yet defined, and which, perhaps for the first time, will be named science of religion.[31]

Our two volumes in the *Religion and Reason* Series published by Mouton entitled *Contemporary Approaches to the Study of Religion* began with the hope of bringing order to the field so that it could be seen, if not as a 'unified science', at any rate as a unified field. Our conclusion was that although Religious Studies is exciting, expanding, academically vibrant, pregnant with new seeds, and an integrally important part of contemporary scholarship as an innovative and linking area of study, it is too early, if we are to do justice to the dispersed multi-religious, multi-cultural, and multi-disciplinary elements of Religious Studies, to talk realistically of a unified field.[32]

How then does Smith's work fit into this wider whole of Religious Studies? Much depends on whether, to use Kuhn's analogy from the philosophy of science, we view Smith's approach as a new paradigm. Is his work the introduction of a paradigm into a field that was formerly without one, is it the introduction of a revolutionary paradigm to supplant another that was formerly dominant, or is the language of paradigm inexact in reference to Smith's creativity? Clearly the answer that is given to this question is contingent not only upon our estimate of Smith's work but also upon our view of what Religious Studies basically is.

We will close this essay by making a shorthand attempt to address our own question in the knowledge that such an attempt deserves a book instead of three rapid paragraphs. In the first place, we salute again Wilfred Cantwell Smith's creativity. It is a moot point as to whether Smith has put into powerful words the expression of a need that was already there unexpressed or whether his originality is such that he has created a need for new thinking *de novo*. Whichever be the case, his thought cannot be ignored, and in the second section of this book seven leading scholars have played variations on Smith's themes of transcendent Reality, global corporate self-consciousness, dialogue and personhood, comparative religion, academic intentionality, truth and Truth, and understanding in relation to evaluation. These themes do not exhaust the range of Smith's work but they represent our salute to its worth. Yet it would appear that Smith's approach does not represent a paradigm in Kuhn's sense by virtue of the fact that it has not been universally received and acted upon.[33]

Kuhn's view was that mature science is governed by a single paradigm such as Newtonian physics or classical electromagnetism. It will normally be imprecise, it will spell out laws and theoretical assumptions, it will structure ways of applying laws to particular contexts, it will admit the possibility of anomolies, it will see itself as a problem-solving activity employing instrumental techniques within wider theoretical principles. According to Kuhn scientific paradigms often dominate the field for a long time because communities of scientists in particular historical contexts are able successfully to use and adapt paradigms for their own benefit and the benefit of the community at large. Eventually, when a more prolonged crisis arises for a paradigm due to the multiplication of serious anomalies and the rise of pressing social needs, it is no longer seen to be normal, it begins to break down, and out of the crisis a new paradigm appears by means of a scientific revolution.[34] It is doubtful whether Religious Studies has ever been dominated by a single paradigm. Early pioneers such as Max Müller, Émile Durkheim, James George Frazer, and Carl Gustav Jung shared no one paradigm, nor do present-day scholars such as Eliade, Lévi-Strauss, Dumézil, Widengren, Pettazzoni, Zaehner, or the scholars contributing to this book. If it be argued that the historical/phenomenological approach has the makings of a paradigm it has to be said that this can only be the case in a weak sense because it is divided within itself, it is not universally approved, and special pleading that it is a paradigm does not constitute it as such. Our provisional conclusion must therefore be that Smith's work is not in itself a paradigm, nor has it supplanted another paradigm in Religious Studies. Indeed the field of the study of religion is in urgent need of further integration whether we formulate this need in terms of the word 'paradigm' or not.[35]

In the second place, it would appear that Smith's work has both enriched and complicated the field of Religious Studies. The west has inherited in the broadest terms two conflicting approaches to the study of religion. On the one hand there is the tradition of scholarship within the Christian and Jewish communities which has a long history and vitality and which looked out upon the world of religion from within the theological and other concerns of the community concerned. On the other hand there was the development of the scholarly study of religion stemming from the Enlightenment and determined by the premises of western critical presuppositions and disciplines which placed the study of religion on a par with the critical study of anything else whether it be aesthetics, politics, economics, literature, sociology, and so on.[36] Smith's point was that to treat religion in the generic sense of the second development was to devalue it by reifying it so that it became an 'it' – a thing out there to be studied – rather than the religious dimension of humankind seen as a living, developing and cumulative response by persons within religious communities to transcendence. His point also was that to treat religion in the particularistic sense of the first development was to devalue other religious traditions and to give to religious traditions of any sort an unwarranted importance. In working out his position between the two extremes, Smith leaned more towards the theological end of the spectrum than to the Enlightenment/social scientific end so that it was felt in some quarters that he was a theologian (which is perhaps debatable) and that he was suspicious of the social scientific and philosophical disciplines (which is more clear). Is it more than facile eirenicism to suggest that Smith's work can be part of a fuller integration that we can anticipate within the wider whole of Religious Studies? In other words, in addition to seeing his enriching and complicating work as constituting a new model with its own presuppositions alongside and over against other models within Religious Studies, in addition to seeing his notions of faith and tradition as capable of extension into a more far-reaching research programme, and in addition to drawing out some of the more obvious insights of his general approach in the way we have done, can we see his work as an element complementary with others within the coming integration of Religious Studies?

In the third place let us attempt briefly to tease out the implications of this suggestion. There is a sense in which historical and phenomenological categories are implicit in Smith's work and the broad enterprise of Religious Studies in the sense that historical religious data supply basic raw material and in the sense that impartiality (implied in the phenomenological notion of *epoché*) and empathy (implied in the phenomenological notion of *Einfühlung*) are basic to the scholar's approach.[37] To this extent, Religious Studies is primarily part of the Humanities. It has to do with the humane. It deals with man in his religious dimension. It cannot be circumscribed by theological value judgments or parochialisms operating from within particular religious traditions, nor can it be delimited by social scientific disciplines whose basic concern is not with man's religiousness. However social scientific researches into religion, although not necessarily the main plank of the social scientific enterprise, are nevertheless valuable. They are supplementary to the work of the historian of religion in analysing what Smith would term the cumulative tradition of the major religions, and they are vital in the analysis of tribal religious traditions that are inaccessible to the historian. Nevertheless social scientific studies of religion are not ends in themselves but are supportive of the basic endeavour to study the history and nature of man's religiousness. Likewise, at the other end of the scale, a concern for transcendence is back on the agenda of Religious Studies. Again it is not an over-riding concern but supportive of the basic endeavour to study the history and nature of man's religiousness. It is revealing, to glance again briefly at the philosophy of science, that scientists such as Polanyi argue that for science to be science it operates with a transcendent reality, irreducibly given, over which we have no control.[38] If natural scientists can begin to speak in such terms why not scholars of religion? Whether it be seen in terms of man's transcendence or a transcendent Reality to which man responds, whether it be seen in terms of the holy or the sacred, whether it be seen in terms of a transcendence that is given or a transcendence that is real for believers, the question of transcendence is in the arena of discussion of Religious Studies. It is within these broad parameters that a new integration within the field of the study of religion is likely to emerge. Perhaps even a paradigm?

It is for Wilfred Cantwell Smith to indicate whether our shorthand is feasible of transformation into a new integration or a possible paradigm for Religious Studies. Indeed it is our hope that scholars throughout the field will use this volume as a vehicle for discussion about the field as a whole. We offer it to Wilfred in honour of his work seen in its own terms, in honour of the creativity of his categories of faith and tradition, and in honour of the significance of his thought for Religious Studies and for scholarship as a whole.

NOTES

1. *Religious Diversity. Essays by Wilfred Cantwell Smith.* Edited by Willard G. Oxtoby. New York: Harper and Row, 1976.
2. W. C. Smith, 'Comparative Religion: Whither and Why?' in *The History of Religions: Essays in Methodology.* Edited by M. Eliade and J. Kitagawa. Chicago University Press, 1959.
3. op. cit., p. 35.
4. op. cit., p. 55.
5. op. cit., p. 58.
6. See Jurgen Habermas, *Theorie und Praxis; Sozialphilosophische Studien.* Neuwied am Rhein: Luchterhand, 1963 (*Theory and Practice,* tr. J. Viertel. Boston: Beacon, 1973); *Erkenntnis und Interesse.* Frankfurt: Suhrkamp, 1968 (*Knowledge and Human Interests,* tr. J. J. Shapiro. Boston: Beacon, 1971); *Legitimationsprobleme im Spat Kapitalismus.* Frankfurt: Suhrkamp, 1973 (*Legitimation Crisis,* tr. T. McCarthy. Boston: Beacon, 1973). Nicholas Rescher, *Conceptual Idealism and Cognitive Systematization.* Oxford: Blackwell, 1973.
   Mary Hesse, *Revolutions and Reconstructions in the Philosophy of Science.* Brighton: Harvester, 1980.
7. See W. C. Smith, *Towards a World Theology.* Philadelphia: Westminster, 1981.
8. Kenneth Morgan was a pioneer in recruiting scholars to write about their own traditions in his edited books: *Religion of the Hindus,* 1953; *The Path of the Buddha,* 1956; *Islam – The Straight Path,* 1958 (all New York: Ronald).
9. See an account of the contribution to the study of religion by these non-western scholars in 'The Study of Religion in a Global Context' by F. Whaling in *Contemporary Approaches to the Study of Religion: The Humanities,* I. The Hague: Mouton, 1984 (edited by Frank Whaling).
10. W. C. Smith, *The Meaning and End of Religion.* New York: New American Library, 1964, p. 141.
11. op. cit., p. 141.
12. op. cit., p. 141.
13. See Martin Buber, *Complete Works: I. Schriften Zur Philosophie. II. Schriften Zur Bibel. III. Schriften Zur Chassidismus.* Munich: Kosel and Heidelberg: Lambert Schneider, 1962–63.
    See Especially M. Buber, *Ich Und Du.* Leipzig: Insel, 1922 (*I and Thou,* tr. R. Gregor Smith. Edinburgh: T. & T. Clark, 1937).
14. W. C. Smith, 'Comparative Religion: Whither and Why?', p. 58.

15. M. Buber, *I and Thou*, p. 112.
16. W. C. Smith, *The Meaning and End of Religion*, p. 17.
17. Ninian Smart here and elsewhere has championed the notion that Marxism should be bracketed with religious traditions as a world view; Geoffrey Parrinder has stressed the primal religions along with the major religions.
18. See the extended discussion of these issues in F. Whaling (ed.), *Contemporary Approaches to the Study of Religion*, I and II. The Hague: Mouton, 1984.
19. J. Hick, *God and The Universe of Faiths*. London: Macmillan, 1973.
20. W. C. Smith, *Towards a World Theology*, illuminates this theme. But insofar as, in Smith's thought, transcendence is given ('seen in global perspective, current anti-transcendent thinking is an aberration' – p. 189), the mere fact that he presupposes transcendence does not of itself constitute him a theologian.
21. Another formulation is found in Huston Smith, 'Perennial Philosophy, Primordial Tradition' in Huston Smith, *Beyond the Post-Modern Mind*. New York: Crossroad, 1982. S. H. Nasr's Gifford Lectures, *Knowledge and the Sacred*. Edinburgh: Edinburgh University Press, 1981 are a working out of the *philosophia perennis* position.
22. *Towards a World Theology*, p. 193: 'As a term I prefer "colloquy"; partly for its multilateral connotations but chiefly to suggest a side-by-side confronting of the world's problems (intellectual and other) rather than a face-to-face confronting of each other'.
23. *The Study of Religion in Indian Universities*. Bangalore: CISRS, 1967.
24. Edward Said, *Orientalism*. London: Routledge and Kegan Paul, 1978.
25. W. C. Smith, 'The Teaching of Religion: Academic Rigour, and Personal Involvement'. Harvard MS; unpublished, 1967.
26. A long account of the many possible ways of comparing religion is found in F. Whaling, 'Comparative Approaches to the Study of Religion' in *Contemporary Approaches to the Study of Religion: The Humanities*, I and this includes a summary of Parrinder's approach.
27. See W. C. Smith, 'Some Similarities and Differences between Christianity and Islam: An Essay in Comparative Religion' in J. Kritzeck and R. Bayly Winder (eds) *The World of Islam: Studies in Honour of Philip K. Hitti*. London: Macmillan; New York: St. Martin's, 1959, 47–59.
28. J. Waardenburg, *Reflections on the Study of Religion*. The Hague: Mouton, 1978.

29. Henry Jordan, *Comparative Religion: Its Genesis and Growth.* Edinburgh: 1905, p. 163.
30. See *Contemporary Approaches to the Study of Religion: The Humanities and the Social Sciences*, I and II (ed. F. Whaling). The Hague: Mouton, 1984.
31. E. L. Burnouf, *La Science des Religions*, 2nd edn., Paris, 1872; trans. *The Science of Religions.* London: 1888, p. 1.
32. See F. Whaling'Introduction' to I of *Contemporary Approaches to the Study of Religion.*
33. Retaining the analogy with the philosophy of science, our suggestion of a fully fledged research programme to work out the implications of Smith's twin notions of faith and tradition would fit in with Imre Lakatos's concept ('Falsification and the Methodology of Scientific Research Programmes' in I. Lakatos and A. Musgrave, eds, *Criticism and the Growth of Knowledge.* Cambridge: Cambridge University Press, 1974) of a well-articulated research programme seen as a structured whole.
34. See Thomas Kuhn, *The Structure of Scientific Revolutions.* Chicago: Chicago University Press, 1962.
35. For an analysis of the possible implications of the relationships between the philosophy of science and the study of religion see F. Whaling, 'Philosophy of Science and the Study of Religion' in F. Whaling (ed.) *Contemporary Approaches to the Study of Religion*, I.
36. A bibliographical analysis in terms of these two strands is offered in John F. Wilson and Thomas P. Slavens (eds), *Research Guide to Religious Studies.* Chicago: American Library Association, 1982. However discussion of basic issues in the field has gone beyond a mere consideration of these two strands, basic as they have been in the past. Smith's position can be seen as a middle way which, while opposed to the exclusivistic tendencies of particularistic theology and particularistic disciplines, is an approach (among others) that affords promise of a wider integration.
37. In spite of clear differences of emphasis between Smith and phenomenologists of religion such as Kristensen, van der Leeuw, and Eliade, there is a sense in which they (and the generality of scholars of religion) share a concern for historical data, for impartiality, and for empathy.
38. Michael Polanyi, *The Logic of Liberty.* London: Routledge, 1951, 40 ff.

Section B

FAITH AND TRADITION IN THE WORLD'S RELIGIOUS TRADITIONS

1

THE HINDU TRADITION: THE VEDIC ROOT

J. L. Mehta

The historical processes and events that lead to the building up of a cumulative religious tradition are complex and often obscure and difficult to unravel and interpret. Each such tradition has a beginning, a provisional origin at a point of time where a community of faith and memory comes to rest, though aware, however vaguely, of unplumbed depths of the past, of an absolute beginning behind that beginning in history. In the Indian case, the historical origin and source goes back to the Ṛgveda, which remains not only the *arché*-text of this religious tradition but the *arché*, the animating source of the religiousness that has generated and sustained the tradition and given it its own unique form and substance. It is likewise the expression of the specific form of faith that it has in turn engendered among the participants and innovators of this tradition, its power and richness in latent possibility undiminished by all that has sprung from it, nor diluted by the hundreds of tributaries of faith that have joined this stream, nor rendered superogatory by the dramatic transformations in the form of religious faith that occurred subsequently. The Vedic religious tradition survived the most cataclysmic, long drawn out intellectual revolution that occurred in Indian history before the modern period: the transformation of Vedic into classical culture and language, which culminated in the work of Pāṇinī of Takṣaśilā (fourth century B.C.) and the rise of Jaina and Buddhist modes of thought and piety. Whether it survives and makes its voice heard during the present such revolution, already in process since the beginning of the last century and in the midst of which we in India live today as participants in ongoing world-historical changes, is not simply a matter now of the life of just one strand in man's religious history being at stake but of mankind's humanity itself.

Some time in the eighteenth century B.C., Abraham, leaving Ur for Canaan, discovered the idea of God – God revealed Himself to him – as the highest whom alone man must serve, and live in conformity with a bond struck between Lord and servant. About the same time, a people living in the Central Asian regions bordering the Oxus and the Jaxartes, and the Aral and Caspian seas, made the discovery of transcendent Truth as the highest and holiest, which the gods themselves serve and guard and body forth, and of which they, bound with man in the intimacy of a sacred compact, bring tidings. A few centuries later, this people, calling themselves Āryans, brought to India their ancient myths and rituals and composed the hymns which were then gathered together in the Ṛgveda Saṃhitā, in which is spelt out their topology of Transcendence, their variegated and friendly intercourse with the gods, and the vibrant and all-embracing richness of their life within the dimension of the sacred. The authors of this first, massive, verbal articulation of human religiousness were Rishis – seers of the Vedic *mantras* and path-makers, craftsmen of the sacred word and revellers in disciplined polysemy – who wove this many-splendoured fabric of words and opened up a well-structured space of sacrality, building pathways between the human and the Divine, busily fashioning the very language of faith and of the sacred over a period of several hundred years.

What happened in the aftermath of this tremendous creative beginning – during *c*. 1000 B.C. to *c*. 500 B.C. – and in consequence of the way this was received, understood, interpreted and creatively developed, was no less astounding: the emergence of sacerdotalism and ritualistic extravagance, of which the possibility indeed lay in the hymns, and their 'proliferation to a point that the world has never seen equalled.' There was nothing inevitable about this development; it happened, as so often in history, especially in religious and intellectual history, that one possibility latent in the beginning was actualized historically by the immediate recipients of the founding event, who understood it, interpreted it and transmitted it in one way rather than another, thus creating a tradition that rested on incomplete 'otherwise'-

understanding and misprision, an inability to hold the original vision in its purity and starkness, a turning away from the reality of that blinding flash.[1] Is it not always the case that an origin, in the very act of starting off a historical process, hides its essence and keeps it to itself, unexpended in the course taken by the emergent stream? A second basic facet of religiousness which is almost focal in Ṛgvedic experience is the majesty, the sacredness and all-pervasive reality of the word (*Vac*; Brahman as sacred utterance and 'formulation').[2] It generated a sensitiveness to the phenomenon of language among the inheritors of the Vedic legacy that resulted eventually in the Grammar of Pāṇinī and the final replacement of Vedic by classical Sanskrit. Much of the philological work relating to the understanding of the Vedic text was done during this period of linguistic transition and the new 'scientific' and scholarly attitude it brought with it, as well as from the altered perspective of a burdgeoning ritualism, half a millenium removed from the closure of the Ṛgvedic canon. Massive and systematic as this work was, it too was a stream that led away from the source, incapable of unveiling its secret. Sanskritic culture swelled and went its victorious way, irresistible in its mainstream splendour, yet conserving always, frozen in memory, the precious gift of the Veda, never severing its link with the origin. This linguistic rapture found exuberant blossoming in classical Sanskrit literature, literary theory and grammatical speculation and inquiry. A third strand in the hymns of the Ṛgveda is the speculative passion that breaks out once in a while, though mostly restrained, often only intimated and expressed by indirection. From this flows the mighty torrent, swirling and surging, of Upaniṣadic thought, made up of a singular quest for the hidden essence and meaning of things, human, cosmic and divine, through mystical insight and logical argumentation, concluding the corpus of Vedic 'knowledge' or Śruti. This in turn becomes the source of the ceaseless and many-sided creativity comprising the various philosophical systems or Darśanas, the Vedānta in particular, which continued well into the middle of second millenium A.D. Religiously, perhaps a more important and intriguing matter, fourthly, may be briefly mentioned here. The Ṛgveda speaks of thirty-three *devatās*, of whom Indra and Varuṇa are respectively the god-'king' and the god-'sovereign', in Louis

Renou's words. But there are two figures of transcendent majesty, hovering above them all, mysterious shadowy presences, one an overarching, beneficent form striding across the spaces, measuring them out; and the other a chill wind, but one of auspicious omen and good promise, blowing through the heavenly mansions: Viṣṇu and Rudra (Śiva). No more than five hymns are devoted to each of them in the Ṛgveda. Yet it is these two inexplicit and enigmatic deities who became the focal points of the two main religious currents, 'the two Indian religions', as J. Gonda has called them, in the post-Vedic age: Vaiṣṇavism and Śaivism, which together constitute the main body of 'Hinduism' as it is known and named today. Finally, a seminal trend in the Ṛgveda is the narrative and mythopoeic, expressed sometimes directly but very briefly, often tangentially and cryptically, which finds some elaboration in subsequent Vedic literature but bears rich fruit only in the massive Epic and Purāṇic traditions of a later day, gathering together the strands and elements above mentioned, and which has provided Hindus with the tales and myths that have nourished and guided their religious imagination, faith and practice. Thus, from the very beginning, the Vedic text, held intact in memory, functioned as a source of other developments it inspired, rather than itself becoming the focus of understanding or of a purely exegetical literature. The unique evidence of interpretive effort of ancient date is represented by the *Nirukta* of Yāska (fourth century B.C.), already separated from the original by some eight centuries. The only full commentary on the Ṛgveda, that by Sāyaṇa, representing the ritualistic school of interpretation, dates from the fourteenth century A.D. The originary text, shining in its remote, solitary splendour, no mere monument but a radiant beacon, still holds back its secret.

The Vedic Age, or Vedism, came to a close about 500 B.C., and 'whatever survived of Vedism has become so integral a part of Indian thought that it is no longer distinguishable as a separate element,' as Renou says.[3] The destiny of the Veda, henceforth and increasingly, was to be 'no more than a distant object, exposed to the hazards of an adoration stripped of its textual substance.' As he puts it in his fascinating *Destiny of the Veda in India*, 'Even in the most orthodox domains, the reverence to the Veda has come to be a simple "raising of the hat", in passing, to an idol by which one no longer intends to be encumbered later on.' It is true that this is 'the oft-repeated fate of great sacred texts, the founders of religions' and shows a tendency which has 'been pushed in India, further perhaps than elsewhere.' Yet, the incredible fact remains that, in the midst of all the polite side-stepping and despite the opacity into which its textual meaning increasingly congealed, the Ṛgveda (along with the other three Vedas) has survived, in complete phonographic accuracy as to text and its pronunciation, accentuation and chanting style, for over three thousand years. This, however did not just happen, was not simply a lucky chance, as a rock-fossil may survive the ravages of time, but was made to happen by generations of institutionalized teacher-pupil transmission, an opalescent rock borne on assiduous memorizing across the millennial stream of time by men of determined faith, even when they did not fully comprehend what this precious cargo of words literally 'meant', apart from its liturgical use. Unencumbered by the modern (but of ancient lineage) myth or superstition of grasping the reality of life through the setting up of a world of objectified 'meanings', of Platonic entities amenable to logical handling and of 'clear and distinct ideas' by which the raw stuff of life can be reduced to conceptual order, these Vedic Brāhmins were content to be simple carriers of an unspent treasure and to let the Veda enjoy the only mode of being appropriate to it and the only perpetuity possible for it – inscribed in the minds and hearts of men of faith. Was there, is there, perhaps a potency, a virtue, an entelechy, or to use a Vedic rather than an Aristotelian term, the majesty of a *svadhā* inherent in the text itself that enabled it to hold its own, create its own destiny through the perils of historical existence and inspire in turn the faith which led the Brāhmins of India to cherish and guard it by dint of unflagging labour and energy? As the *Ur-Dichtung* of the Indian tradition, the Veda is not so much a body of 'meanings' as the source of whatever meaning this tradition has enabled Indians to see in life, as the very opening up of a horizon of meaning, out of which then a whole variety of sacred meanings was constructed in subsequent ages.

It was through this unlocking of such a horizon, releasing the sacred waters, that the multiform and colourful variety of ways was made possible, in which the sacred entered into every aspect of life and experience of the participants in this tradition. For, in the midst of the most dramatic changes and ruptures in their religious history – of which the continuity and unity is all but lost from view – and despite so many broken threads, the one thing to which Hindus clung and never let go, to which they tenaciously held on by dint of continued creative transformation, was their immediate, living relationship with the sacred, articulated in divergent ways from time to time and in forms which changed from one historical epoch to another in response to the challenge and crisis of each. This is sometimes represented in Western scholarly circles as a failure to rise above primitive animism, to move on from *mythos* to *logos*, from magic to reason, or from religion to faith. It is only today, in this age of consummated desacralization in modern world-civilization and our deepening insight into the religious roots of the secularization process emanating from the West, that one can see this phenomenon of Indian religious history for the wonder that it was. For the question today and at this hour in the religious history of mankind, as in reality always, is not whether there are many gods, or two, or the one and only, or whether this religion or that is 'true', but whether human living is not to be irretrievably banished from the dimension of the Holy, within which alone all talk of God and the gods, near or remote, present or absent, transcendent wholly or also immanent, has any meaning.

It is time that we got over the prejudice that Indian religious history, unlike the Western, was no true history, was no more than a series of natural events piled up one on top of another, like geological strata or tree-rings. Proverbially without the historical sense, Indians did not, it is true, seek to objectify their past by recording it (and this includes selective processing and interpretation, both dependent on unexamined presuppositions) in the form of chronologically ordered narratives. But does this imply that they retained no awareness of that past in so far as it continued to be effective in the present, and wrestled with it, or that that past was not itself constituted by remembrance of what was and by acts of free human choice? Who would now maintain, for example, that the Vedic hymns were just simple, spontaneous out-pourings of a devout and warlike people, like battle-cries or cataracts, and not deliberate, artful and sophisticated

38

compositions by Rishis who knew what they were doing? Or, that the Bhakti movement emerged like a glittering sun-set sky, out of nowhere, and not as the outcome of intense creative work, willed in response to a historical crisis, by men who were carriers and re-interpreters of a long religious tradition? Even if the present stage of our historical knowledge may not permit us to reconstruct the precise details of the transition from one phase to the next – especially the change from Vedism to the religious world of the *Mahābhārata*, beyond the highly suggestive speculations of comparative mythologists like Georges Dumézil and Stig Wikander – one can see that an inner logic governs the three millenia of religious change in India, giving it a unity that is intrinsically historical, at least. This inner logic, this thread running unbroken from Vedic times to the present, is constituted by the single-minded, unshaken will to the preservation of the dimension of the Holy in human living at all costs, leaving it to 'history' to reckon these costs as it will. It is well-known that in the Ṛgveda itself there is no evidence to show that the Āryans once left their original home and 'invaded' India. It is for the 'modern' historian to ask why in all these hymns, as also in all later religious documents, they left no indication of the historical situation to which they were responding. If 'the Hebrew religion was hammered out in response to the experience of Egypt,' and 'as an enduring reply to it,'[4] to which 'experience' was Vedism a response and to what counter-claim was it a reply? To any reader of the Veda the question would sound rather odd, as questions about the Zarathustrian reform would not, and it remains for students of religion to ask why this should be so, whatever historians may some day make of it. Does not a 'reply' to a temporary circumstance, contingent both as to its occurrence and to its perception and understanding by contemporaries who felt caught in it, does not a reaction against the adventitious immediacies of a time and a place remain conditioned by them, perpetuating a passing worldly circumstance? The Vedic Āryans defined themselves as 'followers of the Light,' who placed it first, in front (*Aryā jyotiḥ agrāḥ*), the light of which 'the shining ones', refracting the light of the one sacred truth, are embodiments. If there is any experience to which they did their mighty best to respond, and to which they gave an enduring reply, it was to godlessness, worship of false gods and idolatry; to falsity, deceit, conceited scoffing and denial of Divinity, cunning and magic; to the oppressive closure of sacred space, the unyielding resistance of all that covers up the hidden truth of things; to the obduracy of the stone that blocks the well-spring of sacrality and the impediment presented by fortifications against friendly solicitations from the realm of the divine and the true.[5] For the Vedic poet, these are ever-present possibilities to which the mortal condition is subject, and he makes use of the particularities of his ambience, like all poets, to hammer out a language and a ritual of 'making sacred' (sacrifice), and to present a vision that ensures inalienable nearness to the sacred for the children of Manu, for mankind. 'Let the threads that bind us to divinity not be broken, let the sacred threads by which we weave the coloured web of our song remain intact. May we not lose track of the paths that run between the gods and men, nor fail in our contractual hospitality to the Immortal that has come as a guest in the mortal's house. May we not lose sight of the trace left behind by the bird in flight.'[6] That, in sum, was the single, all-overriding concern of the Vedic Rishis, as in every subsequent phase of Indian religious life. The particularities of historical chance are glanced at, sometimes betrayed, but never dwelt on or insisted on. Yet, there was a history: a community of shared vision on the march, with memory of an inauguration, awareness of present crisis, and a voice that spoke into the future.

Is that inaugural voice still heard, making of the Veda-event not an objectified fact to be disposed of historically, as Max Müller wished and hoped, but rather a living presence, an event which still holds us within its amplitude? This pioneering, modern Vedic scholar, first editor and translator of the Ṛgveda, was honoured by Indian Pandits who bestowed on him the name 'Moksha Mular' – 'he who by publishing the Veda for the first time in a printed form gave the root, the foundation, the knowledge of final beatitude';[7] 'received *śrāddha* presents on several occasions, with shawl and sacred thread' from India; and in the concluding fifth volume of the great Poona edition of the Ṛgveda (1951), the last of the five dedicatory verses in Sanskrit is in grateful remembrance of Max Müller, who is placed in line with Yāska and Sāyaṇa, the two greatest Indian interpreters of the Veda. It was not for the Pandits who rendered honour where honour was due to ask what this transformation of the *Śruti* into Scripture might mean for the future, nor to question the kind of value assigned by Max Müller to the Ṛgveda. Let me dwell for a moment on the latter. Max Müller thought and wrote in an age in which the historical outlook had just burst upon the European intellectual landscape, when the genetic and evolutionary approach seemed to hold the key to truth, as Hegel was soon to exhibit, with superb self-assurance, in his account of the advance of the spirit to absolute knowledge. It was, in short, the hey-day of historicism and the gospel of progress, when judgment of the past swayed between the two extremes of Romantic adoration and devaluation in favour of the certainty of a fullness yet to come. Max Müller wrote, 'People do not yet see the full importance of the *Veda* in an historical study of religion', and went on to declare, 'The bridge of thoughts and sighs that spans the whole history of the Āryan world has its first arch in the *Veda*, its last in Kant's *Critique*. While in the Veda we may study the childhood, we may study in Kant's *Critique of Pure Reason* the perfect manhood of the Āryan mind'. We must see, he insisted, 'what the true *historical* value of this ancient religion is . . . Accept the *Veda* as an ancient *historical* document, containing thoughts in accordance with the character of an ancient and simple-minded race of men . . .' He noted with satisfaction how 'in 1850 the Brahma-Samaj solemnly pronounced the dethronement of the Veda' from its position as the word of God. But he did not ask why, after first taking over uncritically the concept of 'Scripture', the Brahmos had to 'dethrone' the Veda, and goes on to remark, 'Even after the fall of the Veda, do not suppose that the religious reformers of India discarded it altogether. They deprived it of its Divine Right, but they seemed to value it all the more.' May the 'fall' have been due to a vague presentiment on their part that somehow the category of 'Scripture' did not quite fit in the case of the Veda? Finally, he expresses the hope that 'the time will come when the scholars of India will study the Veda, as we study it in Europe, namely as an historical record of the highest value in the history of religion; but even then I trust that in India the Veda will always retain its particular position as the oldest book which, for the first time, told the inhabitants of that country of a world beyond this world, of a law beyond human laws, and of a Divine Being in whom we live, and move, and have our being'. Max

Müller had no doubt of 'the intrinsic value of that oldest among all Sacred Books of the Āryan race, however crude, childish, unscientific it may seem to us,' that is, to Christian scholars living in the mid-nineteenth century and in Max Müller's case, at Oxford, the hey-day of British Imperial power and evangelical self-assurance. He saw that 'the life-blood of what there is of natural religion in India still flows from the Veda ... those who know anything of the real issues of religion in India know or ought to know, that they depend today, as three thousand years ago, on the Veda', rightly, except for the doubtful but engaging notion of 'natural religion'. He was convinced, as he wrote to his wife in 1864, that his 'translation of the *Veda* will hereafter tell to a great extent on the fate of India and on the growth of millions of souls in that country. It is the root of their religion, and to show what that root is (no temples, no idols!), is I feel sure, the only way of uprooting all that has sprung from it during the last 3000 years.' Amazing resentment against history in one who bore it so close to his heart! Max Müller's insistence on the 'childish' character, and therefore on the merely historical value, of the Veda, presupposes a conception of history which needs to be examined because, like Hegel's, it is by no means extinct even now. It will take another century, two world wars and other no less traumatic events, above all the present threat to mankind of an all-enveloping catastrophe, for Western trust in the 'law' of progress to be rudely shaken, for a re-valuing, still somewhat suspect in academia, not only of historicism but of the concept of 'history' itself in an attempt to understand what 'has been' and its relation to the predicament of our present and our hopes for the future, and to begin to question what advance and evolution might mean in the realms of thought, art and religiousness. Is the historical process like a becoming explicit of what was implicit in the beginning, an unfolding of what is in bud there, a process of development? Or is it more like the opening up, following that beginning, of one contingent track – the only one perhaps possible at the time – out of several possible tracks, and its pursuit until the force of the original impulse is spent or the path reaches a dead end? Is the beginning *aufgehoben* (conserved, elevated and annulled) into what comes later, so that the end-point of a cumulative tradition is thought of as a privileged vantage point? Or, does the earliest, instead of expending itself in the stream which flows from it, rather keep its bounty unspent? Must the historical process (*Geschichte*) be equated with that which is chronicled (history) or even regarded merely as an object of historiography, presupposing the specifically modern attitude of grasping reality through objectifying representation? Does not the historiographical mode of comprehending a happening rather hide its true nature than reveal it, far from being the only mode of relating ourselves to the past? Are there, in history, any hard facts or brute data to enable the historian simply to 'report' what really happened, and does there not enter, inescapably, an element of interpretation in every attempt to represent the past, thus interweaving and fusing together all the modalities of time?[8] If listened to, the Veda speaks, whether it be to Max Müller the questing man – the 'more' in every historical-philological scholar – or to a modern Hindu even dimly aware of his cumulative tradition.

Three streams flowing down from the heights, three motions in response from the habitations of mortals; a reaching down from a region beyond all regions and from a time before time, and a straining upwards to the voice from beyond, a burst of speech. And, mystery of all mysteries, the triple stream is yet one, the double movement is the one motion itself, the voice calling and responsive speech but the Word itself – and so with the three and the two in their unity. From the timeless, spaceless, region beyond the three regions of heaven, earth and intervening space, from that realm of truth, light and joy where Divinity rests, transcendent and gathered together, there flows, diffracting the One into many divine forms, the triple stream of its largess. The first, the stream of the two way traffic between men and the high gods, born of Aditi, the great mother, with Agni as the messenger of both and himself a god embodying the mediating principle, the Immortal in the midst of mortals, bearing man's offerings to the gods and bringing their presence to his hearth, who dwells also in the human heart as the divine spark – this is the stream of human religiousness itself, the single movement making possible both grace and prayer, with its source in the highest realm of transcendent, sacred truth, and itself the source of the Veda as sacred knowledge formulated in words. Then the other, word-borne stream, with its source in the Ṛgveda as the originative *poiesis*, rushing down the ages, giving rise to countless off-shoots and in turn gathering into itself tributaries of diverse origins, until it builds up a vast network of arteries and itself broadens out into the nourishing river of sacrality for men, herself a form of the divine as Word, the great mother, but for whom man could not know himself as the mortal, nor have news of truth and transcendence. The third stream is that of lived history (*Geschichte*), started off or 'destinated' by the Veda on its erratic, troubled course, bound to the great mother goddess earth; taking various forms and colours under time's exigent needs, yet never letting go of the memory of the source by which to steer its way in dark times, never letting the sacred thread snap or losing sight of that remote star of the Veda. For it is the second stream which, from the human perspective, is *the* Mother, causing the first to shine forth and saving the third from utter loss of meaning and direction. Among the *tīrthas*[9] to which pious Hindus have aspired to make a pilgrimage once at least in their life-time is Gangōtri, the source of mother Gangā (who herself is the earthly form of the great heavenly stream with *its* source in Viṣṇu's seat in the highest heaven) in the Himalayas, symbolizing the totality of the Vedic heritage. The other, more accessible *tīrtha* is Prayāga (modern Allahabad) of the Kumbha fair fame, where there is a confluence of three major streams of the Indian religious tradition: Gangā, representing the central Vedic strand; Yamunā, representing the mystical *bhakti* strand of the Vedic Soma-vision; and the hidden current of Sarasvati, representing the heritage of language-borne 'knowledge', hidden, because existing only in the minds of human carriers. The Veda has itself been a 'destiny' for Indians, and its resplendent presence has been the light by which they have seen life, not just a matter of a polite raising of the hat, except to 'Vedists' unaware of how the Veda enters into the lives of Hindus even today. Whether one talks in terms of 'faith', its loss and possible regeneration, or in terms of the 'sacred', its lapse and possible recovery, it is this perennial three-in-one stream on the banks of which Hindus built their city, out-witting both 'the cunning of reason' in history and the perilous tides of time, unmindful of the ransom that had to be squandered as the guarantee of a total sacralization or sanctification of life.

The first volume of Max Müller's edition of the Ṛgveda was

published in 1849 and the last, sixth volume in 1874. This event marked the transformation of an oral text into a Book and also the formal beginning, after Colebrooke's initial account in 1805, of Western participation in Veda exegesis based on an 'objective' approach, from a background differing both religiously and in respect of scholarly tradition from this alien material. That in turn, along with attempts to translate the Veda, generated fields of 'comparative' scholarship like comparative religion, comparative mythology, and comparative linguistics, for all of which ground had been prepared by Indological scholars during the preceding hundred years (Anquetil-Duperron's translation of the *Avesta* in 1759 being among the most noteworthy of these ground-breaking endeavours). Concerning the task of translating the Veda, Max Müller wrote in 1891, '(The first translators of the Veda) ought to be decipherers, and they are bound to justify every word of their translation in exactly the same manner in which the decipherers of hieroglyphic or cuneiform inscriptions justify every step they take.' We must 'advance step by step, nay, inch by inch, if we ever hope to make a breach in that apparently impregnable fortress.'[10] That is one, the philological, aspect of Vedic scholarship, to which a host of specialists, Vedists and Iranists alike, have been contributing since. Another, of greater interest to students of religion, is that represented by the work of interpreters like Bergaigne, Oldenberg, Bloomfield, Lüders, Renou and (among living Vedists) Thieme and Gonda. In Heinrich Lüders' pregnant words, 'Der Veda will nicht belehren; er schildert nicht, er beschreibt nicht und erzählt nur selten. Er spielt aber fortwährend auf Dinge an, die uns zunächst vollständigunbekannt sind.'[11] To understand these unfamiliar things to which the Veda alludes all the time, we must not, he said, disdain the help of the subsequent religious literature of India, for that would be slavery to the modern standpoint, the principle namely that the Veda must be explained out of the Veda itself, which according to him, rests on an illusion; we must not import into our interpretation ideas from our modern Western religious and intellectual world; we must stop for once believing that the Vedic Rishis always meant something other than what they said and always used language to conceal their thoughts, or that they stood barely on the threshold of civilization. In his monumental (but alas fragmentary) work

Varuna, Lüders demonstrates, systematically and compre-hensively, that in the Rgveda *Rta* has a simple, unambiguous meaning: truth, and that it constitutes the central point of the Vedic religion – 'To have made Truth the highest principle of life, that is a deed for which perhaps even modern peoples might envy those ancients (the Āryans).'

Since this monograph may be regarded as the finest work so far of hermeneutical 'Vedology', let me just point to two major conceptual issues which still bedevil our efforts to understand those ancients. The first concerns the indiscriminate use of the vague, unexamined, alien word 'magic' (from Persian *'magus'*, in bad odour with Greek and Christian alike) by Lüders (and even by Thieme, who tries hard but cannot get rid of the word), and by Western scholars studying non-Christian religions and 'primitive' cultures generally. If magic consists in the attempt to coerce and manipulate nature, or supernatural powers, there is no magic to be found here. How does the 'true word' of the Vedic poet, itself bestowed by the gods, 'cause' Indra to 'cause' rain by virtue of the 'magical power of truth'? Rather than setting up all this rigmarole as a defence mechanism, is it not more reasonable to assume that there is a touch of trope and polysemy in 'rain' here? Whatever the case may be elsewhere, there is no evidence in the Rgveda that the Rishis sought to bring about a purely physical or mental event by the 'magische Kraft' of their observable acts, or speech or thought. Strange vacuity and blindness that comes over, like a *petit mal,* even the best-informed and well-meaning scholars when they come up against, rather themselves raise up, a wall in their attempt to understand what is different, as if they actually needed an excuse to prevent rational agreement! May it not be that all the 'magic' involved here is the magic of bringing, or experiencing, under divine inspiration, some mere 'fact' of life within the dimension of the Holy, of seeing it as part of a sacred cosmic order, of finding and proclaiming its reality or truth to lie in the sacred thus disclosed rather than in the natural causal relation of which, we may be sure, they were not ignorant? Did the Vedic priest, while lighting the sacrificial fire, not really know that it was rubbing two pieces of wood that 'caused' them to ignite, rather than the 'true word' of his chant, that 'the true word' only (?) transformed a merely natural occurrence into a theophany: the becoming manifest, the arrival, of the god Agni? May it not be that the only 'magic' here is the magic of all language: making manifest, rendering present, the gift of being? The other point is philosophical and concerns the idea of 'truth', which in the Western philosophical tradition has been conceived, at least since Plato, as *homoiosis*, or correspondence of a thought or statement with reality. But, how is a statement about God or the gods, or about any metaphysical entity, known to correspond to such reality? In what sense of being *are* such entities? Is there perhaps a primary sense of truth, which all our thoughts and statements presuppose?[12] Secondly, there exists in the West a philosophical tradition, deriving from Greece, and another tradition, the religious, having other roots, with 'truth' as the concern of the former and 'faith' that of the latter (or, as a more illuminating recent proposal has it, two kinds of faith, one in reason, the other in God). The polarity of their relation to each other, and the constant, unresolved tension between the two, has led to the formation of a mode of thinking which appears inappropriate when it addresses itself to a tradition like the Indian, which has not been subject to *that* kind of polarity and dialectical tension. Even in pre-Socratic Greek thought *Aletheia* was thought of as a goddess, in Parmenides for example, and truth was understood as lying within the dimension of the Holy, not yet divorced from the sacred. The Vedic Rishis never made *Ṛta* or *Satya* into a deity nor personified it like the Avestan *Aša* (*Aletheia* in Plutarch's rendering), for its supreme and primordial divinity was the mother of all deity, and yet it remained the sacred origin and goal of all Indian thought, religious or philosophical, without giving rise to the two separate domains of theology and philosophy. Despite his startling discovery of the focal status of truth in Vedic religion. Lüders, and even Thieme, remained caught up in the embarrassments stemming from the never clearly thought out notions of 'truth' and 'magic'.

Another valuable insight gained by modern Western interpreters of the Veda concerns the role of a contractual relationship between truth and the gods, between gods and men, among men, and within the personal life of each human being, between truth and the need for personal integrity. Since truth is the highest reality, the gods have their very being as embodying the bond with truth (for example, Agni is described as having struck the 'friendship of seven steps' with Truth); Varuṇa as sovereign deity keeps guard over it, watching over its presence in the secret places of the human heart; Mitra (the god of contracts between men) gives sanctity to all human bonds and endows them with truth; and Aryamān is the special guardian of the matrimonial bond, sacred because the wedded pair undertake to be true to each other and be friends, bonded together, by walking seven steps together – with Agni, who knows the paths of truth which run between men and the gods, as witness. 'Friendship' is the commonest name in the Ṛgveda of the bond between men and the gods, and so of the bond between man and truth. The lordship of transcendent truth and the ultimate sacredness and sanctifying nature of the 'region of truth' make it the relationship of all relationships, so that 'being true to' is the common sacred measure and norm for man's relationships to the gods, to nature, to other men and to himself. The breaking of any of these bonds is a lie; keeping and cherishing it is truth, integrity, loyalty, fidelity, faith, truing and troth. Truth is the origin and source, the *arché* and ruling principle, of all bonds, of all *religio* and sacrality. The Immortals, born of truth, 'are truth' and provide the measure of truth to man, according to the Vedic conception, and the mortal estate, taken by itself, is one of untruth; only participation in a sacred order, *religio*, and through that in the Great Truth, enables man to be led 'from darkness to light, from untruth to truth.'

Vedic scholarship has indeed 'advanced with giant steps' since Max Müller published his translation of the first volume of the Vedic hymns in 1869, so that Paul Thieme could write in 1951 (with reference to Lüders' achievement) that 'the Rigveda is not (anymore) a book with seven seals,' that even in 'the dark words of the Seer one can find a clear sense.' It would be churlish to deny the new illumination and a breath of fresh air and exotic fragrance offered by modern Ṛgveda philology and foolish to ignore its future possibilities. The modern approach, it is true, brings with it, as it is based on, presuppositions characteristic of the present age (which has its own virtue); it comes to the subject from outside and often treats the Veda as an 'object' and not a living reality; it is more concerned with the historical antecedents of the text than with what it has meant to the people whose faith it has nourished and what it may yet come to mean in the future. Nevertheless, from the point of view of the Vedic faith itself, no light must be spurned, however slanting the angle from which it comes and whatever the nature of the medium through which it is refracted at different times. Within the Indian tradition, the Ṛgveda has functioned as a founding origin and source, and therefore most of the religious literature subsequent to it is in the nature of 'a series of foot-notes' to it, if not a massive commentary on it – not only the Brāhmaṇa and Upaniṣadic literature but also the Epic and Purāṇic, and the philosophical streams flowing from there. In addition, there is the very extensive exegetical tradition of the six Vedāṅgas, specially the *Nirukta* tradition, existing since long before Yāska in the fourth century B.C. and summed up, among others, by Sāyaṇa's entire work eighteen centuries later. Thirdly, there is the Indian Neo-Vedic movement, inaugurated by Dayānanda Saraswatī, carried forward by Śrī Aurobindo and others and elevated to near-completion in the great unfinished work of Anirvan – in Sanskrit, English and Bengali respectively – not to mention the massive editorial and translation activity in various Indian vernaculars during the present century. Western Veda-philologists and Indologists are mostly suspicious and critical, often ignorant, of this whole modern 'Indian' approach and therefore tend to ignore it completely, perhaps too derisively – rightly, perhaps, in order to preserve the purity of their own specific 'scientific' academic tradition. Their purpose is not to discover how the Veda has been historically operative in the life of a people or has been understood within a living tradition, but to find out what it 'really' means, in itself; and they do not pause to ask what that 'really' means. The Western scholar seeks to *understand*, without being religiously involved, material which to him is alien to begin with, he comes to it with prepossessions which are extraneous to it; the Indian *lives* within a cumulative tradition of which the roots are in the Veda and seeks, from the end-point at which he stands, to go back to the Veda and re-experience it in terms of all that has emerged from it in a time of present need. Does he import into it meanings which appeared in a later age, read into this Ur-text retrospectively, or does it really contain those meanings in germ? Would it be right for him to try to get out of this 'circle of understanding'? For him, the Veda is Mother, a

49

deity, and what *he* seeks, if he is modern and not untouched by a sense of historical distance and the variety of alienation characteristic of modernity and its acids, is both to understand this text *and* to experience an epiphany. He must live, truthfully, suffering in full awareness the 'darkness of these times' and with hope in the coming dawn, and assist in its emergence by the only act of worship that is appropriate to the goddess *Vac* (Word, Logos): a prior dedication to the *Śabda-Brahman* (Reality as Word) that the Veda is, to which no word, of whatever provenance, can be alien.

Recent philosophical thought has taught us to see how historical objectification of the past subverts our living relationship to that past and also how a tradition is historically constituted by appropriation of the past through repeated acts of non-objectifying understanding from the perspective of changing present, through 'repetition' (*Wiederholung*). And it is becoming more and more apparent how very much this whole process is like interpreting a text, commenting on it, translating it, re-working it, or taking it apart, fragmenting it, and putting it together again in novel guise. Now, the Ṛgveda is a text, consisting of 'formulations' painstakingly composed by a number of seer-poets at different times and artfully put together to form a rounded whole. It is a sacred text, revealed in the sense that these 'formulations' are a gift of the gods (*devattam brahma*) to the Rishis who 'saw' them, and therefore regarded as not man-made, with its source in the 'highest region' of transcendent truth and speech. Yet it is not a Book or Scripture; like all 'knowledge', its paradigmatic mode of being is to exist in the minds of men (where *esse* and *legere* are at one) and to be recited and chanted by them. The textuality of this text, hence, cannot be understood in terms or categories proper to 'the religions of the Book' but must rather be treated as *sui generis*. It calls, to begin with, for a thorough elimination of Western religious and theological conceptuality from any attempt to understand this text, as well as from the entire tradition rooted in this pre-text. Was Schopenhauer perhaps right when he described Rammohun Roy as a 'Brahmin turned Jew?'[13] Also, appreciation of Vedic 'mythology' requires that we do not allow the Greek passion for the 'eidos' and their conception of the gods and mode of telling their tales about them to obtrude here, and that we do not 'psychologize' the gods, following the all-embracing subjectivism, since Descartes, characteristic of the modern age.

The question, then, is: what kind of text is the Rgveda? More importantly and fully: What may this text be for me, a Brāhmin, by virtue of my initiation *into* this text, and into life *through* this text; what may it mean to me now, at this point of time in world-history when, for the first time in Brāhmin history, the ancient Light seems to have slipped into a total eclipse? For, as W. C. Smith very rightly insists, 'religious *truth* is a function of a personal life lived in that context,' in the present case, in the context of that text. One may then go on to ask what the truth is that this text reveals, that it hints at, alludes to and states in its poetic utterance, of which the saying is itself part of a doing (*sacer + facere*);[14] what 'truth' itself, an *Ur-Wort* of *homo sapiens*, might mean – apart from its opposites, untruth and lie, illusion and deceit, covering up and closure, unfaith and desecration – and whether that which dispenses and makes possible all meanings can itself be defined. For the Veda, it is the movement, from the human perspective, away from untruth, from darkness into light, from mortality to Immortality. Is it then not the task of the future, to which the Veda directs the 'twice-born' and the Western specialist alike, to think the Holy and the True in their intrinsic, indivisible unity and, learning from the thinking of a Martin Heidegger,[15] seek to experience that integral plenitude, in that highest abode of Viṣṇu and seat of *ṛta*, reaching down towards the mortal in a thousand irridescent light-rays drawing him into its healing, liberating dance?

Such, in rhapsodic argument and dense brevity, is the root and such the soil from which it gathers up the sap that sustains Hindu religiousness.

NOTES

1. The idea is central to much of Heidegger's thinking. Harold Bloom's *A Map of Misreading* (New York, 1975) is a widely read charting of the process by a literary theorist.
2. This is Paul Thieme's rendering. See his brilliant article 'Bráhman' in ZDMG, 102 (1952), pp. 91–129.

3. References to Louis Renou in this article are from his *Religions of Ancient India* (New York, 1968) and *The Destiny of the Veda in India* (Delhi, 1965).
4. Walter Kaufmann, *Religions in Four Dimensions* (New York, 1976), p. 29.
5. The references here, almost word by word, are to corresponding ideas in the Ṛgveda and in particular to the 'exploits' of the so-called warrior hero Indra.
6. This again gathers together, in literal translation, thoughts scattered in the Ṛgveda.
7. Actually, it was Max Müller himself who gave himself this title. See Nirad C. Chaudhury, *Scholar Extraordinary* (New York, 1974), p. 140. All quotations from Max Müller in this article are from *The Life and Letters of the Right Honourable Friedrich Max Müller*, 2 volumes, edited by his wife Georgiana (London, 1902) and from *Biographical Essays* (London, 1884).
8. See, apart from the discussion of 'history' running through all of Heidegger's writings, two recent books by professional historians: Hayden White, *Metahistory* (Baltimore, 1973) and Peter Munz, *The Shapes of Time* (Wesleyan University Press, 1977).
9. On this matter Diana Eck of Harvard has been writing perceptively of late. See her *Banaras: City of Light* (New York, 1982), a title which does ring a Vedic bell!
10. *Sacred Books of the East*, XXII (Delhi, 1979), pp. ix and xi.
11. *Varuṇa* I (Göttingen, 1951), p. 2, note. Volume II of this work was published in 1959. The editor of this posthumously published work, Ludwig Alsdorf, did this very hard labour of love because, as he said in his foreword to volume II, 'es schien aber von höchster Bedeutung, ein Werk von so grundlegender Wichtigkeit nicht nur Kreise der Indologen oder gar Vedisten, sondern auch dem weiteren der Religionswissenschaftler und Vertreter von Nachbardisziplinen zugänglich zu machen.' He also drew attention to the 'noch nie eingehend untersuchten Zentralbegriff der vedischen Religion, das Ṛta.' Neither the book nor its central thesis has found, regrettably, any echo among scholars of religion. As regards the meaning of 'Ṛta.', Paul Thieme wrote, in the article referred to at note 2 above (p. 110, note 2), 'Dass ṛta die Wahrheit und nichts als die Wahrheit bezeichnet, muss nach der Erörterungen von Lüders, *Varuṇa I*, 13 ff. endgültig sicher stehen.' Thieme's Review of Lüders' work in ZDMG 101 (1951) and 113 (1963) should be most helpful to the interested reader.
12. Here again, even a student of religion, and in the present context he

especially, may learn from Heidegger's life-long wrestling with the words 'truth' and '*aletheia*,' 'reason' and '*logos*'.

13. See Wilhelm Halbfass' splendid study, *Indien und Europa. Perspektiven ihrer geistigen Begegnung* (Basel/Stuttgart, 1981), pp. 225 and 290, note 12. The author's remark is worth quoting in full: 'andererseits ist Rammohan nich nur von orthodox-hinduistischer, sondern auch von westlicher Seite der Kompromissbereitschaft gegenüber den Christentum beschuldigt worden. Besonders scharf geht Schopenhauer mit ihm ins Gericht. Er bezeichnet ihn als 'Brahmin turned Jew' und beschuldigt ihn, die Upanishads in theistisch-biblischem Sinne verfälscht zu haben.'

14. As Paul Thieme has pointed out (*Gedichte aus dem Rig-Veda*, p. 5. Stuttgart, 1977), Vedic poetry is 'Zweck-Dichtung', in the sense that it was not simply the expression of a vision or of an experience, emotion recollected in tranquillity, and addressed to a potential 'reader', but rather a chant of prayer, invitation and offering; a manifestation of the fire within man and a flame with its tip reaching out to the farthest region above, and meant to accompany the sacrificial rite as a part of it. The sacrifice itself was not so much a symbol of something else as a *rite* of transformation – of the earth-bound mortal into a pure flame, a tongue of fire rising to the region of 'the great Truth' and Soma reservoir – and a hierophany in which the lived 'friendship' between gods and men was confirmed and renewed.

15. My apology for mentioning this thinker here is as follows. Religious thought (including understanding/interpretation of another tradition) involves employment of the most general 'philosophical' notions of God, man, world, thought, reason, language, being, truth and time. If one thinks and talks in a Western language, one inevitably brings to bear the Greek-Christian conceptuality, with which these terms are loaded, upon an alien mode of living and thinking, particularly in the religious context. Almost always this is done naively, unhistorically, dogmatically. One then fails to see the 'other' as he sees himself, and even when one undertakes to study specifically how the other sees himself, one still operates with those same concepts, continuing to take them for granted as self-evident. This kind of philosophical naivety can only be overcome through *philosophical* questioning, not just of single concepts but of the entire complex of metaphysical ideas in its historical becoming, leading to an awareness of the specificity and particularity, the uniqueness, of Western metaphysical thought. The only philosopher who has done this, for the first time in the history of Western thought, is Martin Heidegger, who by no means 'rejects' this philosophical and religious

tradition. Not surprisingly, there is wide-spread 'resistance' to his thinking, showing all the marks of a patient undergoing psychoanalytic treatment. The passion that drove him on in his long 'path of thinking' was to see the dimensions of truth and sacredness in their original unity, best expressed in the following lapidary statement, 'Erst aus der Wahrheit des Seins lässt sich das Wesen des Heiligen denken. Erst aus dem Wesen des Heiligen ist das Wesen von Gottheit zu denken. Erst im Lichte des Wesens von Gottheit kann gedacht und gesagt werden, was das Wort 'Gott' nennen soll.' (*Wegmarken*, 181 f.)

2

THE CONFUCIAN TRADITION:
A CONFUCIAN PERSPECTIVE ON LEARNING
TO BE HUMAN

Tu Wei-ming

In the modern pluralistic cultural context, the Confucian 'faith' in the intrinsic meaningfulness of humanity[1] may appear to be finite, historical, secular and culturally specific. However, to the living Confucian, this faith is an articulation of truth, an expression of reality and, indeed, a view of life so commonly accepted in East Asia for centuries and so obviously rational that it is singularly self-evident. In this essay, I intend to demonstrate, based upon my own understanding of the Confucian project, that this humanistic claim about faith is of profound significance to the study of religion as an evolving and developing discipline which may, in the long run, establish a unity of understanding and appreciation of ultimate concerns despite the seductiveness of sophisticated relativism currently espoused by some of our most brilliant and open-minded colleagues in the social sciences and the humanities.

I. LEARNING FOR THE SAKE OF THE SELF

The Confucian approach to perennial human questions has generally been considered finite, if not miserably parochial. This is partly because Confucius, in response to the queries of his students, refused to speculate on death and spirits on the ground that our understanding of life and human beings should be of primary importance.[2] The Confucian focus on the person living here and now as the point of departure is, however, predicated on a broadly conceived notion of life and human beings in which death and spirits feature prominently as its constitutive elements.

55

In other words, genuinely to appreciate the Confucian perception of the living person necessarily involves attendant knowledge of and sensitivity to death and spirits. The significance of this will be discussed further but it is important to note here that the naive positivistic assertion that Confucius was unmindful of those profound human concerns because he did not overtly answer questions about death and spirits is not only inadequate but misleading. In fact, it is difficult to imagine what shape the Confucian tradition would have assumed had the mourning rituals and the ancestral cult been left out.

Yet, despite the outsider's view that the traditional Confucians were under their ancestors' shadow,[3] the Confucian commitment to the human community is firm and comprehensive. This commitment may mean instrumentally that the person living here and now is where the whole Confucian enterprise begins. It may also mean substantively that the person in ordinary daily existence is the basis for the full realization of humanity. The Confucian insistence that learning is for the sake of the self,[4] an end in itself rather than a means to an end, speaks directly to this. Learning, for the Confucian, is to learn to be human. We are, to be sure, inescapably human. In a naturalistic sense it is our birthright to be so but being human in its aesthetic, moral or religious sense necessitates a process of learning. Learning to be human then means to become aesthetically refined, morally excellent and religiously profound. I am critically aware that the terms and categories I have just used are not Confucian although they can be shown to be compatible with the original Confucian insight. Perhaps, it is simply a matter of emphasis, but the primary Confucian concern of learning is character formation defined in ethical terms.

If the primary Confucian concern is to learn to become a good person, what does this entail? It is vitally important to know, from the outset, that learning to become a good person in the Confucian context is not only the primary concern but also the ultimate and comprehensive concern. Therefore, it does not make much sense to compare and contrast the idea of the good person with that of the wise, strong, sensitive, intelligent or creative person. To the Confucians, the good person is necessarily wise, strong, sensitive, intelligent, creative and more. If we prefer to use the word 'good' to designate a quality that can be distinguished from other desirable qualities such as wise and creative, we may have to redefine the primary Confucian concern in more neutral terms such as to learn to become more authentically or more fully human. With due respect to the interpretative consensus among Sinologists that Confucianism is a form of social ethics, the word 'authenticity' even with its modern existential implications seems to me more appropriate than narrowly conceived moralistic terms such as 'honesty' and 'loyalty' to convey the original Confucian sense of learning for the sake of the self.

To learn to become an authentic person in the Confucian sense is certainly to be honest with oneself and loyal to others, but it also entails a ceaseless process through which humanity in its all embracing fullness is concretely realized. This dimension of Confucian learning is not reducible to any particular virtue; nor is it an aggregate of those that are distinctively Confucian. Yet, the living person here and now as a point of departure inevitably imposes constraints on the Confucian intention to universalize its project: How can a Confucian assume that learning to be human, a process which varies according to country, history, culture, social class and a host of other factors, is a universally valid conception? Traditional Confucians were of course not aware of the significance of this question. They believed that the idea was sound; they put it into practice; they demonstrated its validity through exemplary teaching; they embodied it; indeed, they lived it.

II. UNDERSTANDING THROUGH INQUIRY

The living Confucian in the twentieth century, with heightened critical self-awareness partly as a response to the challenge of pluralistic relativism, cannot take for granted that the Confucian message is self-evidently true. The idea of learning for the sake of the self may have been a reflection of the perceived privilege of the cultural élite in the latter half of the Spring and Autumn period (722-481 B.C.). It may have been an integral part of the ideology of the newly emerging feudal bureaucracy (or the declining slave-owning aristocracy) designed to monopolize the channel of upward social mobility. It may also have been a manifestation of the peculiar Sinic predilection for moral education at the expense of scientific knowledge and institution building.[5] It is difficult, after all, to determine whether the Confucian idea of humanity was really inclusive in a sense comparable to the idea of 'all men are created equal' or whether it signified a rather exclusivistic 'we Chinese' or even 'we the educated classical scholars in the state of Lu.'

Furthermore, the living Confucian is also aware that the idea of learning for the sake of the self could not have meant a quest for one's individuality. Even in the West, individualism as a positive doctrine is a relatively recent phenomenon.[6] Self, in the classical Confucian sense, referred to a center of relationships, a communal quality which was never conceived of as an isolated or isolatable entity. Since the social basis, the cultural background and the ethicoreligious context in which the Confucian idea of learning for the sake of the self emerged were all so radically different from what we experience in the modern West as 'learning' and as 'self', how can we retrieve its meaning without distorting its original intent to make it relevant to us here and now?

The task of trying to understand what Confucius meant when he said that true learning was for the sake of the self requires painstaking archaeological digging. Many disciplines – etymology, textual analysis, exegesis and commentary, just to mention a few of the traditional Sinological tools, will have to be brought to bear on the process. If we extend our task to include an appreciation of the traditional Confucian understanding of the Master's statement over the centuries, other disciplines such as cultural history, comparative religion, hermeneutics and philosophy will also be required. Even then, we can never be sure that we have got it right, for the gap between the two radically different epistemic eras, to use a fashionable expression, may forever remain wide and open. However, the responsibility of the scholarly community is precisely to struggle against overwhelming odds in order to reach an understanding, no matter how partial and how imperfect that understanding turns out to be. For the Confucian, such an intellectual endeavour is not only desirable but necessary for spiritual self-definition.

The matter, however, is complicated by the fact that what is at stake goes beyond the need of the scholarly community to extend its intellectual horizons and the desire of the Confucian to search for his or her meaning in life. The challenge all members of the scholarly community who are actively involved in comparative studies must face is whether or not, in principle, we can really understand such a deceptively simple Confucian statement, 'learning is for the sake of the self,' out of context. The answer, unfortunately, must be in the negative. We cannot know what it means, if we do not situate it in its proper context: Why was the statement made? What did it want to affirm? Was it a response to a different kind of learning prevalent at the time? How central is it to the Confucian mode of thinking? Is it a code for something much more elaborate and significant? Surely there is no guarantee that we can fully appreciate what Confucius meant to convey by that even after we have found satisfactory answers to the questions mentioned above; for there will be numerous other questions that demand our attention, if we are serious about our inquiry.

These issues are also relevant to the Confucian living today. The sort of difficulty that scholars encounter in moving from one linguistic universe to the other pertains to modern Confucians as well. The age of certainty in which the educated person in China would be expected to know what it means to be a Confucian is forever gone. In today's pluralistic world, the Confucian, like his or her counterpart in the Buddhist, Jewish, Christian, Islamic or Hindu community, must learn to live an ethicoreligious life as a deliberate choice. However, unlike those in other faith communities, all Confucians must also try to apprehend the meanings of the statements in the classical texts with the same kind of conscientiousness critical scholars of Confucian learning display. This is partly due to the absence of a functional equivalent of priesthood in the Confucian tradition but the lack of tangible religious institutions that are responsible for the standardization and transmission of Confucian precepts is perhaps a more significant factor. It is therefore interesting to note that the Chinese term for Confucian, *ju*, generically means 'scholar'.[7]

It may not be farfetched to suggest that the modern approximation of the traditional Chinese idea of *ju* is the scholar in the humanities. However, in the highly professionalized academic setting, a scholar in the humanities captures only an aspect of what *ju* purports to stand for. The contemporary use of the term 'intellectual', especially in the sense of one who is engaged in and concerned with the wellbeing of humanity, comes close to the idea of *ju*. In fact, this communal dimension of Confucianism is pre-eminently a social philosophy.[8] Understandably, Confucian learning is often characterized as altruistic, for its primary purpose is thought to be for the sake of others.

III. CENTRALITY OF SELF-CULTIVATION

The prevalent view that Confucianism is a form of social ethics which particularly emphasizes human-relatedness is basically correct, but it fails to account for the centrality of self-cultivation as an independent, autonomous and inner-directed process in the Confucian tradition. Surely, Confucians maintain that one becomes fully human through continuous interaction with other human beings and that one's dignity as a person depends as much on communal participation as on one's own sense of self-respect. But the Weberian characterization of the Confucian spiritual orientation as 'adjustment to the world'[9] because of its alleged teaching of submission to established patterns of human relationships seriously undermines the Confucian ability for psychological integration and religious transcendence. In fact, the strength of the Confucian tradition to undergo profound transformation without losing its spiritual identity lies in its commitment to the inner resources of humanity.

The self as a center of relationships has always been the focus of Confucian learning. One's ability to harmonize human relations certainly indicates one's self-cultivation, but the priority is clearly set. Self-cultivation is a precondition for harmonizing human relations; if human relations are superficially harmonized without the necessary ingredients of self-cultivation, it is practically unworkable and teleologically misdirected. The common Chinese expression that the friendship of the belittled people is as sweet as honey and the friendship of the profound persons is as plain as water suggests that the relationship dictated by need is far inferior to the disinterested fellowship dedicated to moral growth. One enters into communication with other human beings for a variety of reasons, many of which are, to some modern sociologists, morally neutral and thus irrelevant to the inner lives of the persons involved. Confucians recognize that human beings are social beings but they maintain that all forms of social interaction are laden with moral implications and that self-cultivation is required to harmonize each one of them.

The heuristic value of learning for the sake of the self can perhaps be understood as an injunction for self-cultivation. Since self-cultivation is an end rather than a means, learning motivated by reasons other than self-knowledge, such as fame, position and wealth is no longer qualified as true learning. The archer who when failing to hit the mark turns around introspectively to rectify the mistake from within enacts the Confucian concern that to know oneself internally is the precondition for doing things right in the external world.

If human relations are harmonized, it is because the people involved have cultivated themselves. To anticipate a harmonious state of affairs in one's social interaction as a favorable condition for self-cultivation is, in the Confucian sense, not only unrealistic but illogical. Self-cultivation is like the root and trunk and harmonious human relations are like the branches. The priority in terms of both temporal sequence and order of importance is irreversible.[10] Strictly speaking, learning for the sake of others as a demonstration of altruism cannot be truly altruistic, unless it is built on the foundation of self-knowledge. The Confucian Golden Rule, 'Do not do unto others what you would not want others to do unto you'[11] does not simply mean that one should be considerate to others; it also means being honest with oneself. This is the reason, I suppose, that Confucius felt that some of his best disciples still had a great deal to learn in order to put the Golden Rule into practice.

What is the status of the Confucian Golden Rule in self-cultivation if it cannot be uniformly applied? It is certainly not a categorical imperative in the Kantian sense; nor is it a guiding principle for action to which one is enjoined to conform. Rather, it is a standard of inspiration and an experienced ideal made meaningful to the students through the exemplary teaching of the master. Self-cultivation may mean different things to different people at different stages of moral development, and its realization may also assume many different forms. Yet, self-cultivation remains the locus of Confucian learning. Learning to be human, as a result, centers on the self, not the self as an abstract idea but the self as the person living here and now.

IV.   FROM A PERSONAL POINT OF VIEW

One of the most intriguing insights of Confucian learning is that learning to be human entails learning for the sake of the self and that the self so conceived is not the generic self but I myself as an experiencing and reflecting person here and now. To turn the mode of questioning from the impersonal self to the personal I requires intellectual sophistication as well as existential commitment. The safe distance between what I as a person speculate in propositional language and what I speak as a concrete human being is no longer there. I am exposed, for what I think I know is now inevitably intertwined with what I do know. If I am wrong, it is not simply because what I have proposed is untenable but also due to a defect in the way I live. However, the psychoanalytical procedure of allowing my deep-rooted private self to be scrutinized by another intelligence is not part of the Confucian tradition. Confucian self-cultivation presupposes that the self worth cultivating is never the private possession of a single individual but a sharable experience that underlies common humanity.

It is not at all surprising then that despite the centrality of self-cultivation in Confucian learning, autobiographic literature exhibiting secret thoughts, private feelings and innermost desires and drives is extremely rare in the Confucian tradition. Obviously, the cultivated self is not private property that we carefully guard against being trespassed by outside intruders. The ego that has to be protected from being submerged in the waves of social demand is what the Confucians refer to as *ssu* (the privatized self, the small self, the self that is a closed system). The true self, on the contrary, is public-spirited and the great self is the self that is an open system. As an open system, the self in the genuine sense of the word is expansive and always receptive to the world at large. Self-cultivation can very well be understood as the broadening of the self to embody an ever-expanding circle of human-relatedness. However, it would be misleading to conclude that the Confucian self only broadens horizontally to establish meaningful social relations. The concentric circles that define the self in terms of family, community, country and the world are undoubtedly social groups, but, in the Confucian perspective, they are also realms of selfhood that symbolize the authentic human possibility for ethicoreligious growth.

Ethicoreligious growth, for the Confucian, is not only a broadening process but also a deepening process. As I myself resonate with other selves, the internal resources inherent in me are multiplied. I acquire an appreciation of myself through genuine communication with the other; as I know more of myself, I apprehend more of the other. The Confucian dictum, 'in order to establish myself, I establish others; in order to enlarge myself, I enlarge others,'[12] is therefore not only an altruistic idea but also a description of the self in transformation. The quest for inner spirituality as a lonely struggle belongs to a radically different rhetorical situation. Confucian self-cultivation is a deliberate communal act. Nevertheless, the self is not reducible to its social roles. The dramatic image of the modern person who assumes a variety of social roles is definitely unConfucian. The idea of my solely assuming the role of a son in reference to my father and simultaneously assuming the role of the father in reference to my son is unnatural, if not distasteful. From my own experience, as far as I can remember, I have always been learning to be a son. Since my son's birth, I have also been learning to be a father and my learning to be a son has taken on new significance as a result of becoming a father myself. Furthermore, my being a son and a father is also informed and enriched by being a student, a teacher, a husband, a colleague, a friend and an acquaintance. These are ways for me to learn to be human.

Normally we do not talk about these matters in public. They are too personal. We should not reveal too much of our private feelings; they are not intellectually interesting. Yet, at the same time, we are obsessed with what we think, feel and want. We often doggedly assert our opinions, nakedly express our emotions and unabashedly demand our wants. We take rights seriously but we have to be persuaded by authority or law to accept our duties. We humans of the post-industrial societies are estranged from our own traditions and alienated from our own cultures. As we become increasingly subjectivistic, individualistic and narcissistic, we can neither remember the old nor instruct the young. We are politically isolated and spiritually alone. Yet, in our scholarly endeavors we assume that we have to take an impersonal stance in order to reason objectively in the abstract.

V. CONFUCIUS AS AN EXEMPLAR

Confucius was willing to speak as a human being. He opted for an intensely personal style of communication. And, by conscious choice, he shared his thoughts and feelings with those around him: 'My friends, do you think I am secretive? There is nothing which I hide from you. There is nothing I do which I do not share with you, my friends. There is Ch'iu for you.'[13] The openness with which Confucius interacted with his students was not a pedagogical design but a reflection of his attitude toward life. We may suspect that he could afford to reveal himself thoroughly because he spoke from the lofty position of an accomplished sage. The truth of the matter, however, is quite different. Confucius never believed that he had attained sagehood. He was, like us, struggling to learn to be human. His self-image was that of a fellow traveller, committed to the task of realizing humanity, on the way to becoming fully human. As he continued to refine himself in living the life of a *ju*, he frankly confessed that he failed to learn to do the ordinary things that like-minded human beings ought to do:

> There are four things in the Way of the profound person, none of which I have been able to do. To serve my father as I would expect my son to serve me: that I have not been able to do. To serve my ruler as I would expect my ministers to serve me: that I have not been able to do. To serve my elder brother as I would expect my younger brothers to serve me: that I have not been able to do. To be the first to treat friends as I would expect them to treat me: that I have not been able to do.[14]

Confucius' humbleness is also shown in his clear perception of what he could do:

> There are presumably men who innovate without possessing knowledge, but that is not a fault I have. I use my ears widely and follow what is good in what I have heard; I use my eyes widely and retain what I have seen in my mind. This constitutes a lower level knowledge.[15]

By assigning himself to the 'lower level knowledge'; Confucius removed himself from 'the best who are born with knowledge' and allied himself with 'those who get to know through learning.'[16] As a learner, Confucius took himself absolutely seriously as a concrete living person in transformation. He approached his task as a witness of common humanity with sincerity and critical self-awareness:

> In practicing the ordinary virtues and in the exercise of care in ordinary conversation, when there is deficiency, the profound person never fails to make further effort, and when there is excess, never dares to go to the limit. His words correspond to his actions and his actions correspond to his words.[17]

As a seer and an audient, Confucius used his sensory perception wisely to reach a standard of moral excellence in which modesty as a virtue is taken for granted and the vital importance of constantly reflecting on things near at hand is fully recognized. Confucius' genuineness as a person is a source of inspiration to those who share his humanist wisdom not because of its abstract idealism but because of its concrete practicality.

VI. ULTIMATE MEANING IN ORDINARY EXISTENCE

The Confucian project, as exemplified by the lived reality of the Master, is a personal approach to human learning. Its message, simply put, is to realize the ultimate meaning of life in ordinary human existence. What we normally do on a daily basis is precisely the arena in which humanity manifests its highest excellence. To initiate the whole process of learning to be human with the person living here and now is to underscore the centrality of self-cultivation at each juncture of one's moral growth. Implicit in this project is the injunction that we take full responsibility for our humanity. We do so not for any external reasons but because of the very fact that we are humans.

The living person, in the Confucian order of things, is far more complex and meaningful than a mere momentary existence. The idea of an isolated individual who eventually dies a lonely death in the secularized biophysiological sense is not even a rejected possibility in the Confucian perception of human reality. A human being is an active participant of an agelong biological line, a living witness of an historical continuum and a recipient of the finest essences in the cosmos. Inherent in the structure of the human is an infinite potential for growth and an inexhaustible supply of resources for development. Ontologically a person's selfhood embodies the highest transcendence within its own reality; no external help is needed for the self to be fully realized. The realization of the self, in the ultimate sense, is tantamount to the realization of the complete unity between humanity and Heaven. The way to attain this, however, is never perceived as the establishment of a relationship between an isolated individual and God. The self as a center of relationships in the human community must recognize that it is an integral part of a holistic presence and accordingly work its way through what is near at hand.

Mencius, in a suggestive passage, observes:

> All the ten thousand things are there in me. There is no greater joy for me than to find, on self-examination, that I am true to myself. Try your best to treat others as you wish to be treated yourself, and you will find that this is the shortest way to humanity.[18]

The ontological assertion that one's selfhood is totally sufficient does not lead to the existential complacency that self-realization involves no more than the quest for inner spirituality. On the contrary, while through self-cultivation, I, as a person, can take great delight in realizing that I have been in touch with my genuine humanness, I must endeavor to relate conscientiously to others as the most efficacious way of apprehending a commonly shared humanity. The implied soteriology, if we dare can employ such a loaded concept, is found in another Mencian statement:

> For a man to give full realization to his heart is for him to understand his own nature, and a man who knows his own nature will know Heaven. By retaining his heart and nurturing his nature he is serving Heaven. Whether he is going to die young or to live to a ripe old age makes no difference to his steadfastness of purpose. It is through awaiting whatever is to befall him with a perfected character that he stands firm on his proper destiny.[19]

Two terms in the quotation above, 'steadfastness of purpose' and 'proper destiny', deserve our special attention. First, however, a caveat must be noted: the Chinese text cannot be so neatly dissected as the English translation seems to permit in this analysis. Since our goal is a general discussion of the sort of soteriological intent implicit in the Mencian conception of the human condition, the nuanced linguistic features should not concern us here. Mencius fully recognizes the distinctness of the person in his ontological assertion that through knowing one's own nature, one can know Heaven. People are unique. Since there are no two identical faces, there are as many paths of self-realization as there are human beings. There are numerous factors, internal as well as external, that determine the shape of a unique person. Yet, 'steadfastness of purpose,' as Mencius would have it, is the direct and immediate result of a person's will power and is, therefore available to all members of the human community without reference to any differentiating factors. The example that Confucius used to illustrate a similar point is pertinent here: 'The Three Armies can be deprived of their commanding officer, but even a common man cannot be deprived of his purpose.'[20]

This 'steadfastness of purpose' is all that is needed for self-cultivation. All human beings are equal so far as this dimension of human reality is concerned. A severely handicapped person may exert a great deal of effort to coordinate his physical movements, but his will power is absolute, independent, autonomous and self-sufficient. We admire a Helen Keller not only for what she in fact manages to overcome but also for the steadfastness of purpose that makes her awe-inspiring performance possible in the first place. Actually there are numerous cases where self-improvement in the physical sense is an insurmountable task. Many people die before they can realize their potential for a chosen task. We are all, in this sense, fated to be unfulfilled. Confucius' best disciple, for example, died young and the Master lamented: 'There was one Yen Hui who was eager to learn ... Unfortunately his allotted span was a short one and he died. Now there is no one. No one eager to learn has come to my notice.'[21] Yet, one's steadfastness of purpose not only transcends the structural limitation of one's existence but also can transform it into an instrument of self-realization. The case of Yen Hui is particularly suggestive here. His poverty, premature death and lack of any tangible accomplishments by the perceived Confucian standards of public service did not at all deter the Master from praising, time and again, his eagerness to learn, namely his resolve to become a *ju*:

> How admirable Hui is! Living in a mean dwelling on a bowlful of rice and a ladleful of water is a hardship most men would find intolerable, but Hui does not allow this to affect his joy. How admirable Hui is.[22]

In the light of this, one's 'proper destiny' is inseparable from one's willingess and ability to take oneself to task inwardly. One's calling, as it were, is none other than the inner voice that enjoins one to become what one ought to be. This critical self-awareness, informed by one's openness to an ever-expanding circle of human-relatedness, is the authentic access to one's proper destiny. The reality of the human is such that the eagerness to learn in order to give full realization to one's heart, to know one's own nature and to appreciate the meaning of humanity is the surest way to apprehend Heaven. Since our nature is conferred by Heaven, it is our human responsibility to participate in the cosmic transformation so that we can form a trinity with Heaven and Earth.[23] Our proper destiny, personally and communally, is not circumscription. We are not circumscribed to be merely human. Rather, our proper destiny is an invitation, a charge to take care of ourselves and all the beings in the world that is our abode. We must learn to transcend what we existentially are so that we can become what we ontologically are destined to be. We need not depart from our selfhood and our humanity to become fully realized. Indeed, it is through a deepening and broadening awareness of ourselves as humans that we serve Heaven.

The underlying structure of this mode of thinking is analogically presented in a key passage in the Confucian classic, *Centrality and Commonality*, better known as the *Doctrine of the Mean*:

> The Way of Heaven and Earth is extensive, deep, high, brilliant, infinite, and lasting. The heaven now before us is only this bright, shining mass; but when viewed in its unlimited extent, the sun, moon, stars, and constellations are suspended in it and all things are covered by it. The earth before us is but a handful of soil; but in its breadth and depth, it sustains mountains like Hua and Yueh without feeling their weight, contains the rivers and seas without letting them leak away, and sustains all things. The mountain before us is only a fistful of straw; but in all the vastness of its size, grass and trees grow upon it, birds and beasts dwell on it, and stores of precious things (minerals) are discovered in it. The water before us is but a spoonful of liquid but in all its unfathomable depth, the monsters, dragons, fishes, and turtles are produced in them, and wealth becomes abundant because of it.[24]

By analogy, what we see in front of us is but the physical presence of a changing body. However, those who are absolutely sincere in the sense that they, through ceaseless learning to be human, have become witnesses of humanity as such, 'can order and adjust the great relations of mankind, establish the great foundations of humanity, and know the transforming and nourishing operations of heaven and earth.' The reality that the perfect sage symbolizes is not a superhuman reality but genuine human reality: 'all embracing and extensive, and deep and unceasingly springing, these virtues (wisdom, generosity, tenderness, firmness, refinement and so forth) come forth at all times. All embracing and extensive as heaven and deep and increasingly springing as an abyss.'[25]

The Confucian 'faith' in the intrinsic meaningfulness of humanity is a faith in the living person's authentic possibility for self-transcendence. The body, the mind, the soul and the spirit of the living person are all laden with profound ethicoreligious significance. Being religious, in the Confucian sense, is being engaged in ultimate self-transformation as a communal act. Salvation means the full realization of the anthropocosmic reality in our human nature.

NOTES

1. This essay intends to be a response to Wilfred Cantwell Smith's recent treatise on *Faith and Belief* (Princeton: Princeton University Press, 1979) from a Confucian point of view. I am deeply impressed by Smith's assertion: 'Thus it is faith, in a form appropriate to our day, that enables one to cope intellectually and personally with pluralistic relativism – with, for instance, truth as that to which all accounts of it approximate – so that acceptance of diversity enriches rather than undermines one's own apprehension of truth' (p. 170). Although I cannot claim to have understood the theological implications of his historical reflection, I find myself in sympathetic resonance with his thought-provoking observation: 'Truth is ultimately one, although the human forms of truth and the forms of faith decorate or bespatter our world diversely. Our unity is real transcendently; whether history will so move that we approximate it more closely actually in the construction on earth of a world community, not merely a world society already virtually with us, is a question of our ability to act in terms of transcending truth, and love.'

2. 'Chi-lu asked how the spirits of the dead and the gods should be served. The Master said, "You are not able even to serve man. How can you serve the spirits?" "May I ask about death?" "You do not understand even life. How can you understand death?" ' *Analects*, XI:12. All translations from the *Analects* are based on D. C. Lau, trans., *Confucius: The Analects* (Penguin Classics, 1979).

3. The expression is borrowed from Francis L. K. Hsu, *Under the Ancestors' Shadow; Kinship, Personality, and Social Mobility in China* (Stanford: Stanford University Press, 1971).

4. *Analects*, XIV:24.

5. Hou Wai-lu, et. al., eds., *Chung-kuo ssu-hsiang shih* (History of Chinese thought), 5 volumes (Peking: Jen-min Publishing Co.), I, pp. 131–90.

6. See Steven Lukes, *Individualism* (Oxford: Blackwell, 1973).

7. For a discussion of the meaning of *ju*, see Hu Shih, 'Shuo Ju' (On the concept of *ju*) in *Hu Shih wen-ts'un* (Preserved works of Hu Shih; Reprint, Taipei; Yuan-tung Publishing Co., 1953), IV, pp. 1–103.

8. See Étienne Balazs, 'La crise de la fin des Han,' in his *La Bureaucratie céleste; Recherches sur l'économie et la société de la Chine traditionnelle* (Paris: Gallimard, 1968), p. 180.

9. Max Weber, *The Religion of China*, trans., Hans H. Gerth (New York: The Free Press, 1964), p. 235. For a general assessment of Weber's interpretation of Confucianism, see Wolfgang Schluchter, ed., *Max Webers Studie über Konfuzianismus und Taoismus* (Frankfurt: Suhrkamp, 1983).

10. The *Great Learning* states in its main text: 'From the Son of Heaven down to the common people, all must regard cultivation of the personal life as the root or foundation.' See Wing-tsit Chan, trans. and comp., *A Source Book of Chinese Philosophy* (Princeton: Princeton University Press), p. 87.

11. *Analects*, XII:2; XV:24.

12. Ibid., VI:30.

13. Ibid., VII:24.

14. *The Doctrine of the Mean*, Ch. 13. See Wing-tsit Chan, p. 101. A statement comparable in spirit is found in the *Analects*, XIV:28.

15. *Analects*, VII:28.

16. Ibid., XVI:9.

17. *The Doctrine of the Mean*, Ch. 13; Wing-tsit Chan, p. 101.

18. *Mencius*, VIIA:4. See D. C. Lau, trans., *Mencius* (Penguin Classics, 1976), p. 182.

19. *Mencius*, VIIA:1; D. C. Lau, p. 182.

20. *Analects*, IX:26.

21. Ibid., VI:3.

22. Ibid., VI:11.

23. *The Doctrine of the Mean*, Ch. 22; Wing-tsit Chan, pp. 107–108.

24. *The Doctrine of the Mean*, Ch. 26; Wing-tsit Chan, p. 109.

25. *The Doctrine of the Mean*, Ch. 31; Wing-tsit Chan, p. 112.

3

THE JEWISH TRADITION

Louis Jacobs

An inquiry into the relationship between faith and tradition in Judaism must begin with the linguistic problem. The classical sources – the Bible and the Talmudic literature – know neither the Greek-inspired term 'Judaism' nor the term 'religion'. Zangwill put it neatly when he said: the Rabbis were the most religious of men but they had no word for religion. As for 'tradition', while this is roughly equivalent to *masorah* and *kabbalah*, words which are found in the sources, the modern connotation of the word is quite different. In contemporary language a religious tradition generally refers to the practices, forms and rituals of a religious community as the creation of that community in the past. When the community appeals to its tradition the appeal is to the past as a guide for the future. But *masorah* and *kabbalah* refer, respectively, to the handing over and the acceptance of a body of truth independent of the transmission. It is the truth that is said to be binding; those who handed it down and those who received it, to hand it down in turn, are merely the instruments for the conveyance of that truth. Take, for instance, the Biblical appeals to consider the past such as:

> Remember the days of old, consider the years of many generations, ask thy father and he will tell thee, thy elders and they will declare it. (Deuteronomy 32:7).

The father who tells the tale of God's mighty acts in history and the elders who declare these are to be heeded, it is implied, not because there is any virtue in listening to them *per se* but because they are the links in the chain reaching back to the original events. They are reliable witnesses, faithful transmitters and no more than that. Or take the opening section of 'Ethics of the Fathers' (another modern name, for what, in the original, is simply *Avot*, 'Fathers', meaning the teachings of the fathers of the community, the sages). This tractate, *Avot*, records the particular sayings or maxims of the Jewish sages down to the end of the second century and as such constitutes a chain of tradition. But it is noteworthy that the opening passage reads:

> 'Moses received (*kibbel*) a Torah at Sinai and he handed it down (*mesarah*) to Joshua and Joshua to the Elders and the Elders to the Prophets. And the Prophets handed it down to the Men of the Great Assembly'.

The picture is of a body of truth handed down intact from generation to generation, though each generation added something of its own in elaboration of the truth. It is beside the point that, from the historical point of view, the notion of a static truth, uninfluenced by external conditions and communicated in such a neat order, is untenable. The fact remains that this is how tradition is thought of in the sources.

The word for 'faith' – *emunah* – never means, in the early sources, 'belief *that* . . .' but always 'belief *in* . . .'. Naturally, belief in God implies that God exists. Theoretical atheism was, in any event, virtually unknown in Biblical and Rabbinic times. But the explicit meaning of *emunah* is trust in God, confidence in His power to help, acknowledgement of His concern with justice and righteousness. Anselm's famous ontological argument begins with the 'fool' of Psalm 14 who 'hath said there is no God', which Anselm understands as a denial of God's existence. The whole tenor of the Psalm, however, shows that this cannot be correct. The Psalmist continues:

> They are corrupt, they have done abominable works, there is none that doeth good. The Lord looked down from heaven upon the children of men, to see if there were any that did understand, and seek God.

The *naval* of the Psalm is, in reality, not 'foolish' but ethically insensitive. His obtuseness is moral not intellectual. Of the people at the crossing of the Sea it is said (Exodus 14:31):

> And Israel saw that great work which the Lord did upon the
> Egyptians; and the people feared the Lord, and believed in
> the Lord and in Moses His servant.

The people believed in the Lord in the same way in which they
believed in Moses. They had not previously doubted whether
Moses existed. It was their faith and trust in him that had wavered.
Now that they had been delivered they saw that God was reliable
and Moses His true servant. We need only quote one Rabbinic
passage among many to make the point so far as the Talmudic
literature is concerned: 'Rabbi Eliezer the Great said: "Whoever
has bread in his basket and yet says: 'What shall I eat tomorrow' is
of those of little faith" ' (*ketaney emunah*).[1]

Apart from the linguistic difficulties, any attempt to treat
systematically a question of this nature from the Jewish sources is
to impose upon these sources a meaning they simply do not
possess. It is in the nature of neither Biblical nor Rabbinic texts to
explore this, or, for that matter, any other idea in a systematic
way. The very idea of an 'idea' is foreign to Biblical and Rabbinic
modes of thought. These, in the words of Isaac Heinemann and
Max Kadushin, are 'organic'.[2] They grow out of the experiences of
prophets, sages and teachers and are rather like popular proverbs
in which one response is required in one situation, a different
response in another. 'Too many cooks spoil the broth'. 'Many
hands make light work'. Both are true, depending on the
circumstances. This means, in effect, that, until the middle ages,
when the Jewish thinkers were influenced by Greek philosophy in
its Arabic garb, there was no such thing as Jewish theology. The
conclusion to be drawn, however, is not, as Moses Mendelssohn
would seem to have had it in the eighteenth century, that Judaism
has no dogmas. It must have beliefs for it to have an identity. But it
is a valid contention that beliefs of the 'belief *that* . . .' variety are
never too closely defined and that their acceptance (or rejection) is
less cognitive than moral and religious, less due to thought
processes than to personal choice, less the result of reflection than
of response, less because they have been worked out in reason
than because they 'ring a bell'.

To be sure the great mediaeval thinkers were systematic in their
approach. But since they accepted the Bible and the Talmudic

literature as sacred and binding, they were reduced to the attempt, one that could hardly succeed, of incorporating into their system material that, by its nature, defies systematization. The price they paid was to be meta-historical, not to say, unhistorical. They saw no incongruity in reading Greek ideas into the ancient texts, as when Maimonides finds his golden mean in Rabbinic teachings[3] and when he identifies,[4] to the scandal of the traditionalists, the Rabbinic 'Work of Creation' and 'Work of the Chariot' (in the context mystical speculations and reflections on God bringing the world into being and God's providence as seen in Ezekiel's vision of the Chariot) with, respectively, Aristotelian physics and metaphysics.

An instructive illustration of the varying attitudes is provided by the treatment of what amounts to the basic Jewish dogma, the revelation of the Torah. The Mishnah[5] lists among those who have no share in the World to Come one who declares (*ha-omer*, not 'one who does not believe *that*', a form impossible for the Rabbis, as noted above): 'There is no Torah from Heaven'. This statement is elaborated on in an early source mentioned in the Talmud:[6] '*Because he hath despised the word of the Lord* (Numbers 15:31) – this refers to one who declares that the whole of the Torah is from Heaven, with the exception of a single verse which (he maintains) was not said by the Holy One, blessed be He, but by Moses of his own accord, the verse: *Because he hath despised the word of the Lord* still applies to him. And even if he declares that the whole of the Torah is from Heaven, with the exception of a single inference, a single argument from the minor to the major, or a single derivation by means of similar expression (*gezerah shavah*), the verse: *Because he hath despised the word of the Lord* still applies to him'.

The statement about the argument from the minor to the major has puzzled the commentators since it is everywhere acknowledged that this hermeneutical principle is based solely on human reasoning and may be rejected, as happens frequently in the Talmud, by those who advance counter-arguments for its refutation. But anyone familiar with the nature of Talmudic literature will appreciate that what we have here is Rabbinic hyperbole; as if to say, the Torah is a revelation from God and there must be no compromise with this doctrine, not even with the process of inference from the Torah by human reasoning since this is how God wishes His Torah to be interpreted. The one who declares that Moses made up any part of the Torah despises *the word of the Lord*, i.e. he denigrates God's word by declaring it to be the mere human word of Moses. It is the divine character of the Torah that the Rabbis are eager to affirm, that, as it would be expressed today, Judaism is a revealed religion. The Rabbis were certainly not concerned with the question of the Mosaic authorship of the Pentateuch. That was no problem in their day. Even the heretics believed that Moses wrote the Pentateuch, only they declared that some of it was not given by God at all but was made up by Moses out of his own head.

Another passage in the Talmud[7] of similar import tells of the wicked king Manasseh who 'sat and expounded false homilies' (*haggadot shel dofi*). Manasseh said: Had Moses nothing better to do than to record *And Timna was concubine to Eliphaz* (Genesis 16:12)? Krochmal[8] and other modern students of the Talmudic literature have taught us to see that when the Rabbis put words into the mouths of the Biblical characters, especially when, as here, the vocabulary is that of Rabbinic institutions ('sat and expounded false homilies'), they were, in effect, addressing themselves to the faults and offences, as they saw them, of their own times. In all probability there were sceptics in Rabbinic times who refused to believe that God was responsible for every single verse in the Torah, even for verses which seemed quite pointless or which imparted information no one wished to have. There is nothing here at all like a precise theological statement about the content of the divine revelation. It is rather a homiletical device for the purpose of strengthening belief in the sanctity of the whole of the Torah, a free response on the part of the Rabbis to the challenges of their day. The Rabbis are here sermonising. They are not doing theology.

Maimonides, on the other hand, in obedience to his theological stance in which precision is all and totally clear definition an imperative (perhaps in response to and influenced by Islamic claims for the Koran and undoubtedly as part of his dogmatic system-building), states the Rabbinic view[9] (which, for him, is now *the* Jewish view) as: 'The eighth principle of the Jewish faith is that the Torah has been revealed from Heaven. This implies our belief that the whole of the Torah found in our hands this day is the very Torah that was handed down to Moses and it is all divine in origin. By this I mean that the whole of the Torah came to him from before God in a manner metaphorically called "speaking"; but the real nature of that communication is not known to anyone apart from Moses (peace to him!) to whom it came. Moses was like a scribe writing from dictation the whole of it, its chronicles, its narratives and its precepts. It is in this sense that he is termed *mehokek* ("copyist"). And there is no difference between verses like: *And the sons of Ham were Cush and Mizraim, Phut and Canaan* (Genesis 9:6), or *And his wife's name was Mehetabel, daughter of Matred* (Genesis 36:39), or *And Timna was concubine* (Genesis 36:12), and verses like *I am the Lord thy God* (Exodus 20:2) and *Hear, O Israel* (Deuteronomy 6:4). They are all equally of divine origin and all belong to the law of God, perfect, pure, holy and true. In the opinion of the Rabbis, Manasseh was the greatest of all infidels because he thought that in the Torah there is a kernel and a husk, and that these histories and anecdotes have no value and emanate from Moses'. What had previously been exhortation and preachment, directed, in all probability, against some Jewish sceptics in a particular period, now becomes a 'principle of the faith' (the very notion is not found in any of the earlier sources), a dogma eternally binding upon Jews. Under the great weight of Maimonides' authority, this statement was, indeed, accepted by the majority of Jews until the rise of modern historical investigation into the sources of Judaism and of Biblical Criticism. It is still the Orthodox position in Jewry, although, even in the middle ages, thinkers like Abraham Ibn Ezra were prepared to admit to a number of post-Mosaic additions to the Pentateuch, evidently understanding the above-mentioned Rabbinic passages as leaving scope for mild literary criticism of the Pentateuch, provided no actual laws of the Torah were affected.

A few years ago a Swiss scholar, I. S. Lange, published from manuscript a series of Commentaries to the Pentateuch[10] by Judah the Saint of Regensburg (twelfth–thirteenth centuries), a recognised authority for all Orthodox Jews. The book was declared to be heretical on the grounds that it maintains there are (a very few) post-Mosaic additions to the Pentateuch. Attempts were made to suppress the book, one of the rare instances in modern times of Jewish censorship of books alleged to contain heresy. The renowned, contemporary Halakhist, Rabbi Moses Feinstein,[11] fiercely objected that the work could not possibly have been written by the Saint of Regensburg and he refers to both the Talmudic statements and those of Maimonides, whereas it would appear that some of the mediaeval scholars, even if they were 'saints', did not understand the doctrine of 'Torah from Heaven' as precluding entirely every suggestion that this or that Pentateuchal verse may have been added after Moses.

Biblical Criticism and historical investigation in general have presented a mighty challenge to the whole doctrine of 'Torah from Heaven'. If the Documentary Hypothesis is correct and the sources J, E, D and P were put together by a Redactor or a series of Redactors; if many of the textual variants found in the Septuagint and other ancient versions may be a record of a better preserved text; if the Rabbinic teachings and expositions are not seen as having dropped from Heaven directly but as having had a history and best understood in terms of responses to the particular needs of their time; if all this appears convincing, what is to become of the dogma that the whole of the Torah in its present textual form and with all the explications of it in the 'Oral Torah' was delivered by God to Moses? Some Jews in the last century and more in this have been unable to reconcile the new learning with the older tradition, going so far as surrender completely the idea of Judaism as a revealed religion. But, in varying degrees, many other Jews have remained believers in 'Torah from Heaven' by re-interpreting the doctrine in the light of the new knowledge, which, after all, on the believer's own premiss, is also part of God's truth, as is all truth. If I may repeat something I wrote in this connection, it is still possible to believe in 'Torah from Heaven' but it all depends on what one means by 'Torah', by 'Heaven' and, more especially, by 'from'. From one point of view the divide among Jews on this matter is between Orthodoxy on the one hand and Reform and Conservative Judaism on the other. Yet, in reality, the divide is more accurately between the fundamentalist and liberal-critical approach. Orthodoxy itself has sometimes been understood by its adherents more as Orthopraxy, a religious position which does not necessarily mean: 'Believe what you like provided you keep the *mitzvot* (precepts)' but can mean that God did reveal the Torah and its observances, the revelation being seen as not only *to* the people of Israel but *through* them, through their experiences as they reached out for God, reflecting on their history as they encountered Him and sought to do His will. This is a matter of faith not of scholarship; but faith, in any event, is at the heart of religion.

On this point of view it is possible for a believing Jew who adopts the critical approach to be as observant as his fundamentalist brother-in-faith while keeping an open mind on questions to be decided by empirical investigation. For such a believer it is not origins which count but what the observances have become as vehicles for the apprehension of the divine and its expression in daily and holy living. Louis Ginzberg,[12] describing the thought of Zechariah Frankel, who pioneered this approach, writes: 'We may now understand the apparent contradiction between the theory and practice of the positive-historic school. One may, for instance, conceive of the origin and idea of Sabbath rest as the professor of Protestant theology at a German university would conceive it, and yet minutely observe the smallest detail of the Sabbath observances known to strict Orthodoxy. For an adherent of this school the sanctity of the Sabbath reposes not upon the fact that it was proclaimed on Sinai, but on the fact that the Sabbath idea found for thousands of years its expression in Jewish souls. It is the task of the historian to examine into the beginnings and developments of the numerous customs and observances of the Jews; practical Judaism on the other hand is not concerned with origins, but regards the institutions as they have come to be'. In the more existentialist approach of Franz Rosenzweig, the non-fundamentalist believer can gradually approximate towards greater observance of the *mitzvot* as he finds them speaking to his situation, providing him with ways to God. It is reported that Rosenzweig, who increased his observances as he grew older and came to know more about Judaism, was once asked if he wore *tefillin* ('phylacteries'). Rosenzweig is said to have replied: 'I have not *yet* reached *tefillin*'. For Rosenzweig the modern Jew is at the periphery trying to find his way to the centre. Even if he does eventually reach the centre he has done so on his journey from the periphery, unlike the mediaeval Jew who was already at the centre.

From these considerations the question we are examining is, in the language used by Jews, that of the relationship between the Torah and the *mitzvot* and the personal convictions of the individual, faithful and loyal Jew. Put in this way there can only be one answer, the relationship is complicated, with considerable tensions between the two. This is obviously true for the 'liberal' Jew, less so for the traditionalist or fundamentalist. Yet even the Jew who believes that the whole of the Torah is God-given in a direct sense, including the verse *And Timna was concubine*, believes it, presumably, because that is his own personal conviction. Moreover, whatever his actual affirmation, he does see more significance in some verses of the Torah than in some others because his history and traditions have made some verses more significant than others. Throughout the ages devout Jews have been ready to sacrifice life itself for the idea expressed in: *Hear, O Israel* and *I am the Lord thy God*. We have yet to hear of a Jew suffering martyrdom for *And Timna was concubine to Eliphaz*. The principle of selectivity has been at work in the history of Judaism.

Keeping in mind the non-systematic nature of the classical Jewish sources and without expecting to find there too much consistency, we are still able to note how the tension between the Torah and personal faith has been expressed by looking at a number of passages in these and in later sources.

As early as the Song of Moses, God is described as both 'my' God and as God of the fathers (Exodus 15:2):

> He is my God, and I will glorify Him;
> my father's God and I will exalt Him.

The famous French commentator, Rashi (whose commentary is printed in practically every edition of the Pentateuch), no doubt relying on earlier teaching, remarks in exposition of the verse: 'The sanctity did not begin with me but has been established for me by my ancestors'. In other words, the individual is sustained in his belief by the fact that he did not invent it but has received it by tradition. It is noteworthy that Rashi, writing in eleventh century France, speaks of the sanctity (*kedushah*) not the belief. It is the experience of God rather than the mere belief in His existence that is fortified. It is as if Rashi is saying, what I imagine to be an encounter with the holiness of God might have been construed as an illusion were it not that my ancestors have handed down the record of their experiences, encouraging me to regard mine as authentic. Here the tradition fortifies personal faith.

The further idea that the tradition itself becomes significant by the personal choice in which it is appropriated seems to be implied in the Talmudic account[13] of the debate on whether a teacher of the Torah can renounce the honour due to him. The fourth century Babylonian teacher, R. Joseph, argued that he is permitted to renounce his honour, quoting in support the verse: *And the Lord went before them by day* (Exodus 13:21) i.e. God, the Teacher of Israel, renounced His honour to act as their guide. Just as the divine Teacher renounced the honour due to him so, too, an earthly teacher of the Torah may renounce the honour due to him, if he so wishes. To this, R. Joseph's colleague, Rava, objected that with regard to God the whole world is His and the Torah is His and so He can renounce the honour due to Him. It does not follow that a human teacher of the Torah may renounce the honour due to him because of the Torah. Is, then, asks Rava, the Torah his own possession that he may renounce the honour due to him because he is skilled in learning and teaching the Torah? But, the passage continues, eventually Rava came to agree with R. Joseph. Yes, indeed, declared Rava, the Torah is his, the scholar's, quoting in support the verse: *and in his Torah doth he meditate day and night* (Psalm 1:2). That is to say, Rava interprets homiletically the personal pronoun in the verse as referring not to God, as in the plain meaning ('His Torah'), but to the student of the Torah mentioned in the first clause: *But his delight is in the Torah of the Lord*. The student of the Torah makes the Torah his own by his diligent studies. It is no longer something external to him to which he owes allegience. It has become his own; intimate and personal.

The personal aspect of faith finds its expression in the Rabbinic concept of *lishmah* ('literally "for her sake" i.e. for the sake of the Torah'). The motives of the student of the Torah and of the Jew who observes its laws should ideally be purely for the sake of God. The religious act should not be carried out with ulterior motives but solely because it is God's will. Before the performance of a *mitzvah* a benediction is to be recited: 'Blessed art Thou, O Lord our God, King of the universe, who has sanctified us with His commandments and has commanded us to ...', thereby demonstrating the devotional character of the act. It is one performed in obedience to God's will not as a mere mechanical following of the tradition and not in order to acquire a reputation for piety. Faith is expected to infuse constant life into the observances. For all that, there is a realistic appraisal of human nature, an appreciation by the Rabbis that it is demanding too much that the motive for observance must be pure at all times. The early third century teacher Rav is quoted[14] as saying: 'Let a man engage in the Torah and carry out the *mitzvot* even if it is not *lishmah*. For out of engagement that is lacking in *lishmah* he will eventually attain to observance *lishmah*'.

That the motive be pure is, nonetheless, always the ideal. The impure motive is only tolerated because it will eventually lead to observance with pure motive. The oft-quoted and frequently misinterpreted passage in the Midrash[15] notwithstanding, the Rabbis perceived no value in mechanical observance in itself. A secular Judaism, in which the observances are carried out as picturesque folkways, would have been quite repellent to the Rabbis if they had been able to conceive of such a thing. The Midrash in question reads: 'R. Huna and R. Jeremiah said in the name of R. Hiyya bar Abba: It is written: *They have forsaken Me and have not kept My Torah* (Jeremiah 16:11). This means that God says: Would that they had forsaken Me if only they had kept My Torah'. It is preposterous to understand the Midrash as advocating a God-less Judaism. A Judaism without God but with observance of the Torah would have been totally incomprehensible to the Rabbis of the Midrash or to any other representative Jewish teacher in the pre-modern era. Nor is the paraphrase of M. Friedländer, in his popular hand-book of the Jewish faith,[16] anywhere near the mark. Friedländer renders the meaning of the Midrash as: 'theologians would do better if they were less eager to investigate into the essence of God and His attributes and were more anxious to study and to do God's commandments'. There were, in fact, no theologians in Rabbinic times who were eager to investigate into the essence of God and His attributes. That exercise did not emerge in Judaism until the middle ages. What the Midrash means is that even if the people kept the Torah without having their thoughts on God the power and healing force of the Torah would bring them back to Him. It is astonishing how many have quoted the Midrash without noting its conclusion: 'since by occupying themselves with the Torah the light contained therein would have led them back to the good way'. And this conclusion is immediately followed by the statement that the Torah should be studied and the *mitzvot* observed even if it is not *lishmah* because it will eventually lead to *lishmah*.

In Hasidism, the vibrant, mystical movement which arose in the eighteenth century in Eastern Europe, the concept of *lishmah* was deepened. The Hasidic ideal was for the worshipper to have God constantly in mind. This ideal of *devekut* ('attachment'), of a being-with-God in the mind at all times, was held by the Mitnaggedim, the traditionalists who opposed the new movement, to be undesirable. Awareness of God, the Mitnaggedim argued, was an essential preliminary before the Torah is studied and the *mitzvot* carried out but was a hindrance if engaged in during study or observance. Study in particular is impossible unless the mind is directed not to God but is concentrated on the subject studied. How can the student master, say, a difficult passage in the Talmud if his mind is not on its intricacies but on God? To attempt to study the Torah *lishmah* in the Hasidic sense of *devekut* is not to study at all. The would-be worshipper will be left with the *lishmah* without the Torah, or so the Mitnaggedim argued. In Hasidism, too, there are tensions in the matter of *lishmah* and *devekut*. To be with God in the mind at all times is far more difficult than it sounds. Among the later Hasidim the Mitnaggedic critique was partially accepted. Moreover, the Hasidic doctrine of the Zaddik, the Guru-like saint and master, developed in such a way that, it was generally maintained, he alone was fully capable of *devekut*; his followers could only approximate to the ideal by becoming attached to him and through him to God. Yet Hasidic criticism of a blind, mechanical observance continued to be voiced. An early Hasidic text, frequently quoted, shocked the Mitnaggedim. This text remarks that a man should not be over-scrupulous in his observances since this leads to morbidity, obsession and anxiety, all in opposition to Hasidic stress on serving God with joy. A similar Hasidic saying has it that the difference between the

Hasidim and the Mitnaggedim is that the former fear God whereas the latter fear the standard Code of Jewish observances, the Shulhan Arukh. Again, there is the Hasidic tale of the man who repeatedly had a dream in which he saw God. The man took himself off to a professional interpreter of dreams who observed that the interpretation was all too easy. 'You think of God all the time and so, naturally, you see Him in your dreams'. That cannot be the explanation, the man retorted. My whole day is taken up with prayer and worship and study of the Torah. When have I the time to think of God!

On this question of personal faith and the Torah it must be noted that, for the Rabbis, the Torah is never an object of worship. The sixteenth century Italian author, Joshua Boaz, quotes an earlier authority who forbids bowing to the Torah or to the Ark containing the Scrolls of the Torah.[17] It is the custom in many places to bow when the Scrolls are taken in procession around the synagogue but this is understood not as an act of worship but simply a mark of respect as would be paid, for example, to a man of high rank. The Talmud[18] refers to sages who would interpret every single word of the Torah, even the word *et*, which is no more than the sign of the accusative. In their exposition this little word was made to include, in the verses in which it occurs, something not stated explicitly in the verse. But what were these sages to make, in that case, of *thou shalt fear the Lord thy God* (Deuteronomy 6:13), a verse containing the word *et*? What could have been included in a command to fear, that is, to worship, since only God is to be worshipped? Rabbi Akiba is said to have interpreted the *et* to include students of the Torah. They have to be 'feared', that is, treated with respect, just as God is 'feared'. It is interesting to find students of the Torah included but not the Torah itself. Evidently, 'fear' of scholars would not be misunderstood whereas to use such a term of the Torah might give rise to the idea that the Torah is a legitimate object of worship. In fact, to my knowledge, with only one exception, the term 'fear of the Torah' (unlike 'love of the Torah' which is found frequently in the literature) is never found in the whole of the Talmudic literature. The exception is in the Palestinian Talmud[18a] where the word *et* in the above-mentioned verse is said to include both the Torah and its students. But obviously this only means that for the

Palestinian Talmud the term 'fear' can be used of the Torah but only in the sense in which it is used of scholars. There is a prayer in the Zohar,[19] still recited in many synagogues when the Torah Scroll is brought out of the Ark on the Sabbath, which contains the clause: 'I am the servant of the Holy One, blessed be He, before whom I bow and before the glory of His Torah at all times'. In the Kabbalistic thought represented in the Zohar, the Torah is, in a sense, a kind of divine incarnation, at least of one of the *Sefirot*, the powers of potencies in the Godhead. Yet even in this prayer the worshipper who bows to the Torah first declares himself to be a servant of God alone.

It is also at times implied that the sacred institutions of Judaism can act as barriers to faith if they are treated not as means but as ends, though only very rarely do we find this expressed so starkly as in the comment of the unconventional, nineteenth century Hasidic master, R. Jacob of Izbica.[20] The comment is on the second commandment which forbids the making of an image of that which is in the heavens above and the earth beneath (Exodus 20:4). This author first observes that the more highly regarded and spiritually valuable a thing is the greater is the danger of it becoming an object of worship, an idol. That which is in the heavens above refers to the Sabbath, commanded from the beginning of creation and the most sacred institution in time. That which is in the earth beneath is the Temple, the most sacred institution in space. The second commandment, in this interpretation, is an injunction not to make an idol of the institutions of the Jewish tradition. These are instruments to be used for the purpose of coming nearer to God. They are never to be treated as objects of worship and to do so is to be guilty of idolatry. The author finds this thought in the Talmudic saying:[21] 'One does not stand in fear of the Sabbath but of Him who ordered its observance and one does not stand in fear of the Temple but of Him who gave the command concerning the Temple'. Once again, in the Babylonian Talmud, the term fear (*yirah*), denoting worship, is used of God alone.

That priority must be given to faith over the tradition, that it is the former which breathes life into the latter, is implied in the statement in the Mishnah[22] regarding the order of the sections recited in Israel's declaration of faith, the Shema. The first section

(Deuteronomy 6:4–9) deals with God's unity. The second section (Deuteronomy 11:13–21) deals with the performance of the *mitzvot*. Thus the Mishnah records R. Joshua b. Korhah saying, the reason the first section precedes the other is because one is first obliged to take upon oneself 'the yoke of the Kingdom of Heaven' and afterwards 'the yoke of the *mitzvot*'. Faith without its translation into action is meaningless, so it is implied, but practice not infused with faith has similarly little value. There are two 'yokes', that of the Kingdom of Heaven and that of the *mitzvot*, both of which have to be accepted but the first of these has priority in the scale of values.

None of the traditional thinkers ever thought for one moment that it is possible to have Judaism without observance of the Torah. But by the same token they all held mere observance of the law insufficient. Nowhere is this given more powerful expression than in a comment, which became very influential in Jewish religion and ethics, by the great Spanish Talmudist and mystic, Nahmanides (1195–1270). The comment[23] is on the Biblical injunction to be holy (Leviticus (19:2). Nahmanides seeks to analyse the holiness concept. Holiness cannot mean an avoidance of the illicit since that is taken care of by the laws of the Torah, each sinful act being explicitly forbidden. Holiness means, according to Nahmanides, self-denial over and above the demands of the law. It is perfectly possible, he remarks, for a man to be thoroughly disreputable and profligate without actually infringing any law of the Torah. Unless he is a Nazirite he can drink as much wine as he pleases; he can have many wives with whom he can indulge his sexual appetites to excess; he can avoid eating forbidden food but still make a pig of himself when eating kosher food. Such a man, in Nahmanides' pungent formulation, is 'a scoundrel with the full permission of the Torah'. This is why man is commanded to be holy. He is called upon not only to obey the actual dictates of the law but must deny himself even legitimate pleasures where these tend to corrupt his character. There could hardly be a more cogent statement of the idea that the Torah in itself is not sufficient or, better, that the demand of holiness over and above the actual laws of the Torah is itself a demand of the Torah.

A striking passage in the Talmud[24] is indicative of the tension between faith and tradition among the Rabbis. The passage begins with the remark by the third century Palestinian, Rabbi Simlai, that there are 613 precepts of the Torah given to Moses. The later prophets, the passage continues, gave shorter principles for the leading of the good life. (This is without doubt the meaning of *heemidan*, literally, 'they made them stand' i.e. they based all the precepts on certain brief but embracing rules). After describing these 'reductions' of the prophets, the passage concludes: 'Habakkuk based them on one single statement: *But the righteous shall live by his faith* (Habakkuk 2:4)'. Trust in God is thus the basic principle in Judaism from which all else follows.

There is also a recognition that not all men have the same capacity for faith and that apprehension of the divine is arrived at in many different ways. This idea is found in a Midrash[25] on revelation. Psalm 24 verse four is translated as: *The voice of the Lord is with power*, taking 'power' as referring not to God but to the power of the individual to hear God's voice. The voice of God, says the Midrash, was heard by the men according to their capacity, by the women according to theirs. Young men heard it differently from old men. Each individual heard it according to his own capacity. Human nature and individual temperament have a role to play if God's voice is to be heard.

For many of the mediaeval thinkers the way to faith, though supported by the tradition, was to reason for it by the philosophical proofs, particularly the cosmological. The famous moralist and philosopher Bahya Ibn Pakudah, influenced in his work by Sufi ideas, goes so far as to see the tradition itself demanding the attainment of faith through reason.[26] Bahya neatly quotes in his support (though the Biblical knowledge of God is not cognitive, as Bahya would have it, and his rendering of the verse, consequently, is anachronistic): *And thou, Solomon my son, know thou the God of thy father and serve him with a perfect heart* (II Chronicles 28:9). But Judah ha-Levi (*d.* 1141) in his *Kuzari* bases faith entirely on tradition. In reality, as ha-Levi sees it, the appeal to tradition is an appeal to the reasonableness of the tradition. He argues (and in his day, when both Christianity and Islam accepted the truth of the Scriptural narratives, the argument was convincing) that the events at Sinai are attested to by the evidence of two million people, as are the events of the Exodus. The book

Kuzari is in the form of a dialogue between a Jewish sage and the King of the Khazara. The King, troubled by the question of which religion is the true one, invites first a Christian and a Muslim to convince him. They begin their discourse with the creation of the world. But when the Jewish sage is invited to defend his faith he begins not with creation but with the Exodus. The only sure way to faith is by an appeal to history which is why, the sage observes,[27] the Decalogue begins with: 'I am the Lord thy God who brought thee out of the land of Egypt' not with: 'I am the Creator of the world and your Creator'. 'And so did I reply to thee, O King of the Khazara, when thou didst ask me to substantiate the truth of my faith and I informed thee of that which obligates me and which obligates all the people of Israel, that which, in the first instance, the children of Israel became convinced of because they saw it with their own eyes and was then handed down by tradition, the equivalent of seeing with the eyes, from man to man'.

Judaism knows, too, of the mystic's way to faith, that of direct experience. But while the theosophical system known as the Kabbalah is based on mystical speculation and meditation, the mystics were extremely reticent in recording their personal mystical testimonies. Only around thirty of these are extant. The word Kabbalah itself means 'tradition' because the mystics believed that the Kabbalistic gnosis was handed down in a tradition reaching back to Moses or even to Adam. Yet the Kabbalists were fully aware of their originality, stating frequently that the mysteries revealed to them had never before been revealed to man. The link between the traditional gnosis and the new, the device used to bring the personal insights into the Kabbalah, was the figure of the prophet Elijah, who, in Jewish legend, returns to earth from time to time to impart teachings to the saints. For the mystics 'the appearance of Elijah' is a mystical state but since Elijah is a disciple of Moses that which he imparts is both new and at the same time part of the Torah of Moses. In this way personal, mystical experience became part of the tradition.

It was not only the mystics who acknowledged the idea of a developing tradition in which not everything is given and then simply handed down from generation to generation. An oft-quoted Talmudic tale[28] speaks of Moses transported across time to the school of Rabbi Akiba where Moses is unable to understand anything of Akiba's teachings. But when a student asks Akiba how he knows the law he is expounding, Akiba replies: 'I have it by a tradition from Moses at Sinai' and Moses' mind is set at rest. The new Torah taught by Akiba was really new and yet, because implicit in the Torah given to Moses, it is the same Torah. How far this dynamic view of the Torah was preserved in subsequent Jewish thought is a moot point but the idea is present in this and in other Talmudic and post-Talmudic sources.[29]

What of conflicts between the demands of the tradition and personal choice in faith? There are references to the sin for the sake of God (*averah lishmah*), the Biblical prototype being the sinful act of Jael (Judges chapters four and five) who allowed herself to be seduced by Sisera in order to save her people.[30] In circumstances where an individual believes that an act must be carried out for the greater glory of God that act overides the demands of the law. But it must be appreciated that this whole idea occupies a very peripheral place in traditional Jewish thought. It was developed in a radical way by the followers of Shabbatai Zevi, the seventeenth century false Messiah, but that was due to Shabbatai's conversion to Islam which required, for those who still believed in him, theological justification on the lines of the sin for the sake of God. The prevailing attitude was expressed by Hayyim of Volozhyn, the chief disciple of the eighteenth century Gaon of Vilna and leading traditionalist Rabbi, who maintained[31] that once the Torah has been given the doctrine can no longer operate. If it could, he continues, what is the point of the Torah and its laws since the sole guide will be the individual conscience. Where this demands that a certain act be carried out or not carried out, it would depend not on what the Torah says but on whether the motive is pure and for God. The antinomianism implicit in the doctrine of *averah lishmah* is rejected in the name of the Torah.

This has been an attempt at surveying Jewish attitudes to faith in relation to tradition. Since Judaism is not monolithic but consists of the response of a variety of Jewish communities and their teachers even on the idea of revelation, consistency is not to be expected. What we do have is tension between faith and tradition, a tension never completely resolved but which, Jews would hold, has generally been creative. This essay might fittingly conclude with a comment of the Midrash[32] which, perhaps, comes closest to the thinking of Wilfred Cantwell Smith on faith and tradition: '*And ye are My witnesses, saith the Lord, and I am God* (Isaiah 43:12). When you are My witnesses I am God. But when you are not My witnesses I am not God, as it were. Similarly: *Unto Thee I lift up mine eyes, O Thou that art enthroned in the heavens* (Psalm 123:1). If not for me, Thou, as it were, would not be enthroned in the heavens'.

NOTES

1. *Sotah* 48b.
2. Max Kadushin: *The Rabbinic Mind*, sec. ed., New York, 1965; Isaac Heinemann: *Darkhey ha-Aggadah*, Jerusalem, 1974.
3. *Yad, Deot* 1:2–7.
4. *Yad, Yesodey ha-Torah* 4:10.
5. *Sanhedrin* 10:1.
6. *Sanhedrin* 99a.
7. *Sanhedrin* 99b.
8. N. Krochmal: *Moreh Nevukhey ha-Zeman*, ed. S. Rawidowicz, London, 1961, Ch. 14, pp. 238–56.
9. *Commentary to the Mishnah* to *Sanhedrin* 10:1.
10. Jerusalem, 1975.
11. *Iggerot Moshe*, VI, Bene Berak, 1981, Nos. 114 and 115.
12. *Students, Scholars and Saints*, New York, 1958, p. 206.
13. *Kiddushin* 32a–b.
14. *Pesaḥim* 50b.
15. *Lamentations Rabbah*, Proem 2.
16. *The Jewish Religion*, sec. ed., London, 1900, page 3, note 1.
17. *Shiltey ha-Gibborim* to Alfasi, *Kiddushin* 14b.
18. *Pesaḥim* 22b.
18a. *Berakhot* 9:5, 14b.
19. II, 206a.
20. *Bet Yaakov*, Lublin 1906, II, p. 256.
21. *Yevamot* 6b.
22. *Berakhot* 2:2.
23. *Commentary of Ramban*, ed. B. Chavel, Jerusalem, 1960, pp. 115–17.
24. *Makkot* 23b–24a.
25. *Exodus Rabbah* 2:1.

26. *Ḥovot ha-Levavot*, ed. P. J. Liebermann, Jerusalem, 1968, *Shaar ha-Yiḥud*, Ch. 3, p. 97.
27. *Kuzari* ed. Y. Even Shmuel, Tel-Aviv, 1972, I, 25, p. 12.
28. *Menaḥot* 29b.
29. Some of these are given in Louis Jacobs: *We Have Reason to Believe*, third ed., London, 1965, pp. 70–81.
30. *Nazir* 23b.
31. *Keter Rosh* in the Prayer Book of the Vilna Gaon, *Ishey Yisrael*, Tel-Aviv, 1968, p. 539.
32. *Sifre*, ed. L. Finkelstein, New York, 1969, par. 346, pp. 403–4.

4

THE CHRISTIAN TRADITION

George Huntston Williams

INTRODUCTION

Christianity is a congeries of religions, or at least it embraces, over time and regional variations, so great a range of theology, spirituality, and polity that all attempts to get at its essence, even when undertaken by scholars with the greatest grasp in their generation of the whole of Church history, were unsatisfactory because too partisan, too harmonistic, or too intellectualistic.[1] The plenitude and diversity, the fecundity and fissiparous character of the bands and companies that constitute the pilgrim people under Jesus Christ, are such that perhaps all the interpreters of their pilgrimage and sacred memories can do is to acknowledge that they are engaged in the comparative history of a composite entity of ever renewed memory and hope, socio-political, psycho-cultural, and religious with an experienced and compelling Transcendent referent.

In any case, all attempts to characterize Christianity as a people and a faith, whether by ancient or modern foes *from without*, such as Celsus in *The True Discourse*, who had actually read Christian literature, and Ludwig Feuerbach, *Wesen des Christentums* (1841); or *from within*, from Justin Martyr in his *Apology* (165) to Adolf von Harnack in *Das Wesen des Christentums* (1900), have not proved commensurate with the plenitude or adequate to the sometimes paradoxical complexity of the religion that started out as a stumbling block to so many messianic Jews and folly to so many Greeks questing wisdom, even salvific gnosis (I Cor. 1:23).

Christianity was such a congeries from the start. There were at least four gospels about Jesus Christ before the canonization of the canonical four, the latter all modifications of one genre among the four earlier ones with assimilations of motifs of the other three.[2] The holiest writ of Christianity contains, moreover, many seeds for growth and change. Perhaps no other world religion so forthrightly as Christianity allows, within its formative sacred scripture, for more truth to be brought forth from the same ultimate source (John 16:12 f.), for the ongoing presence of the Founder within his community and for his promised Spirit (John 14:16, 26) even unto the end of the world (Matt. 28:20), nor within its sacred text made so express a distinction between the revelation from God and a humanly authoritative doctrine and praxis of a preeminent follower (Paul, I Cor. 7:10, 25): with the consequence that with Matthew (13:52) the Christian, as householder, 'brings out of his treasure [of Scripture] what is new and what is old'; and Church history itself becomes veritably, as Gerhard Ebeling (b. 1912) subtitled his book on Church history (1947), 'the history of the interpretation of Sacred Scriptures.'[3]

Moreover, Christianity is the only religion that has taken over the sacred scripture of another religion and claimed it as its own, while portions of its own distinctive sacred scripture vilified those out of whose midst it came, as a child from the womb. For almost two millennia, Christians denied that the sons and daughters of Abraham and Sarah after the flesh could have a valid interpretation of those elder scriptures. An inbuilt religious effrontery permitted Christians to humiliate and even persecute Jews as Deicides down into the late twentieth century, when in their very own uniquely Christian canon it was evident that one of the twelve closest to Jesus failed to get the purport of the Master's message and betrayed him, while the acknowledged head of these twelve closest to the Lord publicly denied him thrice (Matt. 26:34). Moreover, in those same scriptures, there is little evidence that more than a few of the alleged twelve, as apostles, ever proclaimed the news of their Lord's preaching or resurrection or founded a single community of faith because of their own conviction in Jesus as the Messiah of God, while the chief apostle was not an early follower and eyewitness of the extraordinary finale of the Lord's career but rather a persecutor, Saul/Paul.

The earliest witnesses to Jesus as the Messiah were divided as to whether one had first to become a Jew in order to be counted among his flock (circumcision, dietary laws, heed to the place of the Temple and synagogue), which led to debates as to whether the new community or communities constituted the true or a New Israel.[4]

Beginning with the first Apologists and coming to such great Old Testament scholars as Origen of Alexandria and Caesarea, such 'Church' historians as Eusebius of Caesarea with his *Preparation of the Gospel* as companion to his *Ecclesiastical History*, up through Augustine of Hippo and Otto of Freising in the age of the Emperor Frederick I Barbarossa, many Christians have taken the history of salvation as continuous from Abel onwards. The classical Protestant Reformers went so far as to make pedobaptism and circumcision the counterpart rites of the one covenant in two dispensations. But the Latin Church at the time and almost up to the present also celebrated both the circumcision of Jesus (1 January)[5] and his baptism, Epiphany (6 January), while all liturgical Churches continue not wholly consistently to observe Pentecost, forty days after Easter, as the feast of the founding of the Church in the Upper Room. Only in the last half of the second Christian millennium have major spokesmen of Christianity come to consider the covenant with Israel as abiding (e.g., Reinhold Niebuhr; John Paul II as recently as his communication to the Jews in Mainz, 1980), taking Paul's words seriously in Romans 11:11–32 (especially 29), and thus placing Christianity in a new relationship to the mother religion, much as it was back in the first century.

Because Christianity as a congeries of religions has a canon of Scripture within a somewhat larger canon, also Tradition and traditions, ancient creeds and latter-day confessions, covering, with the Old Testament, roughly four thousand years of history, in various climes and among various peoples of varied temperaments, it is remarkable that observers outside can see in Christianity any kind of a unity in time and space.

Ancient Roman and Greek critics of Christianity could not but see some evasive polytheism or atheism in early Christian devotion to Jesus Christ against the background of Jewish monotheism with its majestic account of creation respected, if not believed, by them, while the renunciation of the ancient civic and fertility gods and above all of the sacral character of the Emperor and the Empire seemed indeed at once atheistic and seditious and bigoted. Nor did these critics understand the interior life of Jews who, having over the centuries learned to combine ethnicity, polity, piety, and worship, lived out their faith in closed communities in the Mediterranean diaspora. Yet the Roman authorities tolerated Judaism as a highly moral and communally disciplined Oriental oddity. They could understand even less the interior life of Christians who laid claim to some of the same prerogatives as the Jews while guarding their own distinctive views as arcane, dismissing even their own catechumens as their worship proceeded to the practice of the central mysteries, all the time professing themselves to be both a new religion and a religion validly in succession to Judaism. Tertullian of Carthage could say that 'the soul everywhere is naturally Christian' (*Apologeticum*, 17), by which he meant a natural knowledge of the Creator.[6]

Muslims, for their part, could never understand in their first confrontations a religion with four Gospels rather than a single Ingil, as they insisted was alone conceivable [comparable to their own Book of oracles and revelations]. Much later the devotees of other world religions would find Christianity, divided into so many jurisdictions and competing missions in the area of their dominance, that Christianity in whatever confessional form seemed to outsiders far more the ideology of imperial colonization and exploitation than the unique revelation of salvation that its disparate missionaries, often backed up with halberds and canon, rifles and regiments, merchants and engineers, claimed to represent.

Moreover, within any given form of Christianity, like Orthodoxy or Catholicism, there also coexists such a range of modalities of faith and practice that several of them constitute in themselves a congeries of religions with quite varying emphases over time and in various tongues. Interestingly, the denizens of the outer circle of one Christian grouping often find themselves spiritually or ethically or theologically actually closer to those at *the interior* of another historically evolved circle of the Christian 'faith' than the one in which they had themselves been nurtured. It is a common intrafaith (Christian) ecumenical experience that Catholics, for example, feel close not so much to the 'ecumenical' Protestants reaching toward catholics as rather toward 'the more authentic' of that same group still abiding near the interior of that tradition as scripturally 'fundamental' and evangelical, while ecumenically motivated Protestants are often yearning in Catholicism for precisely the comprehensiveness and depth and mystery of spirituality in diverse monastic and other traditions and sometimes find their counterpart Catholic ecumenists excessively oriented to the social gospel.

Christianity is like a vast terrain made up of tundra, desert, deciduous forest, tropical rain forest, alpine and arctic sparseness of vegetation, marine coasts and estuaries, rivers, lakes, and ponds. The seeds and spores of its vast literature in liturgy, song, scholarly treatise, conciliar decree, sermon, and prayer, – a religion of the Book indeed, a religion of the Word in truth – that single words in sacred texts can suddenly sprout and prevail and become as the mustard tree of the Dominical parable (Matt. 13:31 f.), sufficient in a single growing season to supply nesting room for several kinds of birds, and then to wither or to be hacked down to spring up another season, that is, in another century. In addition to this enormous fecundity of Christianity with its inherently fissiparous disposition, going far beyond an occasional schism and reunion, Christians in the same tradition, to say nothing of Christians in different traditions often mean the *same thing* by differing words (I refer not to mere differences in vernacular rendering) and actions, while as often they also mean *different things* by identical formulations and ritual actions.[8] There is in Christianity both continuity in the meaning and function of a practice while the formulation or implementation of it may have changed. For example, the American frontier revival had, by another name, much in common with ancient Christian public penance. Conversely, there is functional and even theological discontinuity even though nomenclature remains constant, for example, the changing meaning of 'saint', 'faith', 'salvation'.

In an effort to map out this variegated terrain with its many schismatic faults, plateaus, and drainage systems in diverse regions and successive centuries, the historian may discern four *loci* or moments of Christian salvation: the historic Christ event, eternal election, the presently accessible grace in sacramental and other forms, and the futuristic Kingdom of God. See Part II.

These four moments have been experienced and embedded in four concentric circles of distinguishable modalities, orders, or degrees of faith in the course of Church history. We briefly sketch these.

I FOUR DEGREES OF SPECIFICITY IN FAITH

In its primary degree or dimension faith is a disposition,[9] a posture of mind, heart, soul, and body Godward. Indeed, the bodily postures of standing in prayer with arms outstretched, of bowing, kneeling, rising, prostration, making on oneself the sign of the cross, immersion in baptism, reverentially kissing an Icon, clapping in ecstasy, chanting and singing, coming forward in penitential reaffirmation, etc., all express trust of a person's heart, mind, and will in God: God in Jesus Christ, the divine in the sacraments. Faith in this primary sense is not so much propositional belief as trust or unreasoned assent.

Secondly, faith can be extended to involve clarification of what one in the disposition of faith as trust holds to be true, the propositional belief of the *regula fidei*, the creed, the confession of faith, namely, what prompts one to bow in prayer or to die as a martyr. But the credal formula is relatively brief and integrally bound up with the life of the community of faith and is to be distinguished from organized faith or systematic theology in great *summae* (see below). At first the baptismal *credo* as propositional faith was expanded in conciliar creed. At the time of the Reformation these formularies, presupposing the ancient creeds, became the somewhat longer articles of faith hammered out in colloquy, diet, and parliament.

Faith as propositional is belief in the context of an emerging community of faith, which thus includes the formularies and the practices of the community into which one was anciently baptized, or, in the Reformation Era, to which one adhered.

The first converts to Christianity, being Jews and holding therefore to the belief of Israel: God is One, were baptized after avowing their enhanced belief: Jesus, though crucified, is the long-awaited Messiah of that God. Later Gentile converts presumably expanded the propositional form of faith to the belief in God the Father as Creator and in Jesus, his Son, as the Messiah, and in the

Holy Spirit. Slowly the Apostles' Creed developed the specifics of this belief further. It is true, as Wilfred Cantwell Smith has pointed out instructively, 'belief' and its Germanic counterparts, *credo*: I believe and its Greek counterpart, etymologically mean 'trust in' rather than 'hold that,' these words all rooted in stems for life, love, giving the heart, etc.; but they have come to have the propositional sense, and are used here in a positive sense.[10] They are formulations out of the interior of the community of faith (in the sense of trust) and involve one also in new liturgical practices and deportment, baptism, communion, communal discipline, etc.

It may be observed that faith as a formulary in the propositional sense has usually been short. The original creeds could be committed to memory. They were formulated in the midst of controversy over specific problems successively agitating the community and threatening schism. Hammered out in synods and councils at which the Holy Spirit was invoked at the Mass/Liturgy preceding each session, they tended to cover only controverted aspects of the traditional faith, implicit or explicit. In Orthodoxy there were but two symbols, the Apostles' Creed evolving from the primitive *regula fidei* and the Niceno-Constantinopolitan Creed of 325/381; but the Latin West had in addition the so-called Athanasian Creed, *Quincunquevult*, still part of the Anglican liturgy, and which speaks of Christ as one *Persona* in two substances (instead of two natures). In the Eastern Church the acceptance of the conciliar creeds by 'the Christophorous laity' was part of the process of reception. The addition of the *Filioque* to the Latin version of the Niceno-Constantinopolitan Creed in Toledo in the sixth century, though not accepted in Rome until the eighth, became so contextualized into scholastic terminology by the IV Lateran Council of 1215 that no matter how many gracious acknowledgments might be made by the Western Churches to the Orthodox who preserve the original formulation, the range of problems ensuing from that one change alone will take generations to clear up what is common and what is still different in the Eastern and the Western understanding of Triadology.

The Latin Church furthermore developed, for its part, the ongoing authority of the Bishop of Rome as successor of Peter, as a source of progressively renewed clarification of dogma as to faith (as belief) and morals, finalized as the dogma of papal infallibility (Vatican I, 1870). Although faith as propositional is considered a way of thinking and feeling with the Church, it is much larger than that.

In the era of Western confessional Christianity, faith came to designate the church itself that held to a given set of articles of faith and became synonymous with a church, such as the Catholic faith, the Orthodox faith, the Lutheran, or the Reformed faith. In the age of further fission of the Lutheran and Reformed tradition it becomes indeed a commonly accepted term for sect, denomination, communion, or church. Given its imprecision and fluctuation of emphasis over time and in diaspora, faith in this sense need not be closely attended to by theologians. It is, moreover, far more in English than in other languages an ecclesial-confessional designation.

The status of Christianity as a whole as a faith among the faiths of the world comes out, however, in the well established term 'interfaith' dialogue for the exchange among Jews, Christians, Muslims, and others, in which context Christianity as a whole is construed institutionally and theologically as a single faith. To the extent that faith is no more than an alternative term for church, it represents a devolution in the meaning of faith; to the extent however, that it preserves the communal context in time and space, of memory and hope, of the work of systematic theology and Christian ethics and governance, it should be treated with seriousness.

For the third meaning of faith involves, in the broad context, the relationship of Christian belief and practice to culture, including the philosophy and world view regnant at the time. The third meaning of faith is ordered faith in systematic theology where scripture, creed, tradition, and praxis are comprehensively clarified by the most plausible or accessible constructs of philosophy. To be sure, Christians were off to a bad start with the sole reference to philosophy in the New Testament, Colossians 2:9: 'See to it that no one makes a prey of you by philosophy and empty deceit, according to human tradition, according to the elemental spirits of the universe.' But Apologists and the first systematic theologians managed largely to neutralize this text in favor of that of John 1, etc. that could be construed to support the view that the Eternal Logos/Wisdom had sown in the minds of thinkers a perennial and salvific philosophy. Still, this theological enterprise entailed confidence in the fallen mind's capacity to give ordered expression to belief, *fides quaerens intellectum*,[11] and the reassurance that though one is not saved by reason, reason can be saved. From the first systematic theology, the *De Principiis* of Origen, through the *summae* of the Schoolmen of various schools and the *institutes* of the Reformers to the *Credimus* (1968) of Paul VI and the *Kirchliche Dogmatitik* of Karl Barth (d. 1968), Christianity has commonly sought to give an ordered and, to the extent possible, reasoned account of the faith of the community.

In Greek classical thought, science as encyclical studies, encyclopedic science, was considered ancillary to philosophy. In most Christian theologians in antiquity, the propaideutic or encyclical knowledge and philosophy came to be conjoined, *together* ancillary to faith as belief in the context of church life and culture at large. To be sure, some early theologians, like Tertullian, regarded simple faith, unargued, rationally unexplained, as sufficing for salvation or indeed more meritorious than assent to rationally argued theological propositions; although, despite his claim 'to believe because it is absurd,' he was well trained in philosophy and certain sciences.

The use in the Nicene Creed of the term 'consubstantial' of the Persons of the Trinity is a notable example of the need to resort to a philosophical term to make clear what was implied in scripture, in respect of God as Creator, Jesus Christ as Lord, and the Holy Spirit.

In organized faith, systematic theology, the whole experience of the Christian people must be considered, tradition alongside the succinct credal formulas. Practices, customs, the accumulated body of conventional scriptural interpretation, canon law, the liturgy itself, constitute together the faith and praxis in the communal sense to which at intervals the rational or ordering and clarificatory process is successively applied. In the recurrent process of giving a rational account of the communal faith going beyond the *credo* or *confessio*, Christians retain and develop or lose sight of or drop several items of importance to other groups, for example, Marian doctrine, footwashing, the veneration of icons, the intercession of saints, or become disproportionately preoccupied with that which caused the particular group to have separated in the first place: the single nature of Christ after the incarnation, justification by faith alone, believers' baptism.[12]

As in all religions, so in Christianity, the problem of the rational expression of faith has become complicated not only by the aforementioned accumulation of traditional (handed-down) practices and normative conventions with the acquired status of inspired usage but also eventually by the writings and directives of the renewers, from Martin Luther, through John Wesley, to such great pan-Christian theologians with import far beyond their confession or church, as Karl Barth or Karl Rahner.[13]

Faith also refers fourthly to the political community of the faithful (though never expressly as in Islam), that by its traditions, modes of worship, para-liturgical and seasonal rites and festivals, privately and corporately has exercised a shared faith, almost as much in a cultural as in a religious sense.[14] Polish national identity and the Polonized molding of Catholicism, like the ethnic Greek community or the pregenocide (1915) Armenian Christian communities have all been quasi-political, indeed the latter two under the Ottoman Turks were required so to behave. The Maronites under their Uniate Patriarch in Upper Beirut are almost as much a political party as a confession and in fact, under the Ottoman rule, constituted a jurisdiction. In Northern Ireland the bloody contest of 'faith' is really a mordant conflict of classes, each burdened emotionally by a battered sense of history with which each side identifies from infancy to senility.

Primitively the church, in polemical parallelism with the Roman Empire, conducted itself as an *imperium in imperio*. After the Christianization of the Empire, the Western medieval successor thereof came to be called the *Holy* Roman Empire (*sacrum* first used by Frederick I Barbarossa). At the same time by the sacrament of unction the Christian king was thought of as an epiphany of Christ, the royal *unctus*, even *christus*. Up through the Reformation Era, Christianity tended to be regionally a single people, though in schism. Even in the East where Christianity subsisted under Islam there were several partly ethnic, quasi-political schisms under Patriarchs answerable to Caliphs or Sultans.

Corpus christianum is a modern word (Ernst Troeltsch) for the medieval Latin or Byzantine reality and, by extension for the ethnicized equivalent of Christian communities organized under Islam (a kind of Christian ghettoizing with local autonomy vested in the highest prelate). With the Reformation, classical/magisterial Protestantism was territorialized under national kings, princes, or town councils, while radical restorationist Christianity, taking on sectarian form, sought to replicate the pre-Constantinian *imperium in imperio*. As confessional splits developed in magisterial Protestantism the local political unit became the defender of the faith in the sense of belief formulated in articles at diets or national synods. By the end of the Reformation Era, under the confessional compromise of *cujus regio, ejus religio*, magisterial Protestantism and Catholicism accepted in principle the state supervision of religion very much as emperor, tsar, king, or prince had headed the national churches of Orthodoxy.

Such a quasi-political or fully politicized communal dimension (Anglican and Presbyterian respectively in the kingdoms of England and Scotland in the sixteenth century) represents our fourth dimension of faith. Richard Hooker (d. 1600) said of England that it is like a triangle: placed on one edge, it is the body politic, on another, the body ecclesiastic.

In no part of old Christendom did church, state, and society become so nearly one as among the Spaniards and Portuguese. From a symbiotic relationship with the Muslim conquerors and the Jewish communities, Christians entered upon crusades of reconquest, eventuating in the fall of the last Muslim territory in Spain, Granada, in 1492 and the expulsion of all unconverted Moors and Jews, but not without Iberian Catholics having assimilated many attitudes and institutions of their hereditary foe, like the state control of the episcopacy (*patronato*) which in due course they would impose on the New World and their colonial possessions in Africa and Asia. The last vestige of the *patronato* disappeared from Latin America when John Paul II visited Haiti in May 1983 and formally reasserted full papal power to appoint Haitian bishops.[15]

Such titles as 'Defender of the Faith,' later Governor of the Church (England) or 'Most Catholic King' (Spain) as appellations of the sovereigns of confessionally homogeneous states with inquisitions for non-conformity had far-reaching consequences, not only for those who lived within such domains but also for those who were conquered and colonized. In the Middle Ages the secular arm had defended official Christianity by inquisitions (in Spain up to 1820) and by crusades against heretics (the Albigensian Crusade sanctioned by Innocent III) and against pagans (the Teutonic knights against the Lithuanians) and of course in a succession of crusades against the Muslims, and in passing against Jews. The survival of the latter into modern times is the pogrom and the Holocaust (a secularized pogrom by a secularized messianic Third Reich).

No Catholic today, no Cistercian, could possibly say with St. Bernard of Clairvaux, arbiter of Latin Christendom in his age, preacher of the Second Crusade, formulator of the constitution of an order of martial knights: 'Who drives his sword into the infidel, Christ drives it for him.' But in Reformed-based *apartheid* in South Africa, in the unwavering, inward (uncoerced) support by the Orthodox Church of the peace policy of the officially atheist U.S.S.R., in the self-righteous revival of American 'manifest destiny' to restrain the 'empire of evil' by nuclear superiority, pushed and polled among the Moral Majority, inc. in the United States, we see some of the lingering 'Constantinian' legacy of the fourth sense of faith as the political community perceived by adherents as the instrument best suited to God's providential purposes.

Although it can no longer be said of Christians in the anger of provincial Roman governors and magistrates or authors (Tacitus *Annales*, xv, 14, 6) that Christians display 'hatred of the human race,' it can be said that they have often, alas, hated each other and fought so many confessional wars in the name of their common Lord, and in defense of their schismatic creed and ethnicized church that it often appears in Church history that Christ brought not peace but a sword (Matt. 10:34), enflamed violence in the hearts of his most ardent or his most calculating devotees, the Kingdom being taken by violence (cf. Matt. 11:12), rather than by the peace which passeth understanding (Phil. 4:7). Ancient martyrdom, the martial missions of Charlemagne, the crusades, the confessional wars in France in the sixteenth century, in Germany, Britain, and the Polish-Lithuanian Commonwealth in the seventeenth century, the recrudescence of ancient acrimonies in Northern Ireland, Lebanon (with five kinds of Catholic jurisdictions alone), and Central America all suggest that politicized, or now ideologized, or religiously polarized communities or even classes within a relatively homogeneous Christian culture are the hateful consequence of the wrong ways religion interpenetrates societies and society shapes Christianity.[16] Christian violence no less than Christian philanthropy and other social ameliorations attest to the legacy, for good or ill, of the fourth, the socio-political meaning of nationalized and politicized Christian confessional faith,[17] even though there are few historic instances of a Christian society as a bearer of the particular belief being actually referred to as faiths, although in the French and Indian War Anglais (Yankee) did in this rare instance mean Protestant as much as English, as once Moor and Turk also meant Muslim.

We have now passed from simple faith as trust or assent through faith as propositional belief of the confessional community itself (from infants to the infirm) and the more fully or comprehensively organized systematic theology in relation to philosophy, to the community of faith as the political or quasi-political defender of a particular creed or articles of faith (belief) usually with an accompanying sense of a providential assignment. These four *degrees* of specificity or comprehensiveness of faith are variously related to four soteriological *loci* or moments relative to time: (1) the eternal decree of God, (2) the historically salvific event of Jesus Christ, (3) the recurrently present means of appropriating or of approaching that salvific reality with a sense of divine immediacy, and (4) the eschatological future. Each of these four soteriologically decisive moments has, moreover, two or more variants in emphasis.

II THE FOUR TEMPORAL LOCI OR MOMENTS OF SALVATION: ETERNAL, HISTORIC, EVERPRESENT, AND ESCHATOLOGICAL

The first *locus* of salvation for Christianity, in terms of its advanced *systematic* theology, is the pre-creational grace of election to salvation (cf. Rom. 8:29 f.; Eph. 1:5, 11). Election came to be theologically located in the intradeical decrees of election and reprobation on the analogy of the more historical actions of God in calling forth some for his special blessing (or reprobation) out of the womb of history: Noah and his family over against the scoffers, Abraham from out among polytheists of Ur, Jacob and Esau, Hebrew slaves under Moses freed from bondage to the Egyptian pursuers in the Exodus, and the return of the remnant of the Chosen People from Babylonian Captivity. The Christian doctrine of election and reprobation goes far beyond that of the People Chosen in history in that through Paul, Augustine, certain Schoolmen, and the classical Protestant Reformers, the eternal decrees came to be thought of as fixed without reference to personal merit, perhaps even before the Fall of Adam and Eve (supralapsarianism), and yet with such personal precision that in a sense even the reprobate acquired a kind of cosmic dignity, since both the elect and the reprobate knew that they could never be certain of their salvific status and that, in any case, their eternal destiny was unrelated to their ethical striving or their moral achievement. Nevertheless, by various theological casuistries, such as asceticism, sanctification, pietism, and puritanism, holiness movements, and philanthropies, Christians have variously sought to approach certitude even as to election. Nothing more fearsome, said Oliver Cromwell, than a Presbyterian just off his knees. Believers tried to be holy in order to be worthy of understanding themselves as belonging to the elect. Understanding faith itself as an unmerited gift, Christianity has nevertheless produced over the generations a profusion of martyrs and monks, Mennonites and Methodists with changing theories about attrition and contrition, condign and congruous grace (cf. Vulgate Acts 10:31), strict Calvinism on the decrees and Arminianism (the Remonstrant mitigation thereof).

The central and historic locus of salvation for Christians is, of course, what could be called the Christ Event, although this term, at its modern inception (see below) was introduced as one of the modalities of the salvific now. Traditionally called in theology the Person and Work of Christ, the historic event has called forth from the interior of the Church and around its margins a succession of variant formulations, in both Christology and soteriology. Christology alone involves: the prophetic preparation for the apostles' and the evangelists' recognition of Jesus as the Christ in Israelite history, the assignment of a special role to John the Baptist pointing to Jesus and an interpretation of his own entry into the sect of the Baptist and his never fully clarified divergence from it, the exposition of his brief ministry of preaching by parable and example, the institution of a band of successors and a commemorative meal, remembered by them as identified by him with his imminent crucifixion, and the demonstration of the divine approbation or even initiation of the whole sequence of events from the incarnation to the resurrection/ascension. No other world religion has so complex a theology as Christianity of its founder as person and as divine event. Muhammad was the final Prophet. There is no Muhammadology even if there is something of a theology of the inlibration of the uncreated Koran. So with the other world religions: at most, remote counterparts of Christology.[18]

Then within Christology itself the salvific moment ranges from stress on the incarnation to that on the crucifixion and the ascension. For an Athanasian, the assumption of human nature by the eternally begotten Son of God, neither the mode of generation nor the countenance of that Son, thought of on human analogy (the Son being eternal Word/Wisdom), was itself the salvific moment. In incarnational theology the Manger was in focus, not Mount Calvary. Another Christology will stress precisely the crucifixion as the salvifically effectual moment of the 'Mediator between God and Man, the *man* Jesus Christ,' (I Tim 2:5), of the High Priest (especially in Hebrews), of the Victim/Sacrifice, but also in some theories of the Atonement, of the Victor over Satan. The latter was decisively deceived by the seeming folly of wisdom made flesh, the stumbling block of ultimate Power, of Lordship crucified (cf. I Cor. 1:23). Satan had thereupon to release human nature held in his grasp since the Fall. From antiquity to the present, Christian theology has necessarily worked with both the incarnational and the self-sacrificial moment, but the very fact that Christian theology still speaks of 'theories' of the Atonement (a word stressing incarnational salvation) or of Redemption (a word stressing one of several crucifixional metaphors of salvation) is itself a remarkable fact, when in contrast normative Christianity has clear conciliar or papal *dogmas*, not opinions or theories, about many aspects of faith (as belief) and morals (praxis), such as the conciliar dogma of the Holy Trinity (Niceno-Constantinopolitan, 325/381), the one Person of Christ in two natures (Chalcedon, 451), and the papal dogma *ex cathedra* of the Bodily Assumption of Mary (1950).

Traditionally Jesus has also been understood as having discharged three offices (the *triplex munus Christi*) of Prophet, Priest, and initially largely unacknowledged King. This formula is not in Scripture but could be disengaged from it by Eusebius of Caesarea. It played some role in the Latin Middle Ages. It was made prominent by Erasmus of Rotterdam, taken over by John Laski, Reformer in England and his native Poland, incorporated into the *Institutes* by John Calvin, and spread to all the Orthodox in the *Confessio* of Peter Mohila of Kiev of 1643, to become by the twentieth century even a common conceptualization among post-Vatican II Catholics.[19] But besides the essentially Reformed term, ecumenized, of the *triplex munus Christi* and the disparate and even not wholly interconsistent theories of the Atonement/Redemption, there has developed from within the new Testament itself – Paul himself providing sanction for several subsequent emphases – a succession of diverse views of Jesus Christ and of his Work that were extruded, usually in council, as heretical from a Catholic/Orthodox perspective and which nevertheless live on in schismatic churches within and without the World Council of Churches and other formulations whose fossilized remains survive only in many an *adversus haereses* of one ancient Father or another. Medieval Latin and Byzantine Christendom, not to say Magisterial Protestantism, spawned or called forth further variants of Christianity so variegated that an objective but perspicacious student of these extinct and these still living forms of Christology would find it hard to assert how Jesus of Nazareth was a salvific figure for all these Christians even in some generic sense that all these groups would acknowledge as at least proximate to their own. And Christology is continuously in the process of devolution and reconstruction, perhaps currently most strikingly among Catholic theologians (the Flemish Edward Schillebeeckx).

The third modality of salvation is in the experiential present of any generation of Christians. Experiential Chrisianity has variously stressed the accessibility of Christ or the Holy Spirit or (the Triune) God Himself in conversion (with various forms in antiquity, in adhesion to a religious order, in revivalistic reaffirmation of subliminal faith), in the sacraments, in the sacrament of the eye (the Icon), in strenuous *imitatio Christi*, in saintly lives and through intercession with them after their death or martyrdom, in mystical ecstasy, in the formed conscience (sometimes in prophetic dissent), in the hearing of the salvific word, in the showering of charismatic gifts (healings, tongues, other miracles), in religious edifices, artifacts, and music.

The Holy Spirit or divine grace has been understood as notably mediated by the sacramental system: in the Latin Church, for example, in baptism, confirmation, penance, eucharist, ordination, marriage and extreme unction (reconciliation). Two of these as primordial deserve special notice as to their evolution.

Baptism in Christian antiquity was mostly of adult converts after a period of catechetical instruction. It took place in living water by immersion and it symbolized dying and rising with Christ, while the unction or chrismation that accompanied it symbolized the preparation of the body for possible death as a martyr and as a kind of royal unction, the mark of being part of the royal priesthood (I Pet. 2:9). Baptism was experiential and in the pre-Constantinian age fraught with hazard from the government, harassment and ostracism by former friends and neighbors. Converts by being baptized into Christ no longer conformed to the world (Rom. 12:4). In the course of Christian history pedobaptism became the more common form of the rite and only the sponsors heard the exorcism of the devil and all his pomps amid the crying of infants at the two main liturgical moments for baptism, at Easter and at Pentecost. Its functional and experiential equivalent has been variously: the monastic vow, penance and penitential acts such as pilgrimages or endowments, believers' rebaptism, owning of the covenant even sealed in one's own blood (Scottish Covenanters), the revivalist experience of taking Christ as Lord and Saviour.

Here is not the place to trace the development of the conceptualization or the practice of the eucharist. Suffice it to say that a commemorative and an eschatological note have never disappeared from the observance of the rite, although the vision of the Messianic Banquet is almost submerged in the liturgical churches. In antiquity two theories of the divine presence were formulated: symbolism and metabolism – the former connected with Augustine, the latter with Ambrose – and two theories of the origin of the change in the two elements (*species*) whether subjective or objective; by the priestly repetition of the institutional words of Jesus, as in the Latin tradition; by the invocation of the Holy Spirit in the *epiklesis* as in Ambrose and the Eastern churches. In the Latin development metabolism evolved into the transubstantiation of the elements into the Body and Blood of Jesus Christ virtually formulated at IV Lateran Council, 1215; and this dogma eventuated in the Feast of Corpus Christi (1264) which came to involve not only exposition of the Reserved Host in the church for adoration of the Living Presence but also the annual procession of the Host in an elaborate monstrance in the streets of the town on the first Thursday after Trinity Sunday. From early Christian antiquity up to the present the replication of the Event of the Last Supper foreshadowing the crucifixion, becoming a daily event for a priest, constituted an enormously meaningful experience of the *present* Christ. Medieval and Tridentine theology of the eucharistic action interpreted the central transaction of the Mass as indeed a repetition of the sacrifice on Calvary. While Luther insisted on the once-for-all-ness of that sacrifice on Calvary, his variant of transubstantiation, namely, the impanation of Christ by virtue of his 'ubiquity,' while the bread coexists with the Body (Luther himself did not employ the useful term consubstantiation), preserved for the Lutheran Mass a sacramental Presence, which disappeared in the Reformed versions of commemoration and subjective interpretations of the Real Presence.

A major issue as to the role of faith in the sense of a personal disposition in relation to the sacraments has been whether the faith and moral status of the celebrant and faith on the part of the recipient affect the validity of the sacrament. In antiquity the problem centered in the validity of the ordination of persons who lapsed during persecution; and the subjective view goes by the name of a bishop opposed to any blemish, Donatism. It was Augustine who theologically grounded the validity of a sacrament in the right intention of the recipient alone. The ancient issue of

Donatism, along with medieval and Reformation-Era 'Neo Donatism,' divides even today, for example, the vast majority of pedobaptist Christians from believers' baptists who, taking as *their* model the most conspicuous examples of conversion to Christ in Scripture, opted for the baptism, even perhaps by immersion, of those only who know what *they* believe (Mark 16:15 f.; Matt. 28:19 f.). Rebaptism of adult schismatics from antiquity down to the present (in fewer and fewer instances among Catholics and the Orthodox), the practice of the Waldensians, Anabaptists, Polish Brethren, Baptists, Disciples of Christ, the Pentecostalists follows this line, despite Ephesians 4:5 on one faith (sense two) and one baptism, since explicit faith and the validity of sacral actions has at least as long a history in Christianity as the Augustinian doctrine of sacramental efficacy *ex opere operato*.

This same issue of faith and order is invoked in the ecumenical question of whether schismatic ordinations are valid. Thus the ecclesiological and indeed even the social/ethnic/political dimension of faith are involved in the appropriation of sacramental grace and in other questions of what is to be recognized as licit mediation of grace in the present. Alas, these issues have become convoluted as a result of various historic displacements, complicating the most irenic attempts at rational articulation.

There is also the mediation of grace through various kinds of *imitatio Christi et apostolorum*, from ancient martyrdom, through monasticism and sectarian discipleship, to social gospel activism in the name and by the eschatological ordinance of Jesus Christ (Matt. 25:14–30), and, in marked contrast, also the pious acceptance of the cruciform suffering inherent in the human condition (taking up the personal cross, Matt. 16:24 f.), the gospel of all creatures answered by the Gospel to all creatures (cf. Rom. 8:22, Mark 16:15). *Imitatio* finds expression even in the social/national/political context of the faith community, manifested in such ceremonies as liturgical kingship, royal unction modeled on baptism (see above Faith: 4), associated with the power to heal disease by the royal touch. Thus, even temporal rulers could be conduits of grace or epiphanies of Christ, as in their Maundy Thursday washing of the feet of the poor.

Mysticism, another manifestation of the divine immediacy, was not coeval with the rise of Christianity, but presently developed distinctly Christian forms partly under the influence of Neoplatonism: pneumatic-gnostic, Montanist, Dionysian, Palamite, Gallic (Gersonian), Rhenish, and Iberian forms of mystical spirituality. Often at issue with the Palamite Jesus Prayer (prayer without ceasing, I Thes. 5:17) and disparate Latin mystical formulations, some under medieval Muslim and Jewish influence, was whether in the present life Christians can so prepare themselves inwardly by sensitizing alleged receptors (*apex mentis*, *synteresis*, or *scintilla animae* (*Fünklein*), or the enflamed will) so as to become beholders of the Beatific Vision or recipients of divine ecstasy and even instrumentalities of divine union. Sometimes the imagery is nuptial (bridal). The degree to which mystical ecstasy is wholly the work of God or the devotee's achievement, or the synergism of both, is a recurrent theme of mystical theology. But whatever the experience, it is a present event for the believer in relation to the Holy Spirit or to Jesus Christ as Bridegroom or to the whole Triune God or even to the ultimate Ground of divine Being (*Abgrund*) beyond the Three Persons (Meister Eckhardt, O.P., deemed on this 'excess' heretical).

The receptor of mysticism is also called conscience or is at least related to it. From the point of view of sociology the conscience is only the condensation, interiorization, and individuation of the group consciousness and rises as distinctive only in a matured and individualistic culture. The very etymology suggests a social context (*con* equals *with*). But however explained sociologically and even sociobiologically, in Christianity it has had its own history (cf. I Pet. 2:19, 3:16, 21, etc.).[20]

The conscience throughout most of the tradition, reflecting the socio-ecclesial context and eventually discrete family ambience, is experienced as the accusing conscience. This is true in the Lutheran cultural context. In the Reformed and particularly in the Puritan development conscience comes very close to inner illumination, thought to be from a source higher than that of the ecclesial environment and as a prophetic or a warning or an enabling conscience, giving rise to what is called the non-conformist conscience, which would withdraw from the established church rather than violate what is experienced as a divine directive from within: this within groups as divergent in polity in seventeenth and eighteenth-century Britain as the Quakers and the Independents. The view of the inviolable conscience, presupposed in several American constitutional documents, evolves as eventually conscientious objection to war, guaranteed by the Constitution for members of the historic peace churches and recently extended to conscience even without religious sanction. There is an Anglo-American history of great significance for all societies in a line running well before George Fox through David Thoreau to Martin Luther King, Jr. The conscience is, however, here adduced as another example of the divine voice experienced in the present. It is not an accusing conscience but an emboldening conscience, impelling one to speak and act against the ambient majority. It is scarcely to be considered personally salvific but is another example of the experienced divine presence.

Another sub-locus of the present experience of salvation is in the hearing of the Word. Martin Luther said that 'the ears alone are the organs of a Christian man',[21] for faith comes by hearing the word (Rom. 10:17). This is experiential, though not mystical. To be sure, Luther's first printed work was *Theologie Deutsch* (Wittenberg, 1516) – his name for an anonymous mystical tract in the Rhenish tradition; but Luther and classical Protestantism as a whole programmatically turned against mysticism as just one other form of vain striving for merit. Instead, Luther stressed the present experience of the Word duly preached as a rehearsal of the Christ Event, of Law and Gospel, of *Christus pro nobis*, which experience comes to the hearing congregation mediated through the preached Word from the written Word, by a duly ordained and constituted preacher.

In the ancient Church, there was, of course, the *kerygma*, the proclamation by itinerant apostles and evangelists of the Good News. But within the ancient churches the homily was not preached to save. Celtic and Anglo-Saxon, and Slavono-Greek missionaries to the Slavs to some extent revived the saving sermon. Then the Franciscan and Dominican friars in the twelfth century revived the saving *kerygma* in preaching in the open squares in the growing towns especially among the many marginalized denizens crowded there; and St. Francis of Assisi journeyed with eleven companions to Egypt to convert the Muslims by preaching, and he even approached Sultan El Kamil at Damietta in 1219. The two orders of preaching mendicants were prominent also in the Era of Reformation and Counter-Reform, the Franciscans having by then created several new families of preachers, notably the Capuchins, bent on reclaiming converts to Protestantism and gaining new converts in the Iberian possessions beyond the seas. They were joined by the new Iberian order of the Jesuits, skilled in theological debate but also in great preaching especially at court to convert or to recover for the Catholic fold.

Luther's stress on the preaching and the salvific hearing of the word of God as Christ *pro nobis* became the basis of the immense development of the sermon in Protestantism until at length it would actually leave the pulpit, insisted upon by Luther, to the open air with John Wesley. Against the express injunction of his bishop, he took 'the whole world as [his] parish,' preaching in town squares and open fields, until at length the Evangelical Revival in English-speaking countries and especially in America took on the new forms that have evolved still further into the preaching of the electronic church.

So influential has Luther been on saving faith *ex auditu* that in the Polish National Church, which arose among Americans of Polish ancestry, living among Protestants and reacting against the perfunctory Roman Catholic homily of the time, the preaching of the Word became one of the seven sacraments (baptism and confirmation being conjoined); while in Vatican II the foundations were established for making within the vernacular Mass, amid the enhancement of the readings from Scripture and congregational hymn-singing, the once parish-managerial homily into a saving sermon based on a text from the lectionary.

In the meantime, still very much within the tradition of Luther, Rudolf Bultmann (b. 1884), influenced by Søren Kierkegaard and the younger Martin Heidegger, developed the motif of Luther of the faith *ex auditu*, as both New Testament professor and existentialist theologian, into a very influential and sophisticated form of experienced nowness. Though he was radical in his demythologizing of the three-storey religious world and the theologoumena of the New Testament, he remained faithful to Luther in his stress upon 'the Christ Event' (*Christusereignis*) that continuously replicates itself in the hearing of the Word. Bultmann based this updated doctrine of the present Christ, in part, on John 5:24 f.: 'He that hears my word and believes in him that sent me has eternal life.' Bultmann expressly connected the resultant Christ Event in the existential/experiential present with Luther's doctrine of justification by faith alone. Far, then, from being only a past event prepared for in the history of Israel, the Bultmannian Christ Event is a now-experience with Christ recurrently present in the ministry of reconciliation (II Cor. 5:18 f.).

Of the other modalities of the sense of the divine immediacy in the present, the most compelling are Icons, legitimated against the injunction against images of the divine in the Decalogue by virtue of incarnational theology, clarified decisively at II Nicaea in 787. Further, the diversity of the Christian sense for holy space and the divine presence therein is set forth in the history of Christian edifices for worship and contemplation, as diverse as the hermit's cell, the ancient basilica, the sealed cave of the recluse, the Romanesque or Gothic cathedral, the Rococo monastery, the New England white wooden meeting house, the plain Friends' meeting house without steeple, the post-World War II edifices of architectural daring in devastated Europe, the thatched huts modeled on tribal chieftain's dwellings in Africa for the worship of the King of heaven, the camp meetings with or without tabernacles of the American frontier and their urban equivalents. But only in some of these is there an intended or yearned for sense of the *mysterium tremendum et fascinosum*, for many of the aforementioned edifices for worship stress precisely not the space enclosed but the people gathered. Thus it is perhaps in various liturgical and ecstatic or spontaneous forms of music, from chants to hymns and choruses, popular, traditional, and especially composed of highly structured genres, that for many the sense of the divine presence is most powerfully evoked.[22]

The fourth temporal locus of salvation is in the future, in the *eschaton*. It is the Kingdom of God, whether understood as direct immortality upon death, or at the Second Advent, concurrent with the Resurrection of the Dead and the Last Judgment. To be sure, the sense of the inbreaking Realm of God in history, whether experienced as imminent or as immanent, has its not incidental significance in Christian behavior in a given age or region, as socio-political differences among amillennialists, premillennialists, and postmillennialists make evident. Nevertheless, eschatology is by definition the futuristic locus of salvation.

Besides the prophetic, apocalyptic, and millennialist parts of the Old Testament (notably Daniel) and the apocrypha of the intertestamental period, much of it preserved by Christians in the Septuagint and Vulgate while allowed to drop from the canon of Jewry, the New Testament itself has three not wholly interconsistent eschatologies. In Jesus' word to the forgiven thief (Luke 23:43) there is the strongest single statement about immediate immortality (entry into paradise). Elsewhere there is much more evidence of the sleep of the soul, a euphemism for death, until the imminent resurrection, but this soul sleep came to be read out of the Scriptures by lenses polished and refocused by Platonic and Neoplatonic conviction as to personal immortality. In the case of an Origen, preexistent souls temporally fallen, as it were, by incarnations were thought of as released by faith in Christ for immortality in a larger context that allowed for an eventual universal salvation, even of the fallen angels, Satan at their head. Paul, in contrast, is vivid in his dominating picture of an imminent descent of Jesus Christ to lift up the living and the resurrected deceased in glorified bodies to join him in his kingdom (I Cor. 15:12–58; I Thess. 4:13–17). Yet in one place even that kingdom of Christ is said by him to be subject to God that all may be in all (cf. I Cor. 15:24–28), a subordination of Christ's Kingdom disallowed by the Niceno-Constantinopolitan Creed: ' ... and his kingdom shall have no end' (against Marcellus of Ancyra an ally of Athanasius). It is primarily the Seer of the Apocalypse who imported into Christianity through the canon the intertestamental Jewish idea of the resurrection of the saints (then of all deceased), along with a millennial rule of Christ from Zion, after which would follow a period of final tribulation (Rev. 20:3–6), even for the saints of three and a half years (or its equivalent of 42 months = 6 × 7 or 1260 days or 'time, times, and half of a time': Rev. 11:3, 12:6, 14; 13:5 with support from Dan. 7:25; 12:7).

All four modalities of faith from simple trust in the Gospel, long interpreted as a promise of immediate, personal immortality to the rallying of a community preparatory to the imminent Second Advent and millennial rule of Christ, have filled Church history, as in foregatherings of the expectant Montanist faithful in ancient Papuza; for most of ante-Nicene Fathers a reign, thought of as beginning on Zion; for the militant Hussites in the fifteenth century at Tabor; for Anabaptists in the sixteenth century centered in Münster or Strassburg; for the Fifth Monarchy Men in the seventeenth century in England; for the followers of William Miller (Seventh-Day Advents) somewhere in America in 1843; for the Mormons, though not expressly, Utah, 1847; for the Unification Church possibly in Korea reunified; for some members of the Moral Majority, again starting in Jerusalem after a world struggle at Armageddon (Megiddo).

Modifications and permutations of the two basic eschatologies involving in the medieval west the development of an intermediate state of the departed, Purgatory, and the indulgence system related to it, as well as fascinating theodicies and theologies of history reach from Augustine with his intermingled Cities and Paul Orosius with his decisive identification of the Redeemer as born not only a Jew but also notably as a *subject* of the Roman Empire (which then, with the help of Daniel and II Thess. 2:6–9, acquired soteriological significance), through Joachim of Flora's dispensationalism of the Three Persons and the Letter of the Athonite monk Philotheus about Moscow as the Third Rome, to the dispensationalism of the followers of Cyrus I, and even to current papal eschatology. Scofield, drawing heavily upon the millennialism of the Plymouth Brethren (followers of John Nelson Darby, d. 1882), made of his *Scofield Reference Bible* (1909) the basis for a sharp discontinuity between Israel and the Church and for a premillennialism that allows for a pretribulation (cf Rev. 2:16) rupture of the true Church removed therefrom before the millennium.[23] The eschatological concern is not only sectarian. The present Polish Pontiff, not only in his first encyclical, *Redemptor hominis* with five references to future Advent in some sense, is perhaps the most eschatologically oriented of any Pope since the schismatic bishop of Rome, Hippolytus (d. *c.* 236) who wrote not only his *Refutation of All Heresies* but an *Antichrist* and a *Commentary on Daniel*. The eschatology of John Paul II makes much of the ascetic motif and sees in priests and nuns who have made themselves celibate 'forerunners of the Kingdom' (cf. Matt. 19:12).[24]

III CHRISTIANITY AND THE COMPARATIVE HISTORY OF RELIGION

Christianity in taking over the account of Adam created by God in his image (Gen. 1:26), not only, with the Jews, affirmed the unity of the human race, but also by continuing, as the Jews with the same texts did not, a pervasive aboriginal sin that brought about death for human as well as all other creatures, made Jesus Christ as the Last or Second Adam (Rom. 5:14; I Cor. 15:22, 45) even though 'born of woman' (Gal. 4:4), not expressly of Virgin Birth, the potential basis of redemption, through his Gospel, of the whole human race. Since Jesus Christ was also the incarnation of eternal divine Wisdom/Logos (John 1:1–14; Col. 1:15), even the preexistent Christ (Phil. 2:6–11) as God's *instrument of righteous rule* on earth, Christianity, as no other religion has alike on the anthropological, soteriological, and *theo*logical level a seemingly divine assignment to prevail over all religions and to pervade all peoples. Indeed, as late as in the massive theological work of Karl Barth, Christianity was set forth as the unique revelation of God, destined to 'abolish' all religions. Barth, having interpreted election less individualistically than the classical Protestant Reformers, stressed as primordial God's election of the People of the Old Covenant, of Jesus especially foreseen as the Mediator, the Man, and of the Church of Jesus Christ. Programmatically proselytizing, as it broke out of the chrysalis of what was largely an ethnic Judaism, Christianity has understood itself from Paul to Barth as different from other world religions in not being in fact a religion but the sole valid vehicle of salvation. The Neo-Orthodoxy of Barth was an immensely scholarly repristination of the traditional Christian view and globally influential, not only among Protestants but also among Catholics. However, it no longer prevails in Christian academe and is represented only in sectarian form among Churches called collectively 'the Third

117

Force' by Henry Pitney Van Dusen after a world tour in the service of world Christian missions, and only in certain circles of Catholicism that have not assimilated the implications of the inaugural encyclical of Paul VI, *Ecclesiam suam* with its theology of concentric circles of human faith and of *Lumen gentium* promulgated by Paul VI at the end of Vatican II. Thus for the three major thrusts of historic Christianity, Orthodoxy (overlooked by Van Dusen), Catholicism, and Protestantism-Anglicanism the problem of Christianity among the religions of the world is a pressing problem.

It is well known that the followers of Jesus Christ were first called Christians to distinguish them in Antioch from other Jews who did not accept Jesus as the Messiah (Acts 2:26). It is not so well known that *Christianismus* was used by Tertullian. More to the point is that *Christianitas* goes back to the Theodosian Code in reference to both the *official* Christian religion (some heresies by this time subject to imperial penalties, rebaptism of Donatists, by death) and orthodox/catholic Christendom of the imperially governed *oikoumene* (xv, 5, 5; xii, 1, 123). It is of interest in a comparative context that the basic word for the congeries of religion of the followers of Jesus Christ implies at once orthodoxy or catholicity in the sense of heresy-free Christianity and also already in antiquity suggests the religio-political dimension of correct faith, our fourth sense of that word (above, Part I).

Increasingly it is observed that Christianity is better understood at its interior and on its margins when brought into historic and current comparison with other religions. In the past the study of other religions has been variously motivated. It has grown out of missionary concern to understand the religious culture in preparation for effectual evangelization and to ascertain the criteria to discriminate valid from syncretistic acculturation. It has grown out of an academic concern to understand the ancient religious environment in which the Church vanquished early rivals by both holding itself apart and by appropriate assimilation of Gentile motifs and institutions (*Religionsgeschichtliche*). It has grown out of the Transcendentalist concern in America, with European antecedents and analogues, to discover the common elements in world religions (the Deism of the philosophes; the liberal Christianity of Gotthold Lessing, *Nathan der Weise*, 1779;

Die Erziehung des Menschengeschlechts, 1780).[25] With the rise of state university departments of religion in the United States, various efforts (for example, Samuel Preus) have been made to locate in the Reformation concern to divest pure Christianity from its historic deformities another root of the objective study of religion.[26] Most recently comparative religious dialogue has grown out of the realization of the necessity for Christian theology to adjust inwardly, structurally to the globally perceived limits of internal and interfaith dialogue with the persistent pluralism of religion. Interfaith dialogue is more a felt need of Christians than of their interfaith partners who, with some qualifications respecting Islam, have no such structurally universalizing drive and assignment as is inherent in the Church (Leroy Rouner).[27]

For Christianity the comparative assignment has both an intra-faith and an interfaith agenda. On the intra-faith agenda is surely the recurrent problem of historic truth, and the inveterate tendency of Christians to resist innovation and renovation, despite more sanction for it in the Bible than in any other sacred scripture (above, Introduction).

It is to the discredit of Christianity that while proclaiming to have the absolute truth, the truth that sets men free (John 8:31), it permitted itself such an egregious succession of pseudepigraphic writings amid its most sacred scriptures, then in its tradition, which is filled with Pseudo-Dionysiuses, Pseudo-Athanasiuses, Pseudo-Clementines, Pseudo-Ambroses, Pseudo-Ignatiuses, Pseudo-Augustines, Pseudo-Isidores, and even one or two instances of Pseudo-Thomases. To be sure, it is anachronistic to apply modern standards of scholarly truth-telling to ancient religious documents; but the oldest commandments ascribed to God as given to Moses even appear in two versions (Ex. 20:1–7; Deut. 5:6–21) and are so counted in Christian tradition that the Orthodox, the Reformed, the Anglicans, and the many denominational offspring of these last two groups have one arrangement, while the Roman Catholics and the Lutherans agree on another sequence. Thus even the ancient commandment not to lie is the ninth commandment in one series and the eighth in the other. But it is also to the credit of Christianity and the Hebraism/Judaism that lies behind it and has run parallel with it to the present that a great deal of blemishing truth is preserved and

119

not excised from Church history and the chronicles and archives and monuments on which it rests: about the human condition, human nature and all its vagaries, about sacral kings, about summoned prophets, holy doctors of the Church before their full conversion, even about the personal lives of the incumbents of holy offices. Although Christians once called themselves the saints of the Most High, Christianity has understood sanctity as much in terms of the mighty and sacred acts of God or his Spirit in men and movements as in personal sanctification. Christianity has conscientiously preserved the record of the surds and absurds, the heretical and the horrendous, the hypocrisy in the name of the holy and holiness in the interest of personal or class power.

Some time before our full awareness as Christians of the importance of dialogue with the representatives of other faith communities as a pressing Christian theological problem, we had already come to the point where, from being embarrassed by the profusion of denominations and the fissiparous character of Christianity, we could see that all this was in fact the unfoldment in history of the plenitude of the Christ Event (in the historian's sense of the Bultmannian experiential term). In the intra-Christian ecumenical movement, there is uncertainty, of course, as to whether we as individuals can ever fully participate in the richness of the tradition if we fail to be loyal, in ecumenical openness, to the specificity of our own particular confessional tradition, theology, polity, and praxis, updated for the modern world, lest we become disconnected spiritualizers, vaporized in the steady flow of ecclesiastical development. We cannot be just ecumenical Christians: a specific commitment is the concomitant of capacious sympathies.

Scanning the plenitude of the Christian communities of faith, one has no doubt about the need of defining further the emerging discipline of the comparative study of the Christian religions. In an ecumenical climate it can be undertaken without rancor and partisanship.

The discipline of a comparative morphology of Christianity is not a systematic theology that abstracts from persons and places, movements and monuments, to distill an essence from what is the most history-conscious religion of the world, save Judaism itself. The discipline is aware that what needs clarification and comparison and ecumenical assessment is *more than Christian thought* and some selected Christian doctrines or privileged practices that the historian of Christian thought deigns to bring within the purview of scrutiny or exposition. Church history as the discipline at hand for comparative intra-faith religious morphology is not auxiliary to systematic theology or Christian ethics but an important discipline of *divinity* in its own right, the interpretation of the ideally One Holy Catholic Church and also of all the allegedly malicious heresies and of the communion of saints and of all the spurned rascals and heretics who sometimes turn out to have been not only as earnest but as close to the truth once for all delivered to the saints (Jude 3) as the self-declared catholic, apostolic, and orthodox.

It has been humorously observed by Alfred North Whitehead that one should 'seek simplicity and distrust it.' In the case of Church history or better the historiography of the Church conceived ecumenically in time and in space the intra-Christian scrutiny is insufficient if it turns out to be too simple. One understands in any religion orthodoxy best by grasping the import of the heresy tempting because of its simplicity. And surely one understands the Church in the sense of a congeries of peoples in different traditions by seeing Christianity on the edges of Islam, on the frontiers of secular humanism, on the borders of Marxism, at the interior of a culture essentially Hindu, at the bottom of society where another religion or ideology makes of Christians second-class or even alienated citizens.

The Ultimate behind and within the phenomenon of religion is at work in Christianity and some of that grace, and love, 'wrath' and seeming indifference, the remoteness and the mercy or even the sometimes mystical intimacy when seen in other religions is also experienced differently in one's own. The generic character of religion is such that the Church historian, like the historian of Islam, will wish to lift up his eyes from time to time to the distant blue hill country of some other world religion and he or she should at least once during a career make a scholarly excursion to that unfamiliar region; and returning with sharpened vision as to the cunning of love and grace, he or she will have found that the local hills, rills, and plateaus are probably no higher but also probably no duller or deeper or more profound than those visited and

121

admired from afar; and with renewed diligence he or she can join others in the irrigation of the more parched portions of the long familiar promised land.

CONCLUSION

It is clear from what has been said by a Church historian, in honoring an Islamist and a world figure who has placed the comparative history of religion on a new footing, that there is need both for an intrafaith (i.e., Christian) ecumenism of dialogue and possible merger or union and for an interfaith dialogue without any expectation of union; and that in engaging in either form of dialogue it is quite possible that a believer or a devotee and whole communities of faith will find they also understand themselves better as a result of hearing and being heard by others. The discipline, besides systematic theology, involving intrafaith ecumenism is Church history, not 'the history of [official] Christianity' or 'the history of Christian thought' or 'ecclesiastical history.' Although, to be sure, the meanings of these terms have varied and overlapped over the centuries in different languages, *l'histoire ecclésiastique* and *l'histoire de l'Église*, to resort to another language wherein one term makes the stress on the community of faith especially clear, there is inherent in the discipline of Church history, as it has evolved, the disposition to be ideally comprehensive in its coverage. Although Church history (in Acts, in Hegesippus, in Eusebius of Caesarea) started out as a branch of apologetics and in the Middle Ages sank to the level of chronicle and was revived in the Latin Schism of the sixteenth century as a branch of theological polemics (the *Centuries* of Magdeburg, the *Annales* of Cesare Baronius), the discipline since the eighteenth century has been characterized by *intended* inclusiveness and increasing objectivity in setting forth the multitudes of the Christian people under their variegated confessional banners, not as a postulated corporeal entity divinely injected into human history, 'a reification of a divine idea.' Church history began with an inchoate *ekklēsia* that thought of itself as a sect in Jewry with a world mission.[28]

One does not usually find in 'histories of Christian thought' or 'of Christianity' anything about the Association of Evangelical Baptists in the Soviet Union, the new Prayer People among the Yorubas of Nigeria, about the four jurisdictional groupings of Malabar Christians tracing their origins in Kerala in India to St. Thomas, or about Mormons, Spiritualists, and Christian Scientists as outgrowths of the American transposition of historic Christianity, or about the 'native' *Tridentine* Church of the People's Republic of China with its insistence on the Three Selves, or about the Ibero-Amerindian-African syncretistic groups in Latin America, and their analogues in earlier history except in the regional history of religion. But Church history, as it has evolved under various influences into its comprehensive stewardship for the whole range of Christian faith and its vagaries, in its magnanimous and nonjudgmental posture, is under its emerging canons required to take note of the nonconformist, the marginal, the unofficial versions of Christianity, and those professing to be based upon a book of secondary revelation (e.g., *Science and Health*), as well as of all the thrusts at the interior of the main body of Christians. Church history is the discipline of interpreting the People of Christ who know that Something was folded into history and into the very substance of human nature by the incarnation and the crucifixion and who live not only off the fleeting dynamism of the current culture in part created by them or their ancestors but also out of the fresh vitalities ever irrigating that society and especially that People by grace. In any case, in that interfaith/intrafaith dialogue in time and space of the scholarship dealing with the communities that have called themselves Christian, what we at the outset might well hold to conventionally though perhaps even conscientiously, yet precariously and with ever decreasing satisfaction as to many specifics, becomes enhanced for us both as to our ultimate conviction and, as we have become sensitized in dialogue, as to our mutual compassion in our common human condition before the Mystery that brought us all forth from the darkness of the womb of time. Meanwhile, in our interfaith dialogue in the comparative study of religion, we engage in continuous redefinition of what it means to be creatures of the Creator, subjects of a Realm of grace, and, if Christians, members of a

123

mystical Body in time and space that may well be that in which we *all* 'live and move and have our being,' as Paul said (as reported from Mars Hill, Acts 17:28), quoting himself expressly from an ancient Greek poet.

> Cambridge, Massachusetts, 19 July 1983,
> On the vigil of the Sixth Assembly in Vancouver of the World Council of Churches of Christ,
> In the middle of the papal jubilee for reflection on the 1950th anniversary of the Crucifixion,
> In the midst of fifth-centenary global celebrations of the birth of Martin Luther,
> On the occasion of 180th anniversary of the first comprehensive (six-volume) *Church History* to have been published in the New World, dedicated by Joseph Priestley (b. 1753) to President Thomas Jefferson.

NOTES

1. For Wilfred Smith's discussion of the search for an 'essence of Christianity,' see *The Meaning and End of Religion* (New York: Macmillan, 1963), pp. 47 f.
2. Helmut Köster, 'The Four Primitive Gospels,' *Harvard Theological Review*, LX:2 (April 1968), pp. 203–47.
3. On scripture, see the Honorand's 'The Study of Religion and the Study of the Bible,' *Religious Diversity: Essays of WCS*, ed. Willard G. Oxtoby (New York & London: Harper & Row, 1976), pp. 41–56.
4. WCS holds that the Church was once thought of 'as an idea in the mind of God and as injected ... into history in the first century'. 'With the theological postulate gone,' he concludes a long paragraph, 'I suppose that Ph.D.s in Church History will cease.' 'Muslim-Christian Relations,' *On Understanding Islam: Selected Essays* (The Hague, etc.: Mouton, 1981), pp. 250 f. The Honorand has evidently in mind such conceptualizations of the church as the manifold wisdom of God now made known to principalities and powers (Eph. 3:10), as the body of Christ (Col. 7:18, 24), and as the eschatological Bride adorned (Rev. 21:2). It is also true that Hermas in his *Shepherd* used the metaphor of an Old Lady for the church and

that some Gnostics imagined among the many aeons of their pleroma a preexistent Church. But basically the word was used of individual congregations and only gradually of the congeries of churches called for the first time 'catholic' by Ignatius of Antioch in his Epistle to the Smyrnians, 8, 2. The concept of the preexistently determined elect as constituting a church, as it were, in the mind of God, was notably developed by Augustine, who used for it *civitas* rather than *ecclesia*. It is the gentle thrust of my essay that Church historiography does not rest, as a discipline of divinity or Church history as a discrete and inwardly dynamic and distinctive part of world history, on a phantom postulate. See further n. 29.

5. Since 1969 this has been made a Marian feast, the Solemnity of Holy Mary, Mother of God, a nomenclature marking a shift in Catholic perspective on the Old Testament, closer to that of classical Protestants.

6. In the same, Ch. 1, Tertullian makes clear that 'a man becomes a Christian, he is not born one.' The natural theology of Tertullian, so far as it went, has a venerable Christian history. The English Deist, Matthew Tindal, would later write *Christianity as Old as the Creation* (London, 1730), a conceptualization that far exceeded Tertullian's *anima naturaliter christiana.*

7. On the overlapping circles of faith in various religious traditions, see WCS, *Towards a World Theology* (London: Macmillan; Philadelphia: Westminster, 1981), esp. Ch. 1, 'A History of Religion in the Singular,' pp. 3–20.

8. WCS shows that on the level of individuals religious terms and practices may vary from decade to decade or even from day to day, *Meaning and End*, pp. 190 f.

9. The Honorand devoted a volume to the explication of faith as 'engagement' in religious history with a disparaging view of propositional belief, *Faith and Belief* (Princeton: University Press, 1979).

10. See on Credo in *Faith and Belief*, pp. 69–104, and further on the relation of faith to its rational expression, WCS, *Belief and History* (Charlottesville: University Press of Virginia, 1977).

11. WCS casts the problem of faith and reason in historical rather than philosophical terms: a question of the relation of the classical Greek tradition of faith in reason and the Christian faith in God, *Faith and Belief*, pp. 15 f. I have myself been helped by the distinctions discovered in the meaning of faith in Greek philosophy by Harry A. Wolfson and seen by him to have been replicated and amplified by scriptural faith, *The Philosophy of the Church Fathers*, 3rd ed. (Cambridge: Harvard University Press, 1970, Chs. v and vi.)

12. One may refer here to the Honorand's concept of 'cumulative tradition,' added to, subtracted from, and preserved in such a way that each generation hands down but also shapes and selects, *Meaning and Religion*, pp. 157 ff.; *Faith and Belief*, pp. 17 f.

13. I am aware that in distinguishing from faith as *fiducia*: belief as *credo* or *confessio* and then identifying the community creating the belief as also *a faith*, I seem to be unnecessarily equivocal; but I wish thereby to underscore the great difference between the communal *credo* and the creative and relatively autonomous *summae* and systematic theologies undertaken by individual believers (even though they may call forth schools: Origenist, Augustinian, Thomist, Calvinist, Barthian) and then to lift up, in honor of an Islamist, the approximations to religio-political faith endemic in Church history, comparable to the Submitted Community (church, state, and society of Muslims) that is Islam, even though the term 'faith' rarely covers the societary entity in Christianity, whether churchly or sectarian.

14. On 'faith's expression in community,' see *Meaning of Religion*, pp. 174 ff. and *World Theology*, p. 47.

15. It is of passing interest that it would be in predominantly black Francophone Haiti that the Iberian system would have been adopted and then endured as the last instance. WCS has shown special interest in the 'trilogue' of medieval Spain, see *World Theology*, pp. 90 f. and *Understanding Islam*, p. 234. Since the Pope is the nearest Christians have to a Caliph, I make bold to note my own recent work, *The Contours of Church-State Relations in John Paul II* (Waco, Texas: Baylor University Press, 1983).

16. GHW, 'Four Modalities of Violence [in Church History],' *Journal of Church and State*, XVI (Winter, Spring, 1974), pp. 11–30; 237–61.

17. WCS, with special reference to the crisis of the partition of India, shows vividly how the state is an almost necessary form to be taken by Islam, *Islam in Modern History* (Princeton: University Press, 1957/1977), Ch. 5, esp. pp. 213 ff.

18. One thinks of boddhisattvas and imams, but these are respectively embodiments of great souls who have followed the Buddha and tarry this side of Nirvana to help others on the Dharmapada and in Shiite Islam the imams, as any of the recognized twelve heads of Islam beginning with Ali and his sons. Bahaism holds to a spiritual succession of incarnate imams, like the succession of Tibetan Dalai Lamas. In some Buddhist sutras there are actually three bodies of the Buddha: the cosmic body, the body of bliss, and the transformation body actualized under the Bodhi Tree. For the inlibration of the Uncreated Koran and the preexistent Created Heavenly Koran, I

have found Harry A. Wolfson illuminating. *The Philosophy of the Kalam* (Cambridge: Harvard University Press, 1976), Ch. 3.

19. I had occasion to trace the history of *triplex munus Christi* in '*Translatio Studii*: The Puritans' Conception of Their First University, 1636,' *Archive for Reformation History*, LVII: 1/2 (1966), pp. 152–81, and in 'Erasmianism in Poland 1518–1605, *Polish Review*, XXII (1977), pp. 3–50. The *triplex munus* appears in Mohila's *Confessio* as *quaestio* xxxiv, placed there under Calvinist influence, Philip Schaff, *The Creeds of Christendom*, 3 volumes (New York, 1881–90), III, p. 314.

20. Cf. Krister Stendahl, 'The Apostle Paul and the Introspective Conscience of the West,' *Harvard Theological Review*, LVI:3 (July 1963), pp. 199–215.

21. *Lectures on Hebrews*, April 1517 to March 1518; Weimar Edition, LVII:3, p. 221.

22. The Honorand has long been sensitive to the expression of faith in art: *Meaning and End*, pp. 172 ff., *The Faith of Other Men* (New York: New American Library, 1963), pp. 53 ff.; *Understanding Islam*, pp. 3–25.

23. The most comprehensive collections of eschatological documents are those by LeRoy Edwin Froom, *The Prophetic Faith of Our Fathers*, 4 volumes (Washington, D.C.: Review and Herald Press, 1950–54) and Ernst Staehelin, *Die Veründingung des Reiches Gottes: Zeugnisse*, 7 volumes (Basel: Reinhardt, 1958–65).

24. GHW, 'The Ecumenical Intentions of Pope John Paul II,' part i, *Harvard Theological Review*, LXXV: 2 April 1982), esp. pp. 144–52.

25. For the role of Transcendentalism with special reference to Harvard, see my 'The Attitude of Liberals in New England toward Non-Christian Religions, 1784–1873,' *Crane Theological Review*, IX:2 (Winter 1967), pp. 59–89.

26. Samuel Preus, 'Zwingli, Calvin, and the Origin of Religion,' *Church History*, XLVI (1977), pp. 186–202; 'Religion and Bacon,' *Continuity and Discontinuity in Church History*, ed. by F. Forrester Church and Timothy George (Leiden: Brill, 1979), pp. 267–84.

27. Cf. Leroy S. Rouner, 'Rethinking the Christian Mission in India Today,' *Religion in Life*, XXXV:4 (1968); pp. 530–45; and his forthcoming, *Return Home in Peace: The Christian Contribution to World Community*, esp. Chs. 8 and 9. This thought seems to be closely related to that of the Honorand, who, though *sui generis*, perhaps represents an updated and very much more nuanced version of the Transcendentalist quest for an ultimate unity at the interior of every world facet of faith. Cf. his moving summons in *World*

Theology, p. 129: 'It will not be possible [to build a world community], unless each of us brings to it the resources of his or her mind, and . . . faith.' Cf. the same thought earlier, *Meaning and End*, p. 9.

28. This section may serve as a respectful rejoinder to the Honorand's disparagement of Church History as a divinity school discipline or as a topic of doctoral research. See above, n. 4, in reference to a programmatic paragraph, which seems, in having seen in 'the mediaeval period' the most successful for doctoral candidates, because there Christianity is seen in full historical and cultural context, to have made the Islamic vision of religion normative. Surely the pre-Constantinian Era of the growth of the New Testament canon and the extraordinary formulations of the faith and discipline in the face of imperial persecution in the Ante-Nicene Period, must by all be regarded as being as normative for at least the majority of Christians, including even Catholics, as the medieval period of greatest papal ascendancy. In contrast to Islam, which rose like a storm over the desert and did not calm down until three of the five patriarchates and the corresponding areas of the Christianized Roman Empire had been subdued, Christianity preserves at its core a body of literature, canon and Church Fathers, reflective of believers who lived for almost three centuries as a latently subversive (prophetic) force within the body politic. Ecumenical Christianity, including now Orthodoxy and surely the Catholic Church with its own sovereign patriarch in Vatican City State with a global diplomatic corps of prelates, must continue to be understood within its own scriptural and confessional history and awareness of being a community in time no less than in global space and not a spiritual epiphenomenon of era, nation, and class. And even Islam, with its doctrine comparable to election, has also several other 'postulates' that, for some, may also be 'gone' without Islam's ceasing any more than the Church to be an historic entity requiring its own special methodologies, whether that Christianity be 'official,' as under Theodosius, or illicit as in the Ante-Nicene Era, or separated from the state, beginning among the first, in the spirit of the Enlightenment, in the United States: a separationism that began in earnest in the restorationist movements of the sixteenth century (see my *La Reforma Radical*, Mexico City: Fondo de Cultura Económica, 1983) and is now espoused in principle, and not as a necessary consequence of secularization, by all churches *without exception*. Does the Honorand now rejoin church and state, as it were, in order to be contextual about post-Reformation and

especially post-Enlightenment Christianity? Without the presuppositions that have informed the present essay, I could not have written my 'The World Council of Churches and the Vancouver Theme in Historical Perspective,' *Harvard Theological Review*, LXXVI:1 (January 1983), pp. 1 ff. That Theme for Vancouver, 20 June to 10 August 1983, is 'Jesus Christ *the* Life of *the* World.' I, like our Honorand, have difficulty with the two definite and inclusive articles in the religiously pluralistic context, but I hold with the Council that *the* Church is an historic entity and not a postulate of the first century.

5

THE MUSLIM TRADITION

Annemarie Schimmel

When Wilfred Cantwell Smith decided to leave Harvard for Dalhousie, I jokingly said to him, 'You follow the example of Imam Ghazzali, who left the Nizamiyya in Baghdad in search of a more spiritual life and went into the wide world!' He smiled; but little did I know that the comparison was, after all, not so far off the mark: had Wilfred not always stressed the dynamic and organic quality of *dīn*? And had he not rightly pointed out that Ghazzali's *Iḥyā' 'ulūm ad-dīn*, in its very title, presents *dīn* as something that is alive and that the author's aim was 'to give life to religious theory, not to provide some inanimate pattern'?[1]

Indeed, if I understand correctly Wilfred's concept of Islam, 'the religion with a built-in name,'[2] it is the powerful 'living' quality of this religion which has fascinated him from the beginning of his studies, a quality which is even more evident in the correlative concept *īmān*, 'faith.' As he formulates it, 'Islam is that total framework by being imbedded in which each component part of the lives of the Muslims, each thing that they see, each object that they touch, each sentence that they utter or receive, takes on meaning.'[3] This sentence could have been written only by someone who had lived among Muslims, discussed their problems with them, and experienced their approach to, or, rather, their realization of the whole complex of *islām* and *īmān* (to which one may add, as the Sufis do, *iḥsān*, as the practical expression of one's faith by 'doing everything as beautifully and perfectly as possible'[4] because one knows that one is always in the presence of God the Transcendent who is yet 'closer than the jugular vein' to man [Sura 50/18]). The situation would have been assessed differently by scholars in earlier generations, many of whom avoided going to Islamic lands in order not to disturb their neatly plaited concept of Islam as a kind of depository for various bits and pieces from earlier religious and thought systems, or an Arab cultural-religious entity with a strong hellenistic bias (which basically ended with the fall of Baghdad in 1258 and then lingered on in a state of decay). Their 'Islam' was as removed from the modern world as was the religion of Babylon or ancient China. But according to Wilfred, Islam 'comes alive for the Muslim through faith, which is not an item in a religion but a quality in some men's heart.'[5] It is, as Louis Massignon loved to emphasize, the embodiment of the faith among the three Abrahamic religions, Judaism being centered on hope, Christianity on charity. Indeed, it is this living personal faith which deeply impresses the visitor to Islamic countries and which has found its most typical expression in *tawakkul*,[6] the confidence that 'God knows what is best for His servants in a certain moment.' This personal relationship of the human 'servant' to the Lord makes so-called 'Islamic fatalism' so different from the stoic acceptance of an impersonal, blind fate, and makes the faithful (*mu'min*) willingly attune himself to what he feels to be God's wise plan in what Rūmī and Iqbāl would call *jabr maḥmūd*.[7] Smith has stressed, time and again, that both *amana* and *kafara* are active verbs – 'to have faith in' and 'to refuse' – and have nothing to do with 'believing' or 'not believing' in modern parlance. Faith, in its form as *taṣdīq* is 'a personal relationship to the Truth';[8] it is, as one may circumscribe it, the constant saying of 'Amen' to the short formula uttered after each recitation of the Koran, i.e. *ṣadaqa Allāhu'l-ʿaẓīm*, 'God has spoken the truth.' Such *taṣdīq* goes well together with the way Muslims confess their faith, namely by witnessing that 'There is no deity save God, and Muhammad is his prophet,' a 'witnessing,' *shahāda*, which, according to Smith, forms in Islam 'a religious category worthy of the name.'[9] And he is one of the few, if not the only, Western scholar who has highlighted the musical and calligraphic beauty of the *shahāda*; the rhythmical breathing of *lā ilāha* in exhaling and *illā Allāh* in inhaling; and the breakthrough from the negation to the affirmation of God's existence[10] which, as it were, fills the lungs with new air, the soul with new life.

Wilfred has never tired of highlighting the theocentric character of Islam and the importance of *tauḥīd* (once more an 'active' noun);[11] and he rightly stresses the fact that it is always God who acts, who takes the initiative, who addresses man first. Not in vain did the Sufis constantly dwell upon the Koranic phrase *alastu bi-rabbikum* in which God addresses the not-yet-created souls, 'Am I not your Lord?' and they answered, in what we may call the first *shahāda*, '*Balā, shahidnā*, 'Yes, we bear witness to it.' It is this pre-eternal covenant which is at the basis of Muslim faith, and the Divine address is repeated every moment, be it in the creative word *Kun fayakūn*, in the revelation of His will through prophets and books, or in the experience that even prayer is a divine gift, for 'How else could a rosebud grow out of dust?' as Rūmī asks.[12]

The greatest sin of man in this God-centered world is *shirk*, 'to associate something with God,' and Wilfred's definition sounds like one taken from some early Sufi's work: 'The man who worships money, or devotes himself to the advancement of his own career, or panders to self-gratification is an "associator" not in the sense that he recognizes the existence of these distractions – we all know that they exist – but in that he is associating them with God in ... his scheme of values. ...'[13] Such a person practices what Iqbāl in our day has called 'a new Baal-worship,' which is branded as the greatest evil of modern society, an evil that comprises man's devotion to all the modern 'isms' as well.[14] Was not, according to Iqbāl, even the Prophet's hegira a subtle hint at the necessity of severing relations with one's hometown lest 'narrow nationalism' grow into another 'idol'?[15]

Islam appears, in Smith's work, as faith 'in a God who commands' and therefore as 'the great drama of decision':[16] 'God has spoken His command, and men thereupon are divided, or, rather, divide themselves, into two groups: those who accept and those who spurn ...' and 'since God knows what is right and what is wrong, the terms in which He addresses mankind leave no room for our human epistemological bewilderment. ...'[17] This absoluteness of faith, which seems so natural to the Muslim and yet demands too much courage for the observer who does not dare to undertake the spiritual leap, is reflected in one of the favorite stories of the Sufis, elaborated by Rūmī and taken up by Iqbāl: that of Bayezid Bistami and the Magian. The Magian, overwhelmed by the great Persian mystic's faith and devotion, found such faith too difficult to embrace.[18]

It goes without saying that the emphasis on the Divine command, as expressed in the Koran, demands an attitude toward the Koran different from the one usually found among Western scholars. Smith has the courage to ask all of us, 'Is the Qur'an the word of God?'[19] a question which, as he himself states, is 'a threat both to Muslim and Christian theology.'[20] But is it not so that 'the word of God is or ought to be man's crucial concern'?[21] It is the Koran which 'lifts the Muslim to transcendence'[22] – as a *ḥadīth qudsī* says, 'Whenever someone recites the Koran, it is as if he were talking to Me (*ka'annahu shāfahani*).' Knowing that the Muslims 'believe that it is divine and then they read it' and not vice versa,[23] one will certainly agree with him that 'it is better (more accurate; closer to the truth) to see the Qur'ān as a symbol of the divine in the lives of Muslims . . . than to see it as a purely mundane seventh-century Arabian book written by Muhammad, as Western scholarship used to do, and to insist on doing.'[24] Here, the problem of the translation of the Koran immediately comes to mind;[25] and even though, according to Muslim conviction, a translation can only be an approximation conveying 'the meaning of the glorious Koran' without reflecting the power of the language and the shades of meaning, one would wish that contemporary translators of the Koran, whose versions are replete with useful, learned footnotes, would have had more feeling for the numinous quality of this book, to convey to their uninitiated readers at least 'a slight fragrance' of it, as Rūmī would say, for 'fragrance is allotted to those who do not see Him.'[26]

Since most of Wilfred's later books center around the problem of faith, the Koran stands out prominently in his treatment. What about the Prophet, the messenger mentioned in the second half of the *shahāda*? To say 'and Muhammad is the apostle of God' is 'to commit oneself to a belief, not about the person of Muhammad, but about the validity of what he brought. The personality of Muhammad is essentially irrelevant.'[27] Certainly, phenomenologically speaking, the Koran, as God's word inlibrate, occupies in Islam the same place that Christ as God's word incarnate does in Christianity – a fact emphasized first by Nathan Söderblom, repeated by Friedrich Heiler and Heinrich Frick, and introduced into Anglo-American scholarship by Wilfred Cantwell Smith. Smith is very well aware of the important role of the Prophet, but recognizes, as we just saw, the second half of the *shahāda* more as a statement concerning God's activity than one about the *person* of the Prophet. He follows here Söderblom's remark that in religious phenomenology, 'the prophet is an aspect of God's activity.'[28] Of course he is well aware that it is Muhammad who is the decisive element through which Islam, the eternal religion of complete surrender to God, becomes 'Islam' in its historical form. A central phrase in *Modern Islam in India*, which I always love to quote, states in connection with the revival of the *Leben-Muhammads-Forschung* in Indian Islam around the turn of the century, 'There are atheists and atheistic publications, and rationalist societies; but to disparage Muhammad will provoke from even the most "liberal" section of the community a fanaticism of blazing vehemence.'[29] He may have found the inspiration for this formulation in Iqbāl's verse in the *Jāvīdnāma*:

You can deny God, but you cannot deny the Prophet![30]

However, it seems to me that in *Modern Islam in India* Smith's criticism of the new image of 'a Prophet of whom they can be proud' is somewhat too strong.[31] Many aspects of Muhammad which are treated in his analysis as developments within modern apologetics can be found much earlier in popular and mystical prophetology. Thus, Tirmidhī's *Shamā'il al-muṣṭafā* (to mention just one favorite classic from the ninth century) offers a picture of the Prophet's kindness, goodness, modesty, etc.,[32] which is very similar to what Smith, at that particular point in his own career when he wrote *Modern Islam in India*, considered 'typically bourgeois.' No doubt the re-evaluation of Muhammad's person is typical of modern times (just recently Pakistani newspapers published articles against the 'christianizing trends' in mystical and popular prophetology)[33] but the Prophet as the *uswa ḥasana* seems to me more central for Islam than is visible from Wilfred's analysis. In fact, the term *muḥammadī-yi khāliṣ*, 'sincere Muhammadan,' was used in the seventeenth and eighteenth centuries in Turkey and India for the ideal Muslim,[34] and a pious Naqshbandi leader like the Urdu poet Mīr Dard dared to coin the phrase 'Humanity consists of "muhammadanism," '[35] that is, of faithfully following the *sunna* of God's beloved Prophet (and, on a different level, of aspiring to attain *fanā fi'r-rasūl*). When reading a sentence like Smith's fine definition of the *kāfir* and the *mu'min*: 'The "infidel," the ingrate (*kāfir*) is he who says "no" to God, and the "man of faith" (*mu'min*) is he who accepts, who says "Yes",'[36] one is immediately reminded of a verse by Sanā'ī (d. ca. 1131) who uses this very vocabulary to describe man's relation with the Prophet:

> Those who say No (*lā*) to him become crooked like a *lam-alif* (*lā*)
> And blessed by bounty (*ni'ma*) are those who say Yes (*na'am*) to him.[37]

Islam is, as the Koran states, 'the religion' par excellence, and Smith's thoughts about the various connotations of *dīn*, 'religion' could be compared with similar statements of a modern Shiite thinker, S. H. Nasr, who dwells upon *dīn* as the eternal form of faith.[38]

A random remark. In some Muslim circles I sensed an aversion to the term *ta'rīkh al-adyān* (*tārīkh-i adyān*) for 'history of religions', and one preferred the term *tārīkh-i madhāhib* so as to preserve the word *dīn* for the one true religion. It seems that Wilfred was the first to draw attention to the other term to describe 'reified' Islam in Urdu, and rarely in other languages, i.e., *nizām*, 'order, system.'[39] Among the masses the term was certainly not loved, and I remember angry utterances against the term *nizām-i Mustafā* when it had been introduced in Pakistan after 1979: 'We have Islam – why do we need *nizām-i Mustafā*? Islam is the religion as brought by Muhammad Mustafā!' etc.

In his first major book, *Modern Islam in India*, Wilfred gave a brilliant analysis of the various strands in Indian Islam which led finally to the partition of the Subcontinent – an event which he deeply regretted. His disappointment with the situation becomes particularly evident from the two chapters on Pakistan and India in his later work, *Islam in Modern History* (1957) which has been partly superseded by the political developments during the last thirty years. But it still contains wonderful insights into the workings of different powers inside Islam in its Arabic, Turkish, and Indo-Pakistani variants. *Modern Islam in India*, however, will remain the standard work of reference for any Islamicist interested in the Subcontinent, despite its Marxist approach. I confess that I did not like the book at first but came to appreciate it more and more after numerous visits to the Subcontinent proved how perceptive Wilfred's analysis of many actors in the drama was.

It is often difficult for a foreigner to appreciate the fact that, in Islam, he has to deal with not only the faith relationship of the individual with God in the sense of post-Enlightenment 'religion,' but also a way of life that comprises every activity in life, including the socio-political one. The 'nation-building power' of the Prophet has been stressed by Muslims from the very beginning of 'modern' theology, that is, from the days of Shāh Walīullāh and Maẓhar Jānjānān in eighteenth century Delhi and is highlighted in the works of Iqbāl and other reformers,[40] even though the realization of the ideal Islamic nation is something only to be aspired to. (Wilfred's thoughts about the problem of the 'Islamic State' in *Islam in Modern History* offer a plethora of possible approaches to this central problem of modern Muslim states.) But whatever the outward form of the state, 'the role of the *ummah*, the Islamic community, in Muslim life is distinctive and crucial.'[41] Is not this *umma* the *umma marḥūma*, 'the community upon which mercy has been shown'? And is it not the specific role of the Prophet that, according to the tradition, on Doomsday, when everyone tries to protect himself and exclaims *nafsī nafsī*, 'I myself!' he shall plead for his followers by calling out *ummatī ummatī*, 'My community!'?[42] In this *ḥadīth*, the inseparable relationship of the Prophet and his *umma* is beautifully expressed, and many worried souls have found peace in the conviction that they belong to this blessed *umma* in which the Prophet is 'like the heart.'[43]

A particularly interesting chapter in *Islam in Modern History* is that about Turkey. At a time when Turkey looked like an outright liberalized country, aspiring to complete westernization, Wilfred was one of the few who discovered the strong Islamic undercurrent among the people. There was, and still is, the pride of being 'laicist but not atheist.' In fact, during the five years I lived in Turkey in the 1950s, I found an overwhelming number of people, especially women, living exemplary Muslim lives. As

Iqbāl, otherwise critical of some developments in Turkey, remarked toward the end of his life, 'We hear now and then that the Turks have repudiated Islam. A greater lie was never told.'[44] And at the present moment it seems as if the trend toward a more genuine Islamic attitude is growing in Turkey (as far as this can be in keeping with Ataturk's legacy) in order to steer a course between the two great power blocs, NATO and the USSR. The invisible mystical current in Turkey has always been much stronger than the outsider realized (not only the *Nurcus*, but also the circle around Kenan Rifai, the revival of the Mevlevis, etc.). Thus, when in 1958 a book entitled *Was Hazrat-i Muḥammad a Turk?*[45] appeared in Istanbul, this should not be taken as a ridiculous or preposterous question but as the legitimate concern of a Muslim who wanted to see his dearly beloved Prophet as a member of his dearly beloved Turkish race.

I agree with Wilfred that it certainly was 'startling to hear the name of Luther on many Turkish lips that could scarcely discourse on the works of al Ash'arī or al-Ghazālī or Iqbāl.'[46] This was a constant source of trouble for me who, teaching in the Ankara Ilâhiyat Fakültesi (church history, among other subjects), had to explain to my students that their admired Luther was, alas, not at all a friend of the 'Turkish' religion, as Islam was generally called in sixteenth- to eighteenth-century Germany.[47] (Interestingly, 'to become Muslim' or 'to belong to Islam' was expressed by the same term in Germany, 'turkisch, Türke werden' as in northern Indian languages *turk hōnā* means imply 'being a Muslim.')

Let us return once more to Smith's approach to Islam in India and Pakistan, a field which he knows particularly well but which can barely be exhausted by any single scholar. It seems to me that many phenomena in that area can be explained by referring to the constant dichotomy between the 'high' and the popular Muslim culture, between the 'prophetic,' Mecca-oriented and the mystical, India-centered approaches, as they appear in Baranī and Amīr Khusrau, in Bada'ūnī and Abū'l-Fażl, in Aurangzēb and Dārā Shikōh, in Iqbāl and Abūl Kalām Azād. Muhammad as the *sayyid-i makkī-i madīni 'arabī*, as Qudsī Mashhadī calls him in his beautiful ode (which is still a favorite of the *qawwāls* in the Subcontinent), reminds the Muslims of their loyalty to a center

137

outside India, and each of the numerous reform movements (including that of the Mahdi of Jaunpur) began when a pious man returned from the pilgrimage to Mecca, having imbibed what he felt was unpolluted Arabian Islam in contrast to the various forms of local Indian Islam that had grown up over the centuries. Did not Makhdūm-i Jahāniyān of Ucch (d. 1384) already prohibit the use of Indian names for God in Muslim devotional poetry?

The lively growth of the indigenous languages and, with them, mystical popular literature, contrasts with the almost immobilized Arabic curriculum of the madrasas. When Iqbāl compares the traditional theologian to a 'Qārūn of Arabic dictionaries,'[48] he is not far from the attitude of the popular Sufi singers in Sind or Bengal who loved to ridicule the learned representatives of a religion in which true spiritual life seemed to be suffocated by the letter. The growing tensions between these two major trends in Indian Islam – enhanced by the variety of Islamic sects such as the Shia and Ismailis – contributed to the shift towards partition, but the fate of both communities is still difficult to assess. S. Abid Husain's touching study of *The Destiny of the Indian Muslims*[49] depicts the plight of the Muslim minority in secular India, while the 'Lost Opportunities' for Pakistan have been deplored recently by the leading Pakistani historian and protagonist of the two-nations theory, Ishtiaq Husain Qureshi in a moving article in the *Festschrift* for Maulānā Maudūdī[50] (who, as will be remembered, was once fiercely opposed to the Pakistan envisaged by Quaid-i Azam Jinnah).[51] Thus, thirty six years after Smith published *Islam in Modern History* everything is still in flux – not to mention the numerous sociological and linguistic problems which are now faced by the Muslims in the present three parts of the Subcontinent.

It is certainly easier for the student of Islam to understand and sympathize with the so-called liberal development in modern Islam which is closer to the 'secularized' Western outlook and, for its followers, not so demanding as the full acceptance of Islam as defined at the beginning of this article. Again, we agree with Smith that 'the "modernist" position of Islam has developed severe weaknesses in comparison with the classical tradition.'[52] Recently, the development of the Jamaat-i Islami, of the Muslim Brethren, and, last but not least, the events in Iran have shown that traditionalist approaches to Islam, whose leaders are able to organize large groups under a powerful motto, can attract more people than a well-meaning but unorganized liberalism which lacks the force of cohesion.

There is, however, another interesting development in modern Islam (at least in certain areas) which proves that Smith's analysis is correct when he combines Sufism with romanticism.[53] The names of the mystical leaders of yore, particularly of Ḥallāj, have become, during the last two decades, key words among the modern, usually leftist, writers. The martyr mystic of Islam, Ḥallāj, whose name has loomed large in Muslim, particularly Persian, literature during the last millennium and whose personality was 'rediscovered' by Massignon, appears in our day not only as the one 'who called people to spiritual resurrection' (Iqbāl),[54] but also as a social rebel (as in Ṣalāh 'Abd aṣ-Ṣabūr's drama) or the representative of the unsolvable paradox of religious life ('Abdal Wahhāb al-Bayātī), etc.[55] This 'secularized Sufism,' in which a mystical martyr is converted into a symbol of freedom and progress of any kind, seems to me worthy of mention. Here we find a reversal of Wilfred's basically correct remark that the martyr in Islam, the *shahīd*, is, contrary to the martyr in Christian understanding, the one 'who gave his life fighting not against history but with it,' *fī sabīl Allāh*.[56] Thus the 'martyr' Ḥallāj is now the symbol for those who fight their way against the fossilizing trends in history, against a hallowed system, perhaps against 'reification.' But at the same time, such a development shows how right Wilfred is when he says of Islam, and of religious life in general, 'For religious life, the story of formative centuries is logically subordinate to that of subsequent ages.'[57] To see how a religious figure, such as the Prophet, could grow in the loving hearts of his followers into an almost cosmic being, or how a mystic like Ḥallāj, much maligned during his lifetime, survived centuries and has never ceased to be a model for people in quest of the living truth is more important to him than to discern this or that influence that might originally have been operative on a person or a movement.

The 'cumulative tradition' is certainly an important aspect of each religion, and the development in time and space of the *sharī'a* in all its details, of Islamic calligraphy, of architecture, or of any

art or craft is part and parcel of the whole religious (in the widest
sense of the word) life. The Muslim will, I am sure, see even in this
'handiwork of Muslims'[58] who have been involved in the
development of this constantly growing tradition, a divine pattern
for, after all, 'not a leaf falls from a tree without God's
knowledge.' The Sufis, and mystically-minded thinkers, have
loved the symbol of the tree, the *shajarat al-kaun*; Muhammad
himself sometimes appears as the great cosmic tree.[59] Shāh
Walīullāh, elaborating Sanā'ī's and Rūmī's parable of the blind
and the elephant, has seen the Divine Truth as a tree of which one
can touch only a certain part, be it branch or leaf, trunk or fruit.[60]
One can also see the religions, and among them Islam,[61] as such a
tree, growing, taking nourishment from the soil, the wind, and the
water, and accordingly developing its branches, twigs, and
blossoms. They are enclosed in the bark which hardens year by
year; the soft young stem, in whose seed the whole tree was already
contained, becomes 'reified.' And the historian may then
legitimately compare the shapes of leaves or branches of the
different trees with each other. 'The Qur'ān is significant not
primarily because of what historically went into it but because of
what historically has come out of it'[62] – 'You shall recognize them
by their fruits.' In less poetical metaphors, one may recall that the
leaders of pre-modern and modern Indian Islam, like Shāh
Walīullāh and Iqbāl, judged the validity of the message conveyed
by the Prophet according to the type of humanity and culture that
has evolved from it, that is, in the fruits of the great tree 'Islam.'

Wilfred Cantwell Smith has always restricted his writings
willingly and wittingly to the *word*, to theology in the widest sense,
and yet many of his statements correspond to the verses of the
great Muslim poets. He rarely speaks of art – one regrets this when
reading his superb description of the Islamic mosque in contrast
with the Indian temple. But if one applies his vision of Islam as the
all-embracing expression of the unshakeable faith in the One God
as the Creator, Sustainer, and Judge and the One to whom man
has to give his undivided loyalty from the pre-eternal covenant to
the 'tomorrow' of Doomsday, then one can also understand and
interpret the works of Islamic art as perfect manifestations of this
faith. Wilfred quotes (as it seems, in full agreement) the definition
of 'religion' from the *Catholic Encyclopedia* as pertaining to Islam:

'Religion means the voluntary subjection of oneself to God.'[64] And struggling with the problem that one cannot really say *lastu bi-muslimin*, 'I am not *Muslim*,'[65] he would certainly agree with Goethe's lines in the *West-Östliche Divan*:

> Wenn Islam Ergebenheit in Gottes Willen heisst,
> In Islam leben und sterben wir alle.

NOTES

1. *The Meaning and End of Religion* (New York: Mentor Books, 1964), p. 305, note 116.
2. Ibid., p. 75.
3. *Belief and History* (University of Virginia Press, 1977), p. 25.
4. *Iḥsān* is derived from Sura 7:54, 'Mercy is with those who practice *iḥsān (al-muḥsinūn).*' The explanation of 'doing everything as beautifully as possible' was given by Mian Quṭbuddīn, the *sajjādanishīn* of Shāh Khāmūsh in Hyderabad/Deccan in a long personal communication about *īmān* and *iḥsān*, October 1980.
5. *The Meaning and End of Religion*, pp. 124–25.
6. For the concept of *tawakkul* see Benedikt Reinert, *Die Lehre vom tawakkul in der älteren Sufik* (Berlin: de Gruyter, 1968). He treats the material very scholarly, but purely statistically.
7. This 'active' *īmān* is beautifully expressed in Iqbāl's poem *Duʿā*, 'Prayer' in *Żarb-i Kalīm* (Lahore, 1937), p. 167. See Schimmel, *Gabriel's Wing* (Leiden: Brill, 1963). Typically, Iqbāl's ideal man is not called *insān-i kāmil*, 'the Perfect Man,' but rather *mard-i mōmin*, 'he who has (the dynamic quality) of faith.'
8. *Faith and Belief* (Princeton: Princeton University Press, 1975), p. 48.
9. Ibid., pp. 42–43.
10. *The Faith of Other Men* (New York: Mentor Book, 1965), pp. 52–59.
11. *Belief and History*, p. 24.
12. Rūmī, *Mathnawī*, ed. Reynold A. Nicholson, 8 volumes (London: Luzac, 1925–40), II, line 2443; Schimmel, *Mystical Dimensions of Islam* (Chapel Hill: University of North Carolina Press, 1975), pp. 164–67. See also Schimmel, *The Triumphal Sun* (London-The Hague: East-West Publications, 1978), pp. 352–66.
13. *Faith and Belief*, p. 42.
14. See Iqbāl, *Jāvīdnāma* (Lahore, 1932), 'Sphere of Venus.'

15. Iqbāl, *Stray Reflections* (Lahore: Ashraf, 1961), Nr. 19: 'Islam appeared as a protest against idolatry. And what is patriotism but a subtle form of idolatry? . . . The fact that the Prophet prospered and died in a place not his birthplace is perhaps a mystic hint to the same effect.'

16. *Meaning and End of Religion*, pp. 102–3.

17. *Faith and Belief*, p. 47.

18. Rūmī, *Mathnawī*, V, line 3356 ff.; Iqbāl, *Jāvīdnāma*, line 1122 ff.

19. *Questions of Religious Truth* (New York: Scribner's Sons, 1967), p. 39.

20. Ibid., p. 49.

21. Ibid., p. 43.

22. Ibid., p. 56.

23. Ibid., p. 49.

24. *Belief and History*, p. 24.

25. Cf. *Meaning and End of Religion*, p. 95.

26. Rūmī, *Dīwān-i Kabīr*, ed. Badī'uzzamān Furūzānfar (Tehran: University, 1957 ff.), No. 468.

27. *Islam in Modern History* (Princeton: Princeton University Press, 1957; New York: A Mentor Book, 1959), p. 27, note 18; and similarly often, thus *The Faith of Other Men*, pp. 61 ff.

28. Nathan Söderblom, *The Living God* (Gifford Lectures; London: Oxford University Press), p. 224.

29. *Modern Islam in India* (Lahore, 1947), p. 69.

30. Iqbāl, *Jāvīdnāma*, line 608.

31. Cf. *Modern Islam in India*, p. 69 sequ.

32. See Abū 'Isā al-Tirmidhī, *Ash-Shamā'il al-Muḥammadiyya*, with the commentary of Bājūrī (Cairo, 1276 h/1859–60).

33. Thus *Dawn Overseas* (January 6, 1983) and the controversies about the 'christianizing' *maulūd* celebrations in Egypt and Saudi Arabia. The danger of elevating Muhammad into a more-than-human sphere of which the Muslims were always aware (as already Būṣīrī's *Burda* shows) was expressed very clearly by Sir Sayyid Ahmad Khan in his discussion of the Prophet's *mi'rāj*; 'We do not make our Prophet "God's son" nor do we want him "to sit at God's right".' (*Maqālāt-i Sir Sayyid*, ed. Maulānā Ismā'īl Panipati [Lahore, 1961], vol. 13).

34. Cf. Schimmel, 'The Golden Chain of "Sincere Muhammadans",' in Bruce B. Lawrence, ed., *The Rose and the Rock* (Durham N.C.: University of North Carolina Press, 1978).

35. Khwāja Mīr Dard, *'Ilm ul-kitāb* (Delhi, 1309 h/1891), p. 504; see also Schimmel, *Pain and Grace* (Leiden: Brill, 1976), pp. 78–80.

36. *Faith and Belief*, p. 40.
37. Sanā'ī, *Dīwān*, ed. Mudarris Rażavī (Tehran: Ibn-i Sīnā, 1962), p. 363.
38. Allamah Sayyid Muhammad Husain Tabataba'i, *Shi'ite Islam*, ed. and trans. Seyyed Hossein Nasr (London: Allen and Unwin, 1975), p. 34, note 2.
39. *The Meaning and End of Religion*, p. 77.
40. For more details see Schimmel, 'The Golden Chain of "Sincere Muhammadans".'
41. *The Meaning and End of Religion*, p. 98.
42. See Tor Andrae, *Die person Muhammads in lehre und glaube seiner gemeinde*, pp. 236–38. This idea is expressed in very early *ḥadīth* collections.
43. Najmuddīn Rāzī Dāyā, *The Path of God's Bondsmen from Origin to Return*, trans. by Hamid Algar (Delmar: Caravan Books, 1982), p. 167. See also Iqbāl, *Musāfir* (Lahore, 1936), p. 32, and similarly *Asrār-i khūdī* (Lahore, 1915), line 397.
44. Iqbāl, *Speeches and Statements*, compiled by 'Shamloo' (Lahore, 1945), p. 217. Schimmel, *Gabriel's Wing*, pp. 240–45, deals with his attitude toward the Turks.
45. Kemal Samancïgil, *Hazret-i Muhammad Türk mi idi?* (Istanbul: Mesa Yayïnlarï, 1958).
46. *Islam in Modern History*, p. 206.
47. The enormous output of 'Türckenlieder' and anti-Turkish, i.e., anti-Islamic, literature between the two sieges of Vienna in 1526 and 1683 is an important phenomenon in the German approach to Islam and the Muslim; the inimical attitude of the sixteenth and seventeenth century writers seem to have influenced the German attitude towards the Turks subconsciously to our day, as Turkish 'guest-workers' can tell.
48. Iqbāl, *Bāl-i Jibrīl* (Lahore, 1936). The verse is very appropriate in that it emphasizes the dynamics of the *shahāda*:
    The free man does not possess anything except the two words *lā ilāh (illā Allāh)*
    but the jurist of the town is a Qārūn in Arabic dictionaries!
    under the weight of which he presumably will sink in the dust like Qārūn, instead of rising to the Divine Presence.
49. S. Abid Husain, *The Destiny of the Indian Muslims* (London: Asia Publishing House, 1965).
50. Ishtiaq Husain Qureshi, 'Lost Opportunities. Musings of a Student of History,' in *Islamic Perspectives*. Studies in Honour of Sayyid Abul A 'lā Maudūdi (Leicester: The Islamic Foundation, 1979), pp. 57–74.

51. *Modern Islam in India*, p. 280. Cf. Fazlur Rahman, 'Muslim Modernism in the Indo-Pak Subcontinent,' *BSOAS* XXI (1958), 97. See also Schimmel, *Islam in the Indian Subcontinent* (Leiden: Brill, 1980), 'Epilogue.'

52. *Islam in Modern History*, p. 156. See also the chapter on 'Liberalism' in the same work and the analysis of the Indo-Muslim situation in *Modern Islam in India*.

53. *Islam in Modern History*, p. 203.

54. Iqbāl, *Jāvīdnāma*, 'Sphere of Jupiter.'

55. For this development, see Schimmel, *Al-Halladsch, Martyrer der Gottesliebe* (Cologne: Hegner, 1967).

56. *Islam in Modern History*, p. 37, note 27.

57. 'The Study of Religion and the Study of the Bible' in Willard Oxtoby, ed., *Religious Diversity* (New York: Harper Forum Book, 1976), p. 46.

58. *Meaning and End of Religion*, pp. 146–47.

59. See Arthur Jeffery, *Ibn al-'Arabī's shajarat al-kawn* (Lahore, 1980).

60. Shah Walīullāh, *Lamaḥāt*, ed. Ghulām Muṣṭafa Qāsimī (Hyderabad: Shah Waliullah Academy, 1964), p. 4.

61. Iqbāl uses this image when he asked Khwāja Ḥasan Niẓāmī, who stood in the forefront of the *tablīgh* movement in India, to call the young Pirs of the Panjab and Sind to 'preserve that tree which had formerly blossomed thanks to the work of their ancestors.' *Iqbālnāma*, ed. Shaikh Muḥd. 'Aṭā (Lahore, s.d.), vol. II, p. 384.

62. 'The Study of Religion and the Study of the Bible,' p. 46.

63. *The Faith of Other Men*, p. 50.

64. *The Meaning and End of Religion*, p. 103.

65. 'Christian – noun, or adjective?' in *Questions of Religious Truth* (New York: Scribner, 1967), p. 106. An Indian friend of mine suggested that *muslim* should be used for the one who agrees to the eternal truth of Islam, even though not outwardly a member of the *umma*, while the adherent to the Islamic system should be called *musulmān*. (In German, however, *Musulman* has a deprecative ring to it and was often changed to *Muselmann*, pl. *Muselmänner*.)

Section C

CURRENT APPROACHES TO THE STUDY OF RELIGION

1

RELIGIOUS PLURALISM

John Hick

Wilfred Cantwell Smith in his work on the concepts of religion and of religions has been responsible, more than any other single individual, for the change which has taken place within a single generation in the way in which many of us perceive the religious life of mankind.

Seen through pre-Cantwell Smith eyes there are a number of vast, long-lived historical entities, or organisms, known as Christianity, Hinduism, Islam, Buddhism, etc. Each has an inner skeletal framework of beliefs, giving shape to a distinctive form of religious life, and wrapped in a thick institutional skin which divides it from other religions and from the secular world within which they exist. Thus Buddhism, Islam, Christianity etc. are seen as contraposed socio-religious entities which are the bearers of distinctive creeds; and every religious individual is a member of one or other of these mutually exclusive groups.

This way of seeing the religious life of humanity, as organized in a number of communities based upon rival sets of religious beliefs, leads to the posing of questions about religion in a certain way. For the beliefs which a religion professes are beliefs about God, or the Ultimate, and as such they define a way of human salvation or liberation and are accordingly a matter of spiritual life and death. Looking at the religions of the world then in the plural we are presented with competing claims to possess the saving truth. For each community believes that its own gospel is true and that other gospels are false in so far as they differ from it. Each believes that the way of salvation to which it witnesses is the authentic way, the only sure path to eternal blessedness. And so the proper question in face of this plurality of claims is, which is the true religion?

In practice, those who are concerned to raise this question are normally fully convinced that theirs is the true religion; so that for them the task is to show the spiritual superiority of their own creed and the consequent moral superiority of the community which embodies it. A great deal of the mutual criticism of religions, and of the derogatory assessment of one by another, has been in fulfilment of this task.

This view of mankind's religious life as divided into great contraposed entities, each claiming to be the true religion, is not however the only possible way of seeing the religious situation. Cantwell Smith has offered an alternative vision.

He shows first that the presently dominant conceptuality has a history that can be traced back to the European Renaissance. It was then that the different streams of religious life began to be reified in western thought as solid structures called Christianity, Judaism, etc. And having reified their own faith in this way Westerners have then exported the notion of 'a religion' to the rest of the world, causing others to think of themselves as belonging to the Hindu, or the Confucian, or the Buddhist religion, and so on, over against others. But an alternative perception can divide the scene differently. It sees something of vital religious significance taking different forms all over the world within the contexts of the different historical traditions. This 'something of vital religious significance' Cantwell Smith calls faith. I would agree with some of his critics that this is not the ideal word for it; for 'faith' is a term that is more at home in the Semitic than in the Indian family of traditions and which has, as his own historical researches have shown, become badly over-intellectualized. But I take it that he uses the term to refer to the spiritual state, or existential condition, constituted by a person's present response to the ultimate divine Reality. This ranges from the negative response of a self-enclosed consciousness which is blind to the divine presence, whether beyond us or in the depths of our own being, to a positive openness to the Divine which gradually transforms us and which is called salvation or liberation or enlightenment. This transformation is essentially the same within the different religious contexts within which it occurs: I would define it formally as the transformation of human existence from self-centeredness to Reality-centeredness. This is the event or process

148

of vital significance which one can see to be occurring in individuals all over the world, taking different forms within the contexts of the different perceptions of the Ultimate made available by the various religious traditions.

These cumulative traditions themselves are the other thing that one sees with the aid of the new conceptuality suggested by Cantwell Smith. They are distinguishable strands of human history in each of which a multitude of religious and cultural elements interact to form a distinctive pattern, constituting the Hindu, Buddhist, Confucian, Jewish, Christian, Muslim etc. traditions. These are not static entities but living movements; and they are not tightly homogeneous but have each become in the course of time internally highly various. Thus there are large differences between, for example, Buddhism in the time of Gautama and Buddhism after the development of the Mahāyāna and its expansion northwards into China; or between the Christian movement in Roman Palestine and in medieval Europe. And there are large differences today between, say, Zen and Amida Buddhism in Japan, or between Southern Baptist and Northern Episcopalian Christianity in the United States. Indeed, since we cannot always avoid using the substantives we might do well to speak of Buddhisms, Christianities, and so on, in the plural. A usage consonant with Cantwell Smith's analysis has however already become widespread, and many of us now often prefer to speak not of Christianity but of the Christian tradition, the Hindu tradition, and so on when referring to these historically identifiable strands of history.

These cumulative traditions are composed of a rich complex of inner and outer elements cohering in a distinctive living pattern which includes structures of belief, life-styles, scriptures and their interpretation, liturgies, cultic celebrations, myths, music, poetry, architecture, literature, remembered history and its heroes. Thus the traditions constitute religious cultures, each with its own unique history and ethos. And each such tradition creates human beings in its own image. For we are not human in general, participating in an eternal Platonic essence of humanity. We are human in one or other of the various concrete ways of being human which constitute the cultures of the earth. There is a Chinese way of being human, an African way, an Arab way, a

European way, or ways, and so on. These are not fixed moulds but living organisms which develop and interact over the centuries, so that the patterns of human life change, usually very slowly but sometimes with startling rapidity. But we are all formed in a hundred ways of which we are not normally aware by the culture into which we were born, by which we are fed, and with which we interact.

Let us then enter, with Cantwell Smith, into the experiment of thinking, on the one hand, of 'faith', or human response to the divine, which in its positive and negative forms is salvation and non-salvation and, on the other hand, of the cumulative religious traditions within which this occurs; and let us ask what the relation is between these two realities – on the one hand salvation/liberation and on the other the cumulative traditions.

In various different forms this question has been much discussed within the Christian world, particularly during the last hundred and fifty years or so as Christians have become increasingly conscious of the continuing reality of the other great religious traditions. For this period has seen renaissances within the Hindu and Buddhist worlds – to an important extent, it would seem, in reaction to eighteenth and nineteenth century Christian imperialism – and a resurgence of Islam is currently taking place. These developments have precipitated intense debate among Christian thinkers in which many different options have been and are being canvassed. Both because of the fullness of this discussion within Christianity, and because I am myself a Christian and am concerned with the problem from a Christian point of view, I propose to describe the main options in Christian terms. They are three in number.

The first, which we may call exclusivism, relates salvation/liberation exclusively to one particular tradition, so that it is an article of faith that salvation is restricted to this one group, the rest of mankind being either left out of account or explicitly excluded from the sphere of salvation. The most emphatic and influential expression of such a faith occurred in the Catholic dogma *Extra ecclesiam nulla salus* (Outside the Church, no salvation) and the corresponding assumption of the nineteenth century Protestant missionary movement, Outside Christianity, no salvation. In these developments Christian thought went beyond a mere overlooking of non-Christian humanity – which might perhaps simply be attributed to restricted vision – to a positive doctrine of the unsaved status of that wider human majority. Exclusiveness of this strong kind was supported by a juridical conception of salvation. If salvation consists in a change of status in the eyes of God from the guilt of participation in Adam's original sin to a forgiveness made possible by Christ's sacrifice on the cross, the appropriation of which is conditional upon a personal response of faith in Christ, this salvation can very naturally be seen as restricted to the Christian faith community. If on the other hand salvation is understood as the actual transformation of human life from self-centeredness to Reality-centeredness, this is not necessarily restricted within the boundaries of any one historical tradition. One cannot know *a priori* where or to what extent it occurs; one can only look at the living of human life in its endlessly varied circumstances and try to discern the signs of this transformation. Except in those whom we call saints, in whom the transformation is sufficiently advanced to be publicly evident, such discernment is often extremely difficult; for salvation/liberation, understood in this way, is to be found in many stages and degrees in the varying qualities of true humanity, often realized more in some areas of life than in others, and with advances and regressions, efforts and lapses in all the respects in which human beings develop and change through the experience of life in time. There may of course – as the Hindu and Buddhist traditions generally teach – be a final moment of enlightenment in which the transformation is completed and Reality-centeredness definitively supercedes the last remnants of self-centeredness. But even if this should be a universal pattern, the journey leading towards that final moment must be long and slow; and progress on the journey can to some extent be humanly discerned as the process of salvation gradually taking place. This understanding of salvation/liberation as the actual transformation of human beings is more easily open than is the juridical understanding of it to the possibility that the salvific process may be taking place not only within one tradition but within a number of traditions. Christian exclusivism has now largely faded out from the 'mainline' churches, but is still powerful in many of the 'marginal' evangelical and Pentecostal sects; and it should be added that the

151

'margins' of Christianity are probably more extensive today than ever before.

However we may now turn to a second Christian answer to our question, which can be labelled inclusivism. This can be expressed in terms either of a juridical or of a transformation-of-human-existence conception of salvation. In the former terms it is the view that God's forgiveness and acceptance of humanity have been made possible by Christ's death, but that the benefits of this sacrifice are not confined to those who respond to it with an explicit act of faith. The juridical transaction of Christ's atonement covered *all* human sin, so that all human beings are now open to God's mercy, even though they may never have heard of Jesus Christ and why he died on the cross of Calvary. I take it that it is this form of inclusivism that the present Pope was endorsing in his first encyclical when he said that 'man – every man without any exception whatever – has been redeemed by Christ, and because with man – with each man without any exception whatever – Christ is in a way united, even when man is unaware of it'. (*Redemptor Hominis*, para. 14. Vatican Polyglot Press translation, London: Catholic Truth Society, 1979). This statement could however also be an expression of the other form of Christian inclusivism, which accepts the understanding of salvation as the gradual transformation of human life and sees this as taking place not only within Christian history but also within the contexts of all the other great world traditions. It regards this however, wherever it happens, as the work of Christ – the universal divine Logos, the Second Person of the divine Trinity, who became incarnate in Jesus of Nazareth. Thus we can speak of 'the unknown Christ of Hinduism' and of the other traditions, and indeed the unknown Christ within all creative transformations of individuals and societies. And if we ask how this differs from simply saying that within all these different streams of human life there is a creative and re-creative response to the divine Reality, the answer of this kind of Christian inclusivism is that Christians are those, uniquely, who are able to identify the source of salvation because they have encountered that source as personally incarnate in Jesus Christ.

Both forms of inclusivism do however involve certain inner strains and certain awkward implications. How are they to be combined with the traditional *extra ecclesiam* dogma? The best known attempt is that of Karl Rahner, with his concept of the 'anonymous Christian'. Those who do not have an explicit Christian faith but who nevertheless seek, consciously or unconsciously, to do God's will can be regarded as, so to speak, honorary Christians – and this even though they do not so regard themselves and even though they may insist that they are not Christians but Muslims, Jews, Hindus etc. Rahner's is a brave attempt to attain an inclusivist position which is in principle universal but which does not thereby renounce the old exclusivist dogma. But the question is whether in this new context the old dogma has not been so emptied of content as no longer to be worth affirming. When salvation is acknowledged to be taking place without any connection with the Christian Church or Gospel, in people who are living on the basis of quite other faiths, is it not a somewhat empty gesture to insist upon affixing a Christian label to them? Further, having thus labelled them, why persist in the aim of gathering all mankind into the Christian Church? Once it is accepted that salvation does not depend upon this, the conversion of the people of the other great world faiths to Christianity hardly seems the best way of spending one's energies.

The third possible answer to the question of the relation between salvation/liberation and the cumulative religious traditions can best be called pluralism. As a Christian position this can be seen as an acceptance of the further conclusion to which inclusivism points. If we accept that salvation/liberation is taking place within all the great religious traditions, why not frankly acknowledge that there is a plurality of saving human responses to the ultimate divine Reality? Pluralism, then, is the view that the transformation of human existence from self-centeredness to Reality-centeredness is taking place in different ways within the contexts of all the great religious traditions. There is not merely one but a plurality of ways of salvation or liberation. In Christian theological terms, there is a plurality of divine relations, making possible a plurality of forms of saving human response.

What however makes it difficult for Christians to move from inclusivism to pluralism, holding the majority of Christian theologians today in the inclusivist position despite its evident local instability, is of course the traditional doctrine of the

Incarnation, together with its protective envelope, the doctrine of the Trinity. For in its orthodox form, as classically expressed at the Councils of Nicaea and Chalcedon, the incarnational doctrine claims that Jesus was God incarnate, the Second Person of the Triune God living a human life. It is integral to this faith that there has been (and will be) no other divine incarnation. This makes Christianity unique in that it, alone among the religions of the world, was founded by God in person. Such a uniqueness would seem to demand Christian exclusivism – for must God not want all human beings to enter the way of salvation which he has provided for them? However since such exclusivism seems so unrealistic in the light of our knowledge of the wider religious life of mankind, many theologians have moved to some form of inclusivism, but now feel unable to go further and follow the argument to its conclusion in the frank acceptance of pluralism. The break with traditional missionary attitudes and long-established ecclesiastical and liturgical language would, for many, be so great as to be prohibitive.

There is however the possibility of an acceptable Christian route to religious pluralism in work which has already been done, and which is being done, in the field of Christology with motivations quite other than to facilitate pluralism, and on grounds which are internal to the intellectual development of Christianity. For there is a decisive watershed between what might be called all-or-nothing Christologies and degree Christologies. The all-or-nothing principle is classically expressed in the Chalcedonian Definition, according to which Christ is 'To be acknowledged in Two Natures', 'Consubstantial with the Father according to his Deity, Consubstantial with us according to his Humanity'. Substance is an all-or-nothing notion, in that A either is or is not composed of the same substance, either has or does not have the same essential nature, as B. Using this all-or-nothing conceptuality Chalcedon attributed to Christ two complete natures, one divine and the other human, being in his divine nature of one substance with God the Father. Degree Christologies, on the other hand, apply the term 'incarnation' to the activity of God's Spirit or of God's grace in human lives, so that the divine will is done on earth. This kind of reinterpretation has been represented in recent years by, for example, the 'paradox of grace' Christology of Donald Baillie (in *God was in Christ*, 1948) and the 'inspiration Christology' of Geoffrey Lampe (in *God the Spirit*, 1977). In so far as a human being is open and responsive to God, so that God is able to act in and through that individual, we can speak of the embodiment in human life of God's redemptive activity. And in Jesus this 'paradox of grace' – the paradox expressed by St Paul when he wrote 'it was not I, but the grace of God which is in me' (I Cor. 15:10) – or the inspiration of God's Spirit, occurred at its fullest. The paradox, or the inspiration, are not however confined to the life of Jesus; they are found, in varying degrees, in all free human response to God. Christologies of the same broad family occur in the work of Norman Pittenger (*The Word Incarnate*, 1957), John Knox (*The Humanity and Divinity of Christ*, 1967), and earlier in John Baillie (*The Place of Jesus Christ in Modern Christianity*, 1929), and more recently in the authors of *The Myth of God Incarnate* (1977).

These modern degree Christologies were not in fact for the most part developed in order to facilitate a Christian acceptance of religious pluralism. They were developed as alternatives to the old substance Christology in which so many difficulties, both historical and philosophical, had become apparent. They claim to be compatible with the teachings of Jesus and of the very early Church, and to avoid the intractable problem, generated by a substance Christology, of the relation between Jesus' two natures. But as an unintended consequence, degree Christologies open up the possibility of seeing God's activity in Jesus as being of the same kind as God's activity in other great human mediators of the divine. The traditional Christian claim to the unique superiority of Christ and of the Christian tradition is not of course precluded by a degree Christology; for it may be argued (as it was for example, by both Baillie and Lampe) that Christ was the *supreme* instance of the paradox of grace or of the inspiration of the Spirit, so that Christianity is still assumed to be the *best* context of salvation/liberation. But whereas, starting from the substance Christology, the unique superiority of Christ and the Christian Church are guaranteed *a priori*, starting from a degree Christology they have to be established by historical evidence. Whether this can in fact be done is, clearly, an open question. It would indeed be an uphill task today to establish that we know enough about the inner and outer life of the historical Jesus, and of the other founders of great religious traditions, to be able to make any such claim; and perhaps an even more uphill task to establish from the morally ambiguous histories of each of the great traditions, complex mixtures of good and evil as each has been, that one's own tradition stands out as manifestly superior to all others.

I think, then, that a path exists along which Christians can, if they feel so drawn, move to an acceptance of religious pluralism. Stated philosophically such a pluralism is the view that the great world faiths embody different perceptions and conceptions of, and correspondingly different responses to, the Real or the Ultimate from within the major variant cultural ways of being human; and that within each of them the transformation of human existence from self-centeredness to Reality-centeredness is manifestly taking place – and taking place, so far as human observation can tell, to much the same extent. Thus the great religious traditions are to be regarded as alternative soteriological 'spaces' within which, or 'ways' along which, men and women can find salvation/liberation/enlightenment/fulfilment.

But how can such a view be arrived at? Are we not proposing a picture reminiscent of the ancient allegory of the blind men and the elephant, in which each runs his hands over a different part of the animal, and identifies it differently, a leg as a tree, the trunk as a snake, the tail as a rope, and so on? Clearly, in the story the situation is being described from the point of view of someone who can observe both elephant and blind men. But where is the vantage point from which one can observe both the divine Reality and the different limited human standpoints from which that Reality is being variously perceived? The advocate of the pluralist understanding cannot pretend to any such cosmic vision. How then does he profess to know that the situation is indeed as he depicts it? The answer is that he does not profess to *know* this, if by knowledge we mean infallible cognition. Nor indeed can anyone else properly claim to have knowledge, in this sense, of either the exclusivist or the inclusivist picture. All of them are, strictly speaking, hypotheses. The pluralist hypothesis is arrived at inductively. One starts from the fact that many human beings experience life in relation to a limitlessly greater transcendent

Reality – whether the direction of transcendence be beyond our present existence or within its hidden depths. In theory such religious experience is capable of a purely naturalistic analysis which does not involve reference to any reality other than the human and the natural. But to participate by faith in one of the actual streams of religious experience – in my case, the Christian stream – is to participate in it as an experience of transcendent Reality. I think that there is in fact a good argument for the rationality of trusting one's own religious experience, together with that of the larger tradition within which it occurs, so as both to believe and to live on the basis of it; but I cannot develop that argument here.[1] Treating one's own form of religious experience, then, as veridical – as an experience (however dim, like 'seeing through a glass, darkly') of transcendent divine Reality – one then has to take account of the fact that there are other great streams of religious experience which take different forms, are shaped by different conceptualities, and embodied in different institutions, art forms, and life-styles. In other words, as well as one's own religion, sustained by its distinctive form of religious experience, there are also other religions, through each of which flows the life blood of a different form of religious experience. What account is one to give of this plurality?

At this point the three answers that we discussed above become available again: exclusivism, inclusivism and pluralism. The exclusivist answer is that only one's own form of religious experience is an authentic contact with the Transcendent, other forms being delusory: the naturalistic interpretation applies to those other forms, but not to ours. This is a logically possible position; but clearly it is painfully vulnerable to the charge of being entirely arbitrary. It thus serves the cause of general scepticism, as David Hume noted with regard to claims that the miracles of one's own religion are genuine whilst those of others are spurious.[2]

Moving to the inclusivist answer, this would suggest that religious experience in general does indeed constitute a contact with the Transcendent, but that this contact occurs in its purest and most salvifically effective form within one's own tradition, other forms having value to the varying extents to which they approximate to ours. This is a more viable position than the previous one, and less damaging to the claim that religion is not a human projection but a genuine human response to transcendent Reality. There is however a range of facts which do not fit easily into the inclusivist theory, namely the changed and elevated lives, moving from self-centeredness towards Reality-centeredness, within the other great religious traditions. Presumably there must be a strong correlation between the authenticity of the forms of religious experience and their spiritual and moral fruits. It would then follow from the inclusivist position that there should be a far higher incidence and quality of saintliness in one traditon – namely, that in which contact with the Transcendent occurs in 'its purest and most salvifically effective form' – than in the others. But this does not seem to be the case. There is of course no reliable census of saints! Nor indeed is the concept of a saint by any means clear and unproblematic; very different profiles of saintliness have operated at different times and in different places. But if we look for the transcendence of egoism and a re-centering in God or in the transcendent Real, then I venture the proposition that, so far as human observation and historical memory can tell, this occurs to about the same extent within each of the great world traditions.

If this is so, it prompts us to go beyond inclusivism to a pluralism which recognizes a variety of human religious contexts within which salvation/liberation takes place.

But such a pluralistic hypothesis raises many questions. What is this divine Reality to which all the great traditions are said to be oriented? Can we really equate the personal Jahweh with the non-personal Brahman, Shiva with the Tao, the Holy Trinity with the Buddhist Trikāya, and all with one another? Indeed do not the eastern and western faiths deal incommensurably with different problems?

As these questions indicate, we need a pluralistic theory which enables us to recognize and be fascinated by the manifold differences between the religious traditions, with their different conceptualizations, their different modes of religious experience, and their different forms of individual and social response to the divine. I would like in these final pages to suggest the ground plan of such a theory – a theory which is, I venture to think, fully compatible with the central themes of Cantwell Smith's thought.

Each of the great religious traditions affirms that as well as the social and natural world of our ordinary human experience there is a limitlessly greater and higher Reality beyond or within us, in relation to which or to whom is our highest good. The ultimately real and the ultimately valuable are one, and to give oneself freely and totally to this One is our final salvation/liberation/ enlightenment/fulfilment. Further, each tradition is conscious that the divine Reality exceeds the reach of our earthly speech and thought. It cannot be encompassed in human concepts. It is infinite, eternal, limitlessly rich beyond the scope of our finite conceiving or experiencing. Let us then both avoid the particular names used within the particular traditions and yet use a term which is consonant with the faith of each of them – Ultimate Reality, or the Real.

Let us next adopt a distinction that is to be found in different forms and with different emphases within each of the great traditions, the distinction between the Real *an sich* (in his/her/itself) and the Real as humanly experienced and thought. In Christian terms this is the distinction between God in his infinite and external self-existent being, 'prior' to and independent of creation, and God as related to and known by us as creator, redeemer and sanctifier. In Hindu thought it is the distinction between *nirguṇa* Brahman, the Ultimate in itself, beyond all human categories, and *saguṇa* Brahman, the Ultimate as known to finite consciousness as a personal deity, *Īśvara*. In Taoist thought, 'The Tao that can be expressed is not the eternal Tao' (*Tao-Te Ching*, 1). There are also analogous distinctions in Jewish and Muslim mystical thought in which the Real *an sich* is called *En Soph* and *Al Haqq*. In Mahāyāna Buddhism there is the distinction between the Dharmakāya, the eternal cosmic Buddha-nature, which is also the infinite Void (*śūnyatā*), and on the other hand the realm of heavenly Buddha figures (*sambhogakāya*) and their incarnations in the earthly Buddhas (*nirmāṇakāya*). This varied family of distinctions suggests the perhaps daring thought that the Real *an sich* is one but is nevertheless capable of being humanly experienced in a variety of ways. This thought lies at the heart of the pluralistic hypothesis which I am suggesting.

The next point of which we need to take account is the creative part that thought, and the range of concepts in terms of which it functions, plays in the formation of conscious experience. It was above all Immanuel Kant who brought this realization into the stream of modern reflection, and it has since been confirmed and amplified by innumerable studies, not only in general epistemology but also in cognitive psychology, in the sociology of knowledge, and in the philosophy of science. The central fact, of which the epistemology of religion also has to take account, is that our environment is not reflected in our consciousness in a simple and straightforward way, just as it is, independently of our perceiving it. At the physical level, out of the immense richness of structure and detail around us only that minute selection that is relevant to our biological survival and flourishing affects our senses; and these inputs are interpreted in the mind/brain to produce our conscious experience of the familar world in which we live. Its character as an environment within which we can learn to behave appropriately can be called its *meaning* for us. This all-important dimension of meaning, which begins at the physical level as the habitability of the material world, continues at the personal, or social, level of awareness as the moral significance of the situations of our life, and at the religious levels as a consciousness of the ultimate meaning of each situation and of our situation as a whole in relation to the divine Reality. This latter consciousness is not however a general consciousness of the divine, but always takes specific forms; and as in the case of the awareness of the physical and of the ethical meaning of our environment, such consciousness has an essential dispositional aspect. To experience in this way rather than in that involves being in a state of readiness to behave in a particular range of ways, namely that which is appropriate to our environment having the particular character that we perceive (or of course misperceive) it to have. Thus to be aware of the divine as 'the God and Father of our Lord Jesus Christ', in so far as this is the operative awareness which determines our dispositional state, is to live in the kind of way described by Jesus in his religious and moral teaching – in trust towards God and in love towards our neighbours.

How are these various specific forms of religious awareness formed? Our hypothesis is that they are formed by the presence of the divine Reality, this presence coming to consciousness in terms of the different sets of religious concepts and structures of religious meaning that operate within the different religious traditions of the world. If we look at the range of actual human religious experience and ask ourselves what basic concepts and what concrete images have operated in its genesis, I would suggest that we arrive at something like the following answer. There are, first, the two basic religious concepts which between them dominate the entire range of the forms of religious experience. One is the concept of Deity, or God, i.e. the Real as personal; and the other is the concept of the Absolute, i.e. the Real as non-personal. (The term 'Absolute' is by no means ideal for the purpose, but is perhaps the nearest that we have). We do not however, in actual religious experience, encounter either Deity in general or the Absolute in general, but always in specific forms. In Kantian language, each general concept is schematized, or made more concrete. In Kant's own analysis of sense experience the schematization of the basic categories is in terms of time; but religious experience occurs at a much higher level of meaning, presupposing and going beyond physical meaning and involving much more complex and variable modes of dispositional response. Schematization or concretization here is in terms of 'filled' human time, or history, as diversified into the different cultures and civilizations of the earth. For there are different concrete ways of being human and of participating in human history, and within these different ways the presence of the divine Reality is experienced in characteristically different ways.

To take the concept of God first, this becomes concrete as the range of specific deities to which the history of religion bears witness. Thus the Real as personal is known in the Christian tradition as God the Father; in Judaism as Adonai; in Islam as Allah, the Qur'ānic Revealer; in the Indian tradition as Shiva, or Krishna, or Paramātmā, and under the many other lesser images of deity which in different regions of India concretize different aspects of the divine nature. This range of personal deities who are the foci of worship within the theistic traditions constitutes the range of the divine *personae* in relation to mankind. Each *persona*, in his or her historical concreteness, lives within the corporate experience of a particular faith-community. Thus the Jahweh *persona* exists and has developed in interaction with the Jewish people. He is a part of their history, and they are a part of his; and he cannot be extracted from this historical context. Shiva, on the other hand, is a quite different divine *persona*, existing in the experience of hundreds of millions of people in the Shaivite stream of Indian religious life. These two *personae*, Jahweh and Shiva, live within different worlds of faith, partly creating and partly created by the features of different human cultures, being responded to in different patterns of life, and being integral to different strands of historical experience. Within each of these worlds of faith great numbers of people find the ultimate meaning of their existence, and are carried through the crises of life and death; and within this process many are, in varying degrees, challenged and empowered to move forward on the way of salvation/liberation from self-centeredness to Reality-centeredness. From the pluralist point of view Jahweh and Shiva are not rival gods, or rival claimants to be the one and only God, but rather two different concrete historical *personae* in terms of which the ultimate divine Reality is present and responded to by different large historical communities within different strands of the human story.

This conception of divine *personae*, constituting (in Kantian language) different divine phenomena in terms of which the one divine noumenon is humanly experienced, enables us to acknowledge the degree of truth within the various projection theories of religion from Feuerbach through Freud to the present day. An element of human projection colours our mental images of God, accounting for their anthropomorphic features – for example, as male or female. But human projection does not – on this view – bring God into existence; rather it affects the ways in which the independently existing divine Reality is experienced.

Does this epistemological pattern of the schematization of a basic religious concept into a range of particular correlates of religious experience, apply also to the non-theistic traditions? I suggest that it does. Here the general concept, the Absolute, is schematized in actual religious experience to form the range of divine *impersonae* – Brahman, the Dharma, The Tao, Nirvāṇa, Śūnyatā, and so on – which are experienced within the eastern traditions. The structure of these *impersonae* is however importantly different from that of the *personae*. A divine *persona* is concrete, implicitly finite, sometimes visualizable and even capable of being pictured. A divine *impersona*, on the other hand, is not a 'thing' in contrast to a person. It is the infinite being-consciousness-bliss (*saccidānanda*) of Brahman; or the beginningless and endless process of cosmic change (*pratītya samutpāda*) of Buddhist teaching; or again the ineffable 'further shore' of Nirvāṇa; or the eternal Buddha-nature (*dharmakāya*); or the ultimate Emptiness (*śūnyatā*) which is also the fullness or suchness of the world; or the eternal principle of the Tao. It is thus not so much an entity as a field of spiritual force, or the ultimate reality of everything, that which gives final meaning and joy. These non-personal conceptions of the Ultimate inform modes of consciousness varying from the advaitic experience of becoming one with the Infinite, to the Zen experience of finding a total reality in the present concrete moment of existence in the ordinary world. And according to the pluralistic hypothesis these different modes of experience constitute different experiences of the Real as non- or trans-personal. As in the case of the divine *personae*, they are formed by different religious conceptualities which have developed in interaction with different spiritual disciplines and methods of meditation. The evidence that a range of *impersonae* of the one ultimate reality are involved in the non-theistic forms of religious experience, rather than the direct unmediated awareness of Reality itself, consists precisely in the differences between the experiences reported within the different traditions. How is it that a 'direct experience' of the Real can take such different forms? One could of course at this point revert to the exclusivism or the inclusivism whose limitations we have already noted. But the pluralist answer will be that even the most advanced form of mystical experience, as an experience undergone by an embodied consciousness whose mind/brain has been conditioned by a particular religious tradition, must be affected by the conceptual framework and spiritual training provided by that tradition, and accordingly takes these different forms. In other words the Real is experienced, not *an sich*, but in terms of the various non-personal images or concepts that have been generated at the interface between the Real and different patterns of human consciousness.

These many different perceptions of the Real, both theistic and non-theistic, can only establish themselves as authentic by their soteriological efficacy. The great world traditions have in fact all proved to be realms within which or routes along which people are enabled to advance in the transition from self-centeredness to Reality-centeredness. And since they reveal the Real in such different lights, we must conclude that they are independently valid. Accordingly, by attending to other traditions than one's own one may become aware of other aspects or dimensions of the Real, and of other possibilities of response to the Real, which had not been made effectively available by one's own tradition. Thus a mutual mission of the sharing of experiences and insights can proceed through the growing network of inter-faith dialogue and the interactions of the faith-communities. Such mutual mission does not aim at conversion – although occasionally individual conversions, in all directions, will continue to occur – but at mutual enrichment and at co-operation in face of the urgent problems of human survival in a just and sustainable world society.

There are many topics which I have not had space to take up in this paper. I have spoken of 'the great world traditions'; but what about the other smaller ones, including the many new religious movements which are springing up around us today? And what about the great secular faiths of Marxism and Maoism and humanism? Again, I have spoken of salvation/liberation as the transformation of human existence from self-centeredness to Reality-centeredness; but what about the social and political dimensions of this transformation? These are among the many important questions which any complete philosophy of religious pluralism must answer. But I hope that in this paper I may have said enough to indicate the possible fruitfulness of this general standpoint, a standpoint to which Wilfred Cantwell Smith's work has contributed so centrally and so notably.

NOTES

1. See Michael Goulder and John Hick, *Why Believe in God?* (London: SCM Press, 1983).
2. *An Enquiry Concerning Human Understanding*, Section X, Part II, Para. 95.

2

THE CRITICAL APPROPRIATION OF TRADITIONS: THEOLOGY AND THE COMPARATIVE HISTORY OF RELIGION

George Rupp

The thought of Wilfred Cantwell Smith both illustrates and abets a renewed convergence of study in the history of religion and theology. I think this convergence is a very significant development. Accordingly, I want to focus this essay on the issues I see involved in it.

Smith's detractors on occasion assert that this convergence of the history of religion and theology in his thought results only from his resistance to focusing on methodological questions. Among historians of religion, this assertion takes the form of observing that Smith has always directed his historical and comparative work toward finally theological concerns. He has, in short, always been a theologian. In turn, theologians maintain that Smith attends insufficiently to systematic and normative issues because he submerges theology into history.

Certainly also his admirers will agree that Smith has combined interest in both theology and the history of religion throughout his work. But the convergence in his thought of the history of religion and theology is not simply a function of his idiosyncratic personal interests or a consequence of aversion to methodological discussions. Instead, it expresses a powerful historical development, one that Smith characterizes eloquently and that continues to shape study in both the history of religion and theology. To elaborate and defend this contention, I will first outline Smith's description and interpretation of the development, then discuss its implications for both the history of religion and theology, and finally sketch an approach to constructive religious thought or theology that is viable in this emerging situation.

I

Smith's most recent book, *Towards a World Theology*, is his most systematic and sustained statement of the themes that illustrate the convergence of theology and the history of religion in his thought. Accordingly, this book provides a convenient point of reference for summarizing his views. It is the first of his books in which 'theology' appears in the title. But his explicit attention to theological concerns is integrally related to the comparative and historical emphases suggested in the subtitle, *Faith and the Comparative History of Religion*.

Not surprisingly for anyone familiar with the tenor of his thought, Smith begins the exposition of his proposal for a theology of the comparative history of religion with a discussion of the historical context for that proposal. He maintains that this context is the historical fact of the unity of the religious history of humankind. He notes that 'at one level, this unity is a matter of empirical observation' (p. 3). But neither this unity nor its significance – including its theological significance – has been clearly recognized in the past. In contrast to this relative lack of awareness of the interconnectedness of religious history in the past, 'a new, and itself interconnected, development is that currently humankind *is* becoming aware of it, in various communities' (p. 6). Smith himself seeks to contribute to this historical awareness. His general contention – illustrated through an impressive series of specific examples – is that religious communities must be understood in relation to each other:

> What the communities have had in common is that their several histories, individually already complex, can be understood, and indeed can be understood better, and in the end can be understood only, in terms of each other: as strands in a still more complex whole (p. 6).

In the context of this emphasis on the unity of human religious life, Smith expounds two conceptions which underlie his proposal for a theology of the comparative history of religion: participation; and corporate critical self-consciousness. The processes which the conceptions of participation and corporate critical self-consciousness describe are certainly not confined to the context of increasing awareness of the unity of religious life. Participation as Smith expounds it is the process through which members of any and every community partake of their shared life in history. Similarly, corporate critical self-consciousness as Smith construes it is the mode of knowing appropriate to and even presupposed in all of what he terms the humane sciences. But despite this deliberate generality of reference, what is decisive for the distinctive direction in which Smith develops the conceptions of participation and corporate critical self-consciousness is increased contemporary awareness of interconnections across historical traditions.

This pattern is evident in the order of Smith's own exposition. In the instance of participation, he proposes the term as descriptive of the mode of religious life for members of every community:

> In each community religious persons participate in that on-going historical process of which the contemporary life of their community is the current phase (p. 42).

But he then also focuses attention on the extent to which persons may participate in the ongoing process of a neighboring community. Smith notes intriguing examples of this cross-tradition participation. Among the more massive instances are the medieval trilogue among Jews, Christians, and Muslims or of all of them with the thought of Aristotle; the commingling of the 'three teachings' – Confucian, Buddhist, and Taoist – in medieval China; and the role that the nineteenth-century Christian missionary movement in Asia played in the religious development of the non-Christian world.

Smith observes that 'the question is delicate and intricate as to whether and to what degree the concept "participation" may be used' to refer to involvement not only in one's own community but also in the traditions of others (p. 43). He recognizes that the term 'participation' may carry connotations of loyalty and reverence and of self-conscious choice. In the case of connotations of loyalty and reverence, Smith notes that participation even in one's own community has often included relating negatively as well as positively. Consequently, to use the term 'participation' in referring to involvement in the traditions of others likewise need not be simply affirmative – even as, one can nonetheless hope, deliberate negativity or hostility in the self-definition of one community over against others becomes more and more a pattern of the past. More telling still are the connotations of self-conscious choosing carried in the term 'participation.' This set of connotations has what Smith regards as the salutary effect of calling attention to the transition from a time of being implicated unwittingly in the ongoing process of a neighboring community to a dawning era of self-conscious engagement with that process:

> What is beginning to happen around the earth today is the incredibly exciting development that will eventually mean that each person, certainly each group, participates in the religious history of humankind – as self-consciously the context for faith (p. 44).

As in the instance of his discussion of participation, so also in his interpretation of corporate critical self-consciousness, Smith focuses attention on the transition toward increasing awareness of interconnections across nominally discrete historical traditions. Indeed, Smith argues that in principle the very conception of corporate critical self-consciousness entails reference to all humankind.

Smith uses the conception of corporate critical self-consciousness to refer to what he calls the mode of humane knowledge – human knowing of the human as distinguished both from human knowing of non-human objects and from the putative subjective awareness of individuals. Smith locates this interpretation of corporate critical self-consciousness in the context of a general evolutionary scheme in which the transition from consciousness to self-consciousness represents the emergence of the human as such and the development of critical consciousness marks the appearance of science. In this context, he locates the development of critical self-consciousness:

> The emergence of critical self-consciousness is the major transition through which the human race is perhaps now in a position to be about to go (p. 59).

The distinctive quality in Smith's interpretation of this emerging critical self-consciousness is evident in the modifier 'corporate.' The force of 'corporate' is to claim for humane knowledge the appropriate equivalent to the requirement that scientific knowledge of objects in principle be available to all other observers. In the case of human knowing of the human, this appropriate equivalent is, Smith argues, 'knowledge that is in principle apt both for the subject himself or herself, and for all external observers; or, in the case of group activities, for both outside observers and participants' (p. 59). Only through this inclusion of participants as well as observers does human knowledge of the human extend in principle to all humankind.

Corporate critical self-consciousness is, then, the disciplined awareness which the human community has of itself. This community is 'constituted at a minimum by two persons, the one being studied and the one studying, but ideally by the whole human race' (p. 60). Consequently, to study the human 'is to study oneself – even when one person studies another (or one society, another) separated by much space, or time, or both' (p. 79). When the paradigm of objective knowledge is applied to humans as the objects of knowledge, it sets observer and observed over against each other. In contrast, corporate critical self-consciousness presses toward a knowing common to both observer and observed because it is construed as knowledge of that whole of which both the subject and the object are a part:

> In principle, then, for all humankind to know each other . . . is for all humankind to become one community. And *vice versa*: only as we move towards community can we come to know (p. 79).

Or, as Smith puts it even more aphoristically, 'the truth of all of us is part of the truth of each of us' (p. 79).

II

Insofar as humans are becoming increasingly aware of the unity of religious life and insofar as the conceptions of participation and corporate critical self-consciousness aptly characterize dimensions of this developing awareness, there is more and more common ground in the fields of theology and the history of religion. Indeed, insofar as this complex historical transition is the context for contemporary understandings and expressions of religious communities, sharp distinctions between theology and the history of religion become less and less tenable. In this sense, Smith's thought is itself an illustration of the historical development he describes. But beyond his own position, this development has definite implications for both theology and the history of religion.

It is worth noting how recent and uncharacteristic in human history is a clear differentiation between theology and the history of religion. In the West before the Enlightenment and throughout the histories of virtually all other traditions, theologians or those in similar positions of intellectual responsibility in other religious traditions were presumed to have such knowledge as was available or desirable concerning what has come to be understood as the history of religion. That there should be a separate scholarly guild to provide information about other religious traditions is an innovation of the Enlightenment in the West. Even more recent is the intention that this information should be objective as distinguished from either serving the apologetic purposes of a religious community or debunking the pretentions of one tradition through unfavorable comparison to another.

Despite its relatively brief duration, a clear differentiation of the history of religion from theology has, however, been enormously productive. The aim of accurately and systematically describing the religious traditions of others in principle apart from both apologetic and iconoclastic interests has contributed immeasurably to the linguistic and historical understanding of the data of religious history. Indeed, this study has often been in the forefront of cross-cultural understanding as Western universities have only gradually moved out of very provincial conceptions especially of the humanities. Missionary concerns and other forms of religious or anti-religious motivation no doubt provided much of the energy for this study. But the development of a discipline in principle differentiated from the theological or ideological interests of any one community has supported and accelerated the remarkable collection of data in the history of religion from the Enlightenment on and especially in the last century and a half.

To note and to applaud a contemporary convergence of study in the history of religion and theology need not and should not entail any interest in simply reversing the very productive differentiation of the two in the recent history of Western universities. But the contemporary context of increasing awareness of interconnections across religious traditions does provide the opportunity to consider again the relations between theology and the history of religion. In particular, the recognition of greater common ground in the two fields allows a moving beyond the mutual stereotypes that have become both inaccurate and counterproductive.

The mutual stereotypes have arisen in the first instance because of the concern on the part of the history of religion to differentiate itself from theology. The result has been a self-characterization of the history of religion as objective study of other traditions in their own right rather than for apologetic purposes. In this self-characterization is the implied and not infrequently also explicit contrast to the traditional theological disciplines, which are suspect insofar as they combine the historical description of data with concern for the normative commitments of a particular religious community. In its sharpest form the contrast is, in short, between objective and value-free study on the one hand and ideologically determined apologetics on the other.

This self-characterization of the history of religion has been influential in providing academic legitimation for the study of religion, especially in American colleges and universities – a process of legitimation that is not without its ironies. Faculty members and departments have argued for the academic respectability of their efforts on the basis of linguistic and historical rigor and objectivity in contributing to understanding both other cultures and earlier periods of Western traditions. At the same time, the greatest interest of students – and of many faculty members as well – has been in offerings that relate such studies to current issues of personal values and public policy. Thus even when the emphasis on the objectivity of the study of religion has been most pronounced, concern with normative questions has been considerable.

171

This apparently irrepressible interest in normative questions is not, of course, confined to the study of religion. But the recurrent expression of such concerns provides the opportunity to criticize the conception of academic study as value-free inquiry – instead of appealing to that very conception in attempting to secure respectability for the study of religion. In sum, the study of religion should aspire to become a model of responsible attention to normative questions, especially because such questions have received insufficient careful study in the modern secular university.

In the context of increasing awareness across religious traditions, normative questions become all the more salient. Historical study of developing traditions that interact with one's own almost unavoidably raises comparative questions about relative adequacy to an increasingly shared experience. The process works in both directions: appraisal is directed toward what is observed and also reflected back on the values of the observer. In Smith's terms, the student participates in both traditions in the mode of corporate critical self-consciousness.

There is, to be sure, the amply illustrated limiting case of investigators who insist that they are only describing what they see and are interested neither in assessing it nor in allowing it to impinge on their own views. This orientation has contributed extensively to the accumulation of data about other traditions and in this regard is worthy of respect. But the stated intention of this approach to understand another tradition on its own terms has the effect of refusal to entertain even the possibility of its truth. Of course, the further result is that the adequacy of the investigator's own views is simply presumed. Ironically, this uncritical stance toward one's own values and disinterest in the normative claims of others is not altogether unlike the position of theologians who want only to commend their own views in comparison to the commitments of others.

To participate self-consciously and self-critically in two or more traditions as parts of a more inclusive whole is, then, a rejection of every such presumed adequacy of one's own views. For the historian of religion – and certainly for the comparative historian of religion – the result is that study becomes fully cross-cultural as inquiry directed toward understanding the other also invites reexamination of one's own traditions. Similarly, for the theologian, exposition and advocacy of his or her own position cannot proceed on the basis of authorities simply presumed to be incommensurate with those of other communities and inaccessible to participants in other traditions. Instead, in this case, too, understanding other traditions and representing one's own are intimately involved with each other because they are directed toward only provisionally separate streams of an increasingly shared history.

This situation of increasing awareness across traditions poses a fundamental challenge to the whole enterprise of theology. In this sense, the situation of theology is different from that of the history of religion. Even if historians of religion cannot uncritically presume their own values, they do not have the professional responsibility to represent the position of a particular tradition. But theologians and those in analogous positions in non-theistic traditions at least in the past typically have had precisely this responsibility: to represent the traditions of a particular community so as to interpret and in turn also to shape the experience of its members. How is this responsibility of the theologians to be executed in the context of an emerging world culture in which participants in any one tradition also increasingly participate self-consciously in the religious life of humanity as a whole?

III

As it always has at least in its monotheistic forms, theology is grounded in particular traditions and seeks from that base to understand what is universally true. The foundation in particularity and the universality of reference continue to be definitive of the enterprise properly construed. But both terms of this polarity also assume a distinctive character in the context of an emerging world culture.

The images, the ideas, the norms and injunctions, the ritual and institutional patterns that constitute the traditions of his or her particular community decisively shape the experience that the theologian interprets. But as theologians and their counterparts in non-theistic traditions become increasingly aware of religious and ideological communities other than their own, they also are at least indirectly and peripherally influenced by those other communities. In short, they participate in multiple traditions even when they affirm their own community as fundamental to their particular identity.

A similar insinuation of multiplicity or plurality characterizes the universality of reference of theology. The aim of the undertaking is still to seek to understand the ultimate conditions of human life, to interpret the whole of experience in its most encompassing context. Included in that whole of experience are, however, an imposing array of alternative symbolizations of the ultimate conditions or the most encompassing context of human life. Even such almost completely formal terms as 'the ultimate' and 'the whole' entail elaborate traditions of assumptions and implications. So, too, of course, do more particular terms – 'God' or 'śūnyatā,' for example. In sum, in the context of increased awareness across traditions, even to formulate the universalistic intention of theology and its analogues in non-theistic traditions already unavoidably involves a comparative dimension.

The novelty of the contemporary situation should not be overstated. After all, awareness of differences among religious traditions on virtually every issue, including the question of how the ultimate is most appropriately conceived or addressed or realized, is scarcely an unprecedented development. Within nominally unified communities, there have always been controversies among competing alternative interpretations of shared traditions. Similarly, conflict between clearly distinguished communities has been an only too characteristic feature of the religious landscape over the centuries. But what is new is the increasingly widespread recognition both of substantial change over time within continuing communities and of systematic parallels in the development of historically only remotely related traditions.

Both change within a continuing community and apparent similarities across distinct communities allow of traditionalist interpretations. Change over time is in this case construed as a series of heretical deviations from what can be identified and must be affirmed as the strictly maintained standard of orthodoxy.

Similarly, the impression of parallels in quite different traditions is resisted because it is held to result from a comparison of positions that are, when rightly viewed, incommensurable. In short, increased awareness both of change within and parallels between religious communities is countered through reiterated appeals to an inerrant authority that guarantees unique truth.

This assertion of traditional authority continues to exercise impressive and at times volatile power, perhaps especially in the face of anxiety over change within and parallels between communities. It cannot, however, alter the increasing recognition of the comparative context of such appeals. The Theravāda Buddhist who relies on the inerrant authority of the Pali Canon, the fundamentalist Christian who bases his or her certainty on the verbally inspired Word of God, and the Wahhabī Muslim who cites the infallible Qur'ān all may give each other pause – the more so as they become aware of extraordinarily impressive figures in their own traditions who have not shared their appeal to inerrantly authoritative, verbally inspired, and infallibly accurate texts. Similarly, appeals to supernatural events or precisely prescribed ritual practices or incommunicable self-authenticating experiences have less self-evident authority as there is increased awareness of differing interpretations within a single community and intriguing parallels in other traditions.

The effect of the historical and cross-cultural awareness is, then, frequently – even characteristically and in the end perhaps unavoidably – to call into question every appeal to a putatively inerrant authority. Awareness which has a comparative dimension and in that comparison is not only appreciative but also critical and self-critical in effect relativizes every such appeal. Diversity within a tradition renders problematical every sharply delineated standard of orthodoxy; and comparison among communities invites appeal to considerations not confined to any one tradition. Thus in practice even if not consistently in theory, the authority of any one tradition is subjected to appraisal on the basis of criteria that are arguably applicable over time and across traditions. The criteria on which such comparative appraisal is based are themselves subject to evaluation. There is, in short, also a plurality of positions on the issue of how most adequately to construe those criteria. But however diverse may be the specific

175

criteria employed, they are all expressions of the general recognition that appeal to the authority of tradition alone does not suffice.

Here again, the novelty of the contemporary situation should not be overstated. Even cursory reading in the history of any religious community offers ample evidence that the truth of particular positions has been commended not only through appeals to traditional authorities but also through claims to illumine and in turn to influence contemporary experience. References to the tradition and either implicit or explicit claims to represent that tradition on the one hand and arguments about the capacity to interpret and shape life today on the other of course appear in greatly differing ratios. But both forms of appeal are almost always present. In Christian traditions, for example, dogmatic and philosophical theology suggest poles between which there is spectrum of approaches. Even in those traditions for which the designation 'dogmatic' is invariably pejorative, there is also a combining of appeals to authoritative traditions and contemporary experience. Similarly, the most insistently dogmatic theology still at least tacitly claims to focus and clarify the ultimately crucial features of lived experience.

But while claims to illumine and influence contemporary experience have ample precedents in virtually all religious traditions, such claims have not been the focus of attention to the extent that they are in the context of increased awareness of change within and parallels between communities. In sum, as this double awareness in effect relativizes the authority of tradition, it at the same time increases the force of claims to interpret and in turn shape the whole of human experience. As a result, the question of criteria for adjudicating the relative adequacy of such claims becomes an inescapable issue for theology and its counterparts in non-theistic traditions.

The criteria employed must address the two sets of considerations implied in references not only to interpreting but also to shaping the whole of human experience. The criteria must, in short, focus attention on both descriptive and normative adequacy.

To aspire to interpret the whole of human experience entails a commitment to comprehensiveness that precludes retreat into a private or even a socially and culturally provincial sphere. Standards of descriptive adequacy thus seek to measure the extent and the depth to which the symbolic resources of a tradition have the capacity to incorporate into that frame of reference any and every datum of experience. Included here are, of course, the perennial questions, crises, and transitions which all religious traditions address: the relationship of the human to the natural, the cosmic, the ultimate; the realities of evil and suffering, of compassion and liberation; the meaning of life itself from birth through the struggles for and support of various communities to its end in individual and perhaps also collective death. But also included are particular historical developments – the missionary success of Islam, the economic power of capitalism, techniques for family planning, organ transplants, nuclear annihilation. The criterion of adequacy to experience measures the capacity to interpret this entire range of data through the symbolic resources of the tradition, a capacity which in turn requires the vitality to accommodate new insights not anticipated in the tradition itself.

Important as is the capacity to interpret all of life, this descriptive adequacy is incomplete apart from its normative dimension. Indeed, mutual assessment of religious positions probably more often than not focuses on this dimension of implications for shaping the world. What is the hierarchy of values presupposed in religious positions that take the goal of religious discipline or devotion to be deliverance to a realm or an existence sharply distinguished from life in space and time? What are the consequences of construing the individual self as an illusion or as an infinitely valuable personality with an eternal destiny or as only provisionally discrete from the ultimate reality of which it is an expression? What is the impact on human being and value of trust in a deity who governs the whole of history or of commitment to a moral order that elicits fervent obedience or of insight into the ultimate emptiness of all reality?

Interaction among traditions that includes both comparative understanding and also at least tacit mutual appraisal will not, of course, reach easy or early agreement on judgments of relative descriptive and normative adequacy. Indeed, the least of the benefits of such interaction is any anticipated agreement. But what may and will occur is an acceleration of the ongoing process of development within each of the communities involved. For example, members of a community may discover that their tradition has attended insufficiently to the implications of contemporary astronomy or physics or genetics in its representation of the human condition and may, therefore, seek to take those data more thoroughly into account. Or others may seek to develop new emphases to counteract traditional tendencies toward tolerating or even legitimating social inequities which on reflection they do not want to affirm. Still others may conclude that the insistent iconoclasm of their traditions requires rethinking in view of the beauty of painting and sculpture evident in other communities but proscribed from theirs.

Such interaction and change does not require prior agreement on criteria for mutual appraisal. Instead, members of the various communities may bring to the process quite different and perhaps very particular criteria for assessing descriptive and normative adequacy. Differences in the criteria employed are not, however, disabling insofar as the initial and probably the most crucial outcome of the process is change in one's own position. For in the case of such reflexive change, the criteria guiding the process are precisely the ones that are compelling to those who are modifying or developing their own positions.

Nor does this process of reflexive change – change in one's own position – preclude two other responses to interaction among traditions: a bracketing of the question of relative adequacy in favor of a scrupulous recording of positions in their historical particularity; and conversion from one community to the other. Those responses have been and may well continue to be frequent and influential. But neither a programmatic resistance to allowing judgments of adequacy or an insistence on transferring allegiance from one tradition to another will eliminate the ongoing and almost certainly accelerating process of reflexive change already underway among all traditions as they participate together in an increasingly common history.

The process of interaction among communities may be especially influential insofar as it serves to intensify the self-consciousness of minority or even submerged tendencies in a tradition. Hence the result of such interaction may be an increase in the diversity within traditions. For example, traditions that have focused almost exclusively on petitionary prayer may recover patterns of meditation and contemplation through contact with communities that have centered spiritual discipline on such practices. Or traditions that have emphasized individual religious attainment may through interaction with other religious or secular traditions develop resources for supporting a sense of corporate responsibility. But each such provisional increase in diversity also affords the prospect of a commonality transcending traditional divisions as members of the various communities reinterpret and even modify their positions so as to accommodate further ranges of experience.

There are, of course, limits to the elasticity and adaptability of religious traditions. Thinkers may simply ignore those limits. They may, that is, commend the positions they advance exclusively on the basis of their capacity to interpret and their power to shape human experience as such quite apart from any special reference to particular religious traditions. But for those theologians and their counterparts in non-theistic traditions who do claim to represent a particular religious community, the situation is more complex. On the one hand, they maintain that the position they hold satisfies the need for orientation and response in the contemporary world. On the other hand, they also affirm that position as consistent with and expressive of the traditions they claim to represent. In sum, they interpret and in turn also shape contemporary experience through the symbolic resources of particular traditions which they receive from others, to which they contribute, and for which they then take responsibility.

This ongoing process I call the appropriation of traditions. It is the process through which participants in religious communities identify with and live out of the traditions of those communities. In short, they make those traditions their own. In the context of increased awareness of change within and parallels between religious communities, this process is more and more self-consciously both comparative and critical. It is therefore not simply acceptance of what is passed on through authoritative channels. Instead, appropriation is a constructive process which requires critical engagement with the commitments of a particular community and comparative assessment of alternative positions in multiple traditions. Comparative and critical appropriation of tradition is, therefore, an approach to theology and its non-theistic analogues available to those who, in Wilfred Smith's terms, participate in the religious life of the human community in the mode of corporate critical self-consciousness. As such, this process is both a crucial dimension of the comparative history of religion and a critically important resource for religious communities worldwide.

THE *PHILOSOPHIA PERENNIS* AND THE STUDY OF RELIGION

Seyyed Hossein Nasr

One of the most remarkable characteristics of the current academic study of religion as such and religions in their relation with each other is that, despite the enormous theological difficulties encountered by Western scholars of comparative religious studies who are also interested in religion itself, so little attention has been paid in academic and religious circles to the approach of the traditionalist school which is none other than that of the *philosophia perennis*. One would imagine that at least in cases where one's current conceptual framework does not do justice to the subject at hand, one would be willing at least to consider seriously another point of view which has dealt in such a universal and comprehensive fashion with the study of religion both in itself and in the multiplicity of forms in which it has manifested itself in human history. It is therefore especially appropriate that in a volume dedicated to Professor W. C. Smith, who is at once a celebrated scholar of comparative religion and concerned with the study of religion as religion and not as philology, history, sociology or some other discipline, an essay should be devoted to the *philosophia perennis* and its approach to the study of religion.

It is first of all necessary to clarify what is meant in this essay by *philosophia perennis* which could also be called, from the point of view adopted here, *sophia perennis*, although the two terms are not completely identical, one emphasizing more the intellectual and the other the realized aspect of the same truth.[1] Since 'perennial philosophy', the English equivalent of the Latin term, has been used widely by groups ranging from contemporary neo-Thomists to Aldous Huxley whose celebrated book bearing this name[2] made the term famous for many non-specialized students of religion and philosophy, it is necessary to clarify its meaning in the context of this study. By *philosophia perennis* to which should be added the adjective *universalis*, as insisted upon so far by A. K. Coomaraswamy, is meant a knowledge which has always been and will always be and which is of universal character both in the sense of existing among peoples of different climes and epochs and of dealing with universal principles. This knowledge which is available to the intellect[3] is, moreover, contained at the heart of all religions or traditions,[4] and its realization and attainment is possible only through those traditions and by means of methods, rites, symbols, images and other means sanctified by the message from Heaven or the Divine Origin which gives birth to each tradition. Although theoretically it is possible for man to gain this knowledge at least on a more outward level by 'himself' because of the nature of the intellect, that 'supernaturally natural' faculty which is ingrained in the very substance of man, the norm is such that the attainment of this knowledge depends upon the grace and the cadre which religion or tradition alone provides. If there are exceptions, they are there to prove the rule and bear witness to the well-known dictum that 'the Spirit bloweth where it listeth.'

The *philosophia perennis* possesses branches and ramifications pertaining to cosmology, anthropology, art and other disciplines, but at its heart lies pure metaphysics if this latter term is understood as the science of Ultimate Reality, as a *scientia sacra*[5] not to be confused with the subject bearing the same name in post-medieval Western philosophy. Metaphysics understood in the perspective of the *philosophia perennis* is a veritable 'divine science' and not a purely mental construct which would change with every alteration in the cultural fashions of the day or with new discoveries of a science of the material world. This traditional metaphysics, which in reality should be used in the singular as metaphysic, is a knowledge which sanctifies and illuminates; it is gnosis if this term is shorn of its sectarian connotations going back to early Christian centuries. It is a knowledge which lies at the heart of religion, which illuminates the meaning of religious rites, doctrines and symbols and which also provides the key for the understanding of both the necessity of the plurality of religions and the way to penetrate into other religious universes without reducing either their religious significance or our own commitment to the religious universe to which we who wish to study other religions belong.

The approach of the *philosophia perennis* to the study of religion, as understood in this essay, is none other than the traditional approach as the term tradition has been understood and explained by masters and expositors of the teachings of what one can call the traditional school,[6] that is, such men as R. Guénon, A. K. Coomaraswamy, M. Pallis, T. Burckhardt, M. Lings, Lord Northbourne, L. Schaya, W. N. Perry and most of all F. Schuon. The point of view of this school should not be identified with either that sentimentalism that sees all religions as being the same or that neo-Vedantism which spread in America after the Second World War and which despite the passing interest of some of its leading figures in the *philosophia perennis* and tradition, should not be confused with the traditional perspective. If there is one principle which all the traditional authors in question repeat incessantly, it is orthodoxy which they, however, do not limit to the exoteric level but also apply to the esoteric. They are orthodox and the great champions of universal orthodoxy. This point alone should clarify their radical difference from the neo-Vedantists and similar groups with whom they are often identified by opponents who have taken little care to examine in depth what the traditionalists have been saying.[7]

Those who have spoken from the perspective of the *philosophia perennis* have concerned themselves with every aspect of religion, with God and man, with revelation and sacred art, with symbols and images, with rites and religious law, with mysticism and social ethics, with metaphysics and theology. This school is concerned with religion in its trans-historical reality refusing to accept the historicism of the academic approach to *Religionswissenschaft* developed in Europe in the nineteenth century. Yet, in contrast to the later school of phenomenology, it is not impervious to the historical unfolding of a particular tradition or the significance and value of a distinct religious 'phenomenon' in the cadre of a tradition which has its own distinct history. Even from the outside it can be seen that the traditional school in fact encompasses more of the field of religion and allows a meaningful understanding of a greater portion of the very complicated reality of religion than any other available approach.[8] As for those who speak from within this perspective, they believe that only this school is able to provide the key for the understanding of the full length and breadth of both religion and religions, of the complexities and enigmas of a single religion and the significance of the plurality of religions and their interrelationship.

It is not possible to deal in detail in such a short essay with the teachings of this school concerning all these issues. It would need a separate book simply to summarize what the traditional authors have written on the different aspects of religion.[9] What can be dealt with somewhat more fully is the approach of this school to the study of *religions*, that is the field which has come to be known as comparative religion or the history of religion, a field to which Prof. W. C. Smith has devoted most of his later scholarly life after beginning as an Islamicist.

To understand the approach of the traditional school or the *philosophia perennis*, as here understood, to the study of religions, as well as religion as such, it is necessary to point to certain fundamental features of the vision of reality or metaphysics which underlies all the teachings of this school.[10] According to the *philosophia perennis*, reality is not exhausted by the psychophysical world in which human beings usually function nor is consciousness limited to the everyday level of awareness of the men and women of present day humanity. Ultimate Reality is beyond all determination and limitation. It is the Absolute and Infinite from which issues goodness like the rays of the sun which of necessity emanate from it. Whether the Principle is envisaged as Fullness or Emptiness depends upon the point of departure of the particular metaphysical interpretation in question.[11] If some critic asserts, as in fact has been done, that according to this or that Oriental sage *māyā* is *Ātman* or *saṃsāra* is *nirvāṇa*, one can answer that such an assertion is only possible if one first realizes that *māyā* is *māyā* and *saṃsāra* is *saṃsāra*. The Principle can also be envisaged as the Supreme 'I', considering the subjective rather than the objective pole in which case ordinary consciousness is then seen as an outward envelope of the Supreme Self rather than its descent into lower realms of the universal hierarchy. But in either case, whether seen as the Transcendent or the Immanent, the Principle gives rise to a universe which is hierarchical, possessing many levels of existence or states of consciousness from the Supreme Principle to earthly man and his terrestrial ambience.

It is in this hierarchic universe that man's life takes place and possesses meaning. Religion is not only the key for the understanding of this universe, but also the central means whereby man is able to journey through these lower stages of existence to the Divine Presence, this journey being nothing other than human life itself as it is understood traditionally. The doctrines, symbols and rites of a religion possess therefore a meaning which is not confined to the spatio-temporal realm. In contrast to most modern theologians and philosophers and scholars of religion who have either consciously or unconsciously adopted the scientistic view which reduces Reality as such to physical or 'historical' reality, the traditionalists refuse to reduce the existence of religion to only the terrestrial and temporal realm. Religion for them is not *only* the faith and practices of a particular human collectivity which happens to be the recipient of a particular religious message. Religion is not *only* the faith of the men and women who possess religious faith. Religion is of Divine Origin. It has its archetype in the Divine Intellect and possesses levels of existence like the cosmos itself. If a religion were to cease to exist on earth, that does not mean that it would cease to possess any reality whatsoever. In this case its life cycle on earth would have simply come to an end while the religion itself as an 'Idea' in the Platonic sense would subsist in the Divine Intellect in its trans-historical reality. The efficacy of its rites here on earth would cease but the archetypal reality which the religion represents would persist.

The traditional school does not neglect the social or psychological aspects of religion, but it refuses to reduce religion to either its social or psychological manifestations. Religion comes from the wedding between a Divine Norm and a human collectivity destined providentially to receive the imprint of that norm. From this wedding is born religion as seen in this world among different peoples and cultures. The differences in the recipient are certainly important and constitute one of the causes for the multiplicity of religions, but religion itself cannot be reduced to its terrestrial embodiment. If a day would come when not a single Muslim or Christian were to be left on the surface of the earth, Islam or Christianity would not cease to exist nor lose their reality in the ultimate sense.

The radical difference between the traditionalists and most other schools of thought concerned with the study of religions comes precisely from this vast difference in the views they hold concerning the nature of reality. The traditionalists refuse to accept as valid that truncated vision of reality currently held in the Western world and arising originally from the post-medieval rationalism and empiricism in Europe which forms the background for much of religious studies today especially in academic circles. It must be remembered, however, that the perspective held by the traditionalists is the same as the world view within which the religions themselves were born and cultivated. That is why the traditional studies of religion are able to penetrate into the heart of religion in such fashion and also why these studies, in contrast to those of most modern scholars of religion, are so deeply appreciated by the traditional authorities of different religions outside the modern Western world and its cultural extensions into other parts of the globe.

The school of the *philosophia perennis* speaks of tradition and traditions. It believes that there is a Primordial Tradition which constituted original or archetypal man's primal spiritual and intellectual heritage received through direct revelation when Heaven and earth were still 'united'. This Primordial Tradition is reflected in all later traditions, but the later traditions are not simply its historical and horizontal continuation. Each tradition is marked by a fresh vertical descent from the Origin, a revelation which bestows upon each religion lying at the heart of the tradition in question its spiritual genius, fresh vitality, uniqueness and the 'grace' which make its rites and practices operative not to speak of the paradisal vision which constitutes the origin of its sacred art or of the sapience which lies at the heart of its message. But because the Origin is One and also because of the profound unity of the human recipient despite important existing racial, ethnic and cultural differences, the fact that there is the Primordial Tradition and also traditions does not destroy the perennity and universality of the *philosophia perennis*. The anonymous tradition reflects a remarkable unanimity of views concerning human life and thought in worlds as far apart as those of the Eskimos and the Australian Aborigines, the Taoists and the Muslims.

The conception of religion in the school of the *philosophia perennis* is vast enough to embrace the primal and the historical, the Semitic and the Indian, the mythic and the 'abstract' types of religions. Tradition, as understood by such masters of this school as Schuon, is such as to embrace within its fold all the different modes and types of Divine Manifestation, making it possible to develop a veritable theology of comparative religion – which in reality should be called metaphysics of comparative religion – able to do theological justice to the tenets of each religion while enabling the student of religion, who is at once interested objectively in the existence of religions other than his own and is at the same time of a religious nature himself, to cross frontiers as difficult to traverse as that which separates the world of Abraham from that of Kṛṣṇa and Rāma or the universe of the American Indians from that of traditional Christianity.

In the same way that the rejection of the reality of hierarchy in its metaphysical sense by so many modern scholars has affected their world view and methodology in every field and domain, the acceptance of this principle constitutes an essential feature of the traditionalist school in its study of religion in its different aspects. Religion itself is hierarchically constituted and is not exhausted by its external and formal reality. Just as the phenomenal world necessitates the noumenal – the very word phenomenon implying a reality of which the phenomenon is the phenomenon – the formal aspect of religion necessitates the essential and the supraformal. Religion possesses at once an external, outward or exoteric dimension concerned with the external and formal aspect of human life but being religion, it is in itself sufficient to enable man who follows its tenets and has faith in its truths to lead a fully human life and to gain salvation. But religion also possesses an inner or esoteric dimension concerned with the formless and the essential with means to enable man to reach the Supernal Essence here and now. Moreover, within the context of this most general division, there are further levels within both the exoteric and the esoteric so that altogether there exists within every integral religion a hierarchy of levels from the most outward to the supreme Center.

There is also a hierarchy of approaches to the Ultimate Reality in religion which can again be summarized in a schematic fashion in the ways of work, love and knowledge, the famous *karma mārga*, *bhakti mārga* and *jñāna mārga* of Hinduism or *al-makhāfah*, *al-maḥabbah* and *al-ma'rifah* of Islam. Likewise, there is a hierarchy among followers of religion or human types seen from the religious perspective corresponding to these modes of approach to the Ultimate Reality. It is to these types that the sapiential tradition of the ancient Greeks referred as the *hylikoi*, *psychoi* and *pneumatikoi*. Islam also distinguishes between the *muslim*, the *mu'min*, as well as the possessor of spiritual virtue or *iḥsān* who is referred to in the Qur'ān as *muḥsin* although this latter term is not as common in later religious literature as the first two.[12]

The hierarchy of ways to God or of human types in their religious quest is innate to the paths or ways in question, the higher comprehending the lower in the sense of both understanding and encompassing it, but the lower not able to comprehend what stands beyond and above it. Hence the inner tension between various religious schools and paths even in traditional settings. These traditional oppositions, however, are very different in nature from the modern attack against the whole hierarchic perspective of the traditionalist school on the charges that it is 'élitist' or something of the sort. If by this charge is meant that the traditional school accepts the saying of Christ that 'many are called but few are chosen', then yes, it is élitist. This school asserts that not everyone is able to know everything but it also affirms strongly that all levels of religion are precious and from Heaven, that all human beings can be saved if only they follow religion according to their inner nature and vocation. It also asserts that as far as the possibility of being able to go beyond the human to ultimately reach the Divine, all human beings are equal by virtue of being human without this equality destroying the hierarchy mentioned or obliterating the obvious distinctions between human types, their aptitudes and capabilities. Being based on the primacy of knowledge, the *philosophia perennis* is 'élitist' in the sense of distinguishing between those who know and those who do not according to the famous Qur'ānic verse, 'Are those who know and those who know not the same?' which the

Qur'ān answers with a strong nay. What is difficult to understand is why this charge of élitism is even made by certain scholars unless it be to keep up with current fads but in this case one wonders why modern physics is not called élitist.

The *philosophia perennis* sees a unity which underlies the diversity of religious forms and practices, a unity which resides within that quintessential truth at the heart of religions which is none other than the *philosophia perennis* itself. But this unity is not in the external forms. All religions do not simply say the same thing despite the remarkable unanimity of principles and doctrines and profound similarity of applications of these principles.[13] The traditionalist school is opposed to the sentimental ecumenism which sees all religions as the same at the expense of reducing them to a least common denominator or of putting aside some of their basic teachings. On the contrary, the traditionalists respect every minutiae of a sacred tradition as coming ultimately from Heaven and to be treated with reverence as should every manifestation of the sacred. They are fully aware of the particular spiritual genius of each religion and its uniqueness and insist that these features are precisely proof of the transcendent origin of each religion and the reality of its archetype in the Divine Intellect. These characteristics also demonstrate the falsehood of the view which would reduce a religion to simply historical borrowing from an earlier religion.

The unity of which the traditionalists speak is properly speaking transcendental unity above and beyond forms and external manifestations.[14] The followers of this school would accept the current criticism of academic scholars against that levelling 'unity of religions' movement that emanated mostly out of India during the last decades of the nineteenth and early decades of the twentieth century. Wherein they differ from most academic scholars of religion is that the traditionalists breathe within the traditional universe in which the reality of something, most of all religious forms, rites and symbols, is not exhausted by its spatio-temporal aspect. Each form possesses an essence, each phenomenon a noumenon, each accident a substance. Using the language of traditional Western philosophy hallowed by its employment by the representative of the *philosophia perennis* in the Latin Middle Ages and even later, the traditionalists distinguish between the external form and the essence which that form manifests or form and substance in which case the external forms of a religion are seen as accidents which issue forth from and return to a substance that remains independent of all its accidents.[15] It is only on the level of the Supreme Essence even beyond the Logos or on the level of the Supreme Substance standing above all the cosmic sectors from the angelic to the physical within which a particular religion is operative that the ultimate unity of religions is to be sought. If as the Sufis say 'the doctrine of Unity is unique' (al-tawḥīd wāḥid), one can also say that the transcendent unity underlying the diversity of religion cannot be but the Unique or the One Itself. Below that 'level', each religion possesses distinct qualities and characteristics not to be either neglected nor explained away.

Within the particular genius and structure of each religion, however, one can discern certain features which are again universal. There is at the heart of every religion what Schuon calls the *religio perennis*,[16] consisting ultimately of a doctrine concerning the nature of reality and a method for being able to attain what is Real. The doctrinal language varies from one religion to another and can embrace concepts as different as those of *śūnya* and Yahweh. The method can also vary in numerous ways ranging from Vedic sacrifices to Muslim daily prayers. But the essence and goal of the doctrine and method remain universal within every religion.

The traditionalist school does not, moreover, simply place all religions along side each other in the manner of a certain type of phenomenological approach which· would collect religious phenomena without any normative judgement as if one were collecting molluscs. Basing itself on the knowledge provided by the *philosophia perennis*, the traditional school judges between grades of Divine Manifestation, various degrees and levels of prophecy, major and minor dispensations from Heaven, and lesser and greater paths even within a single religion. It possesses a normative dimension and studies religions in the light of a truth which for it is truth and not something else but it does so without falling into subjectivism. On the contrary, this truth alone permits the individual scholar to escape from the prison of subjectivism and the passing fads of a particular period within which the scholar in question happens to live, for this truth is supra-individual in nature, being a *sophia* that is at once perennial and universal.

It is in the light of this truth embodied in the *philosophia perennis* that the traditionalist school can also speak about truth and falsehood in this or that religious school as well as greater and lesser truth. The presence of this truth is also the reason why this school is able to be judgmental about a particular religious phenomenon and speak about authentic and pseudo-religion without falling into a narrow dogmatism on the one hand or simply indifference to truth on the other, two alternatives which dominate much of the religious scene in the modern world.

Based on the vision of the truth as such as contained in the *philosophia perennis*, this school not only distinguishes between religion and pseudo-religion and different types of manifestations of the Divine Principle, but it also penetrates into each religious universe to bring out the meaning of its teachings in comparison with other religions and in the light of the perennial *sophia* without ending up in the relativization of religious truth. Today one of the major problems for man in a world in which traditional boundaries and borders of both a physical and religious nature are removed, is how to study other religions sympathetically without losing the sense of absoluteness in one's own religion which is a *sine qua non* of the religious life and which reflects the fact that religion does come from the Absolute.

The traditional school insists on the study of religion religiously and opposes all the relativization that characterizes much of the modern academic study of religions, while also opposing that parochial conception of the truth which sees a particular manifestation of the Truth as the Truth as such. This school insists upon the principle which as a tautology should be obvious but is often forgotten, the principle being that only the Absolute is absolute. All else is relative. There is also a key concept, again developed most of all by Schuon, of an 'apparently contradictory' nature but metaphysically meaningful, the concept of the 'relatively absolute'. Within our solar system our sun is *the* sun while seen in the perspective of galactic space, it is one among many suns. The awareness of other suns made possible by means as abnormal to the natural and normal human state as the 'existential' awareness of several religious universes, does not make our own sun cease to be *our* sun, the center of *our* solar system, the giver of life to *our* world and the direct symbol of the Divine Intellect for *us* who are revivified by its heat and illuminated by its light.

In the same way within each religious universe there is the logos, prophet, sacred book, avatar or some other direct manifestation of the Divinity or messenger of His Word and a particular message which, along with its 'human container', whether that be the Arabic language of the Qur'ān or the body of Christ, are 'absolute' for the religious universe brought into being by the revelation in question. Yet, only the Absolute is absolute. These manifestations are 'relatively absolute'. Within each religious universe the laws revealed, the symbols sanctified, the doctrines hallowed by traditional authorities, the grace which vivifies the religion in question are absolute within the religious world for which they were meant without being absolute as such. At the heart of every religion is to be found the echo of God exclaiming 'I'. There is only one Supreme Self who can utter 'I', but there are many cosmic and even metacosmic reverberations of the Word which is at once one and many and which each religion identifies with its founder. As Jalāl al-Dīn Rūmī, speaking as a Muslim saint, says:

> When the number hundred has arrived, ninety is also present.
> The name of Aḥmad (the Prophet of Islam) is the name of all prophets.

The traditional school studies the ethics, theology, mysticism or art of each religion in the light of the absoluteness of its Divine Origin without either negating the other manifestations of the Absolute or the possibilities of change and transformation which all things that exist in time must of necessity undergo. This school does not, however, identify the reality of religion only with its historical unfolding. Each religion possesses certain principial possibilities contained in its celestial archetypes. These possibilities are realized or become unfolded in the historical period and within the humanity providentially determined to be the temporal and human containers of the religion in question.

Each religious phenomenon is both a phenomenon of religious character in itself not to be reduced to any other category, and a phenomenon which reveals its full meaning only in the light of the archetypal reality of the tradition in question along with its historical unfolding. Not all religions therefore possess all of their possibilities in a state of actuality at a given moment of human history. Religions decay and even die in the sense that their earthly carrier terminates. They can also become revived as long as the nexus between their earthly manifestation and their celestial origin remains. For the traditionalist school there is not the question of which religion is 'better' since all authentic religions come from the same Origin, but there does exist the question from the operative and practical point of view of what possibilities are available at a particular juncture of history, of what one can in practice follow and what is no longer in fact available within a particular religion.[17]

The range of subjects within the field of religion treated by the followers of the *philosophia perennis* is very wide and their treatment is always in depth and in relation to what is essential. Studies emanating from this school have ranged from those concerning the most subtle aspects of Christianity to Jodo-Shin Buddhism, from the ancient Egyptian religion to contemporary Islam. Such major subjects in religious studies as Tibetan Buddhism and the Sufism of the school of Ibn 'Arabī were first dealt with in their fullness in the modern West by the traditionalists.[18] The meaning of the sacred art of the Orient in general and Hindu and Buddhist art in particular were first brought to the attention of the West by A. K. Coomaraswamy, one of the foremost figures of the traditionalist school while the rapport between Islamic and Christian spirituality in its multifarious dimensions has never been treated with such amplitude and depth as in the works of Schuon. The religious subjects dealt with by this school range from metaphysics and cosmology to sacred art with which they are especially concerned since only through the sacred form can one reach the Formless,[19] from traditional psychology and anthropology to ethics and social structure.

The followers of this school all emphasize the importance of scholarship and some like Coomaraswamy have been among the greatest scholars who have ever lived. They pay much attention to philological considerations and historical facts, but they are neither philologists nor slaves of some form of historicism. They distinguish between historicality and historicism and do not follow the implicitly accepted guideline of many a modern scholar for whom what one does not observe in physical or archaelogical historical records simply does not exist. The approach of the traditionalists is, rather, metaphysical. They go from principles to their applications, but their religious studies are no less scholarly, scientifically accurate or logical than that of those academic scholars who pursue other conceptual frameworks and methods of research. It could in fact be said that from the point of view of logical rigor, few academic works can match those of the traditionalist school whose major figures are all at once metaphysicians, theologians, logicians and scholars.

Nowhere is the combination of those qualities more clearly observable than in the works of Schuon who is certainly the greatest figure of this school in the field of religion. In his work is to be found a remarkable combination of metaphysical penetration and 'theological concern' in the sense of traditional Christian theology, poetic sensitivity and trenchant logic, objective concern for the truth and love and compassion for that immortal being who is the subject of all religious injunctions and the recipient of the Divine Message.[20] Among the traditional authors it is especially he who has given the most extensive and comprehensive exposition of religion from the point of view of the *philosophia perennis* including a large number of studies devoted to the spiritual significance of the *anthrōpos* and the role of what he calls 'the human margin' in certain aspects of religious life and thought which cannot be understood or explained except by means of the comprehension of the nature of the human recipient and the ambiguities of the human soul.[21]

Since the traditionalist school encompasses so much and has dealt with so many aspects of religion in depth in such a unique fashion, it might be asked why it is not better known in academic circles. Why is it that in France where the books of Guénon are still reprinted regularly fifty or sixty years after their appearance, he is passed over nearly completely in silence in university circles and why in other countries where there is not the same planned conspiracy of silence the situation is not much better? The reason must be sought in the nature of the *philosophia perennis* itself. To accept to follow it demands not only the dedication of the mind of the scholar but his whole being. It needs a total *engagement* which is more than many scholars are willing to give except those who speak as committed Christians, Jews, Muslims, etc. from the vantage point of their own particular religion. In the academic world of religious studies, however, such a total *engagement* does not come easily. For the traditionalist school the study of religion and religions is itself a religious activity and of religious significance. In this point they share the lifelong concern of Professor W. C. Smith himself. For them, as for him, all study of religion can only be meaningful if it is itself of religious significance. And their studies are indeed religiously significant and often 'disturbing' for those with ultimate concerns. There are therefore fewer scholars attracted to a doctrine and a method which demands so much.

Nevertheless, as other contemporary maps of the high seas of theology and religion lead ships into the bosom of debilitating and mortally dangerous storms and fashionable 'isms' remain incapable of either explaining major features of religion or of providing serious orientation even of a purely theoretical nature in the field of comparative religious studies, more and more the teachings of the followers of the *philosophia perennis* gain the attraction of scholars in the academic world especially in America and Great Britain where there is greater openness academically in the field of religious studies than elsewhere. During the past years not only have some well known scholars of religion adopted the traditional perspective as their own,[22] but to an ever greater degree other notable scholars become attracted to this school as at least one of the schools of religious studies to be considered seriously.[23]

The interest in this school is also bound to grow as the need for ecumenism is felt to an ever greater degree while most current ecumenism leads to a lessening of religious fervor and the diluting of the Divine Message, making worldly peace rather than the Divine Peace which surpasseth all understanding the goal of religion. The followers of the *philosophia perennis* charter a course which makes possible authentic ecumenism which can in fact only be esoteric, for religious harmony can only be achieved in the

'Divine stratosphere' to quote Schuon and not in the human atmosphere where so many seek it today at the expense of reducing the Divine stratosphere to the human atmosphere.

The traditional school, far from being a modern innovation drawn from some neo-Vedantic strand of modern Hinduism, bases itself upon that ancient and venerable wisdom – which in fact was sometimes called in the West *philosophia priscorium* – the *sanātana dharma* of Hinduism or the *al-ḥikmat al-khālidah* of the Islamic tradition known also under its Persian name *jāwidān-khiṟad*.

This *philosophia perennis* has always been present. What the expositors of this school have done is to forge certain keys from its enduring substance in order to open the doors which block the way of modern man today. The solutions they propose for the questions which arise from the study of both religion in the context of the modern secular world and religions in relation with each other deserve to be considered seriously by all who are interested in the religious significance of religious studies today and in the nature and destiny of men and women as beings whose very substance is molded with those realities with which religion has been concerned perennially and which are and will be real as long as humanity lives and breathes in this earthly abode.

NOTES

1. On these terms and the history of the usage of *philosophia perennis* see S. H. Nasr, *Knowledge and the Sacred*, New York, 1981, pp. 68 ff.; and C. Schmitt, 'Perennial Philosophy: Steuco to Leibnitz', *Journal of the History of Ideas*, XXVII, 1966, pp. 505–32.
2. See A. Huxley, *The Perennial Philosophy*, New York, 1945.
3. One of the most basic doctrines of the *philosophia perennis* is that *intellectus* is not to be confused with *ratio*. Reason as currently understood is the reflection upon the plane of the mind of the Intellect which is able to know God and which is at once divine and of access to human beings provided they are aware of who they are. On the distinction between intellect and reason as understood in the perspective in question see F. Schuon, *The Transcendent Unity of Religions*, trans. P. Townsend, New York, 1975, pp. xxviii and 52; also F. Schuon, *Stations of Wisdom*, trans. G. E. H. Palmer, London, 1961, Ch. 1.

4. Throughout this essay the term tradition is used, not as custom or habit, but as a truth and reality of Transcendent Origin with its manifestations in history not only as religion which lies at its heart but also as art, philosophy, science, etc.

> It will already be apparent to the reader that by tradition more is meant than just custom long established. ... All that can usefully be said of it at the moment is that wherever a complete tradition exists this will entail the presence of four things, namely a source of inspiration or, to use a more concrete term, of Revelation; a current of influence or Grace issuing forth from that source and transmitted without interruption through a variety of channels; a way of 'verification' which, when faithfully followed, will lead the human subject to successive positions where he is able to 'actualise' the truths that Revelation communicates; finally there is the formal embodiment of tradition in the doctrines, arts, sciences and other elements that together go to determine the character of a normal civilization.

M. Pallis, *The Way and the Mountain*, London, 1960, pp. 9–10.

See also Nasr, *Knowledge and the Sacred*, Ch. 2, 'What is Tradition?'.

5. See Nasr, *Knowledge and the Sacred*, Ch. 4.

6. In reality the traditional perspective cannot be considered from its own point of view as simply one school among others. But in the context of the contemporary world with numerous 'schools', methodologies and philosophies for the study of practically any subject save science which insists upon the monopoly of its approach to the study of nature, it is legitimate to speak of the 'traditional school' identified with the names mentioned above as well as others who cannot be cited here because of limitation of space. On the traditional school and its representatives see Nasr, *Knowledge and the Sacred*, pp. 100 ff.

7. A case in point is the criticism of the late R. C. Zaehner against the writings of F. Schuon in his *The Comparison of Religions*, Boston, 1958, p. 169. Zaehner's uneasiness with Schuon's theses and in fact with gnosis or sapiential wisdom in general, a concern which is found also in Zaehner's study of Sufism, reflects more than anything else his own religious life and the inner fear he had of losing his faith in exoteric religion through the attraction of the esoteric to which he was drawn by an inner sympathy and which he nevertheless sought to avoid because of the history of his own inner religious struggles and the fear of recurring skepticism.

8. It is interesting to note that one of the foremost American scholars of religion, Huston Smith, who has adopted the point of view of the

philosophia perennis has written that one of the factors which first drew him to this school and especially the works of F. Schuon was that the perspective of this school makes it possible to include so much of the religious universe within its all-inclusive embrace. This quality does not of course imply the indifference of the traditional point of view to pseudo-religion or falsehood, theologically speaking. On the contrary no school in the contemporary world has insisted as much as this school on the necessity to emphasize the question of truth and therefore falsehood, without any sentimentality or rationalistic relativizing.

9. For the works of traditional authors on religion in its more exclusive sense and also the comparative study of religion see R. Guénon, *Introduction to the Study of Hindu Doctrines*, trans. R. Nicholson, London, 1945; and his *Man and His Becoming according to the Vedanta*, trans. R. Nicholson, London, 1945; A. K. Coomaraswamy, *The Bugbear of Literacy*, Bedfont, 1979; and his *Hinduism and Buddhism*, New York, 1943; M. Pallis, *The Way and the Mountain*; Lord Northbourne, *Religion in the Modern World*, London, 1963; and W. N. Perry, *A Treasury of Traditional Wisdom*, Bedfont, 1979.

   As for the writings of F. Schuon all are related to the domain of religion but those which are most directly concerned with religion and wherein is to be found the most universal and penetrating study of religion from the perspective of the *philosophia perennis* include *The Transcendent Unity of Religions*, *Formes et substances dans les religions*, Paris, 1975; *Esoterism as Principle and as Way*, trans. W. Stoddart, Bedfont, 1981; *Christianisme/Islam: Visions d'Oecuménisme ésotérique*, Milan, 1981; and *Approches du phénomène religieux*, (in press).

10. For a synopsis of this metaphysics see F. Schuon, *From the Divine to the Human*, trans. G. Polit and D. Lambert, Bloomington (Indiana); also R. Guénon, 'Oriental Metaphysics' in J. Needleman (ed.), *The Sword of Gnosis*, Baltimore, 1974. For a more facile approach to these metaphysical doctrines as far as the general American public is concerned see H. Smith, *Forgotten Truth*, New York, 1976; and E. F. Schumacher, *A Guide for the Perplexed*, New York, 1977.

11. For the traditional school the Buddhist or Taoist vision of the Void does not at all negate the universality of the metaphysics enshrined in the *philosophia perennis* and in fact provides a most powerful expression of this metaphysics in a language which is complementary but not contradictory to that of, let us say, Hinduism and Islam.

12. The Qur'ān distinguishes between *islām*, *īmān* and *iḥsān*, literally 'surrender', 'faith' and 'virtue'. These terms in the traditional context

refer definitely to a hierarchy. All Muslims, that is those who accept the Qur'ānic revelation are *muslim* but only a smaller number who possess great piety and intensity of faith are *mu'mins* and even a smaller number, identified later with the Sufis, possess *iḥsān* and are *muḥsins*. See F. Schuon, *L'Oeil du coeur*, Paris, 1974, pp. 91–94; also S. H. Nasr, *Ideals and Realities of Islam*, London, 1979, pp. 133–34.

13. *The Treasury of Traditional Wisdom* of W. N. Perry is a monumental testament to this truth.

14. That is why perhaps the most important work of this school on the relation between religions, namely *The Transcendent Unity of Religions* of Schuon was in fact entitled *De l'unité transcendante des religions* in its original French and not simply 'de l'unité des religions.'

15. See F. Schuon, *Formes et substances dans les religions.*

16. One of his last books in fact is entitled *Sur les traces de la religion pérenne*; see also his *'Religio Perennis'* in *Light on the Ancient Worlds*, trans. Lord Northbourne, London, 1965, pp. 136–44.

17. As far as the crucial question of the practice of religion is concerned with which this essay cannot deal, it must be emphasized that for the traditionalist school the goal of the study of religion is the participation in a tradition and the practice of religion. Otherwise religious studies would be as fruitless as studying musical notes without ever having the music performed, without ever hearing the actual music. As far as practice is concerned, the followers of the *philosophia perennis* insist first of all that one can practice only one religion and stand opposed to all forms of eclecticism and syncreticism of religious rites. Secondly they repeat that while the intellectual study of other religions has become a necessity today, the practice of one integral religion is both necessary and sufficient for as Schuon has stated to have lived one religion fully is to have lived all religions.

18. We have in mind the *Peaks and Lamas* of M. Pallis and *La Sagesse de prophètes* (*Fuṣūṣ al-ḥikam*) of Ibn 'Arabī annotated and translated by T. Burckhardt, respectively.

19. Some of the most luminous pages on sacred art are to be found in the works of Schuon, while those of T. Burckhardt are the first to make the spiritual significance of Islamic art fully known to the West.

20. On his writings and their significance see the introduction of H. Smith to Schuon, *The Transcendent Unity of Religions*; and Nasr, *The Writings of Frithjof Schuon – A Basic Reader* (in press).

21. For a synthesis of Schuon's spiritual anthropology see his *From the Divine to the Human*, pp. 75 ff. As for the question of the 'human margin' see 'La marge humaine' in Schuon's *Forme et substance dans*

les religions, pp. 185 ff.; and *Esoterism as Principle and as Way*, part II.

22. We have in mind such scholars as J. E. Brown, V. Danner and H. Smith in America and P. Moore and R. J. W. Austin in Great Britain.

23. For example in a recent work, the Canadian theologian and scholar of religion P. J. Cahill writes, 'Perhaps the most provocative theory to explain and maintain the unity and diversity of religion . . . is that of Frithjof Schuon. . . . If we accept Schuon's hypothesis, and it makes more sense than any other with which I am acquainted, then what is at work in diverse religions are symbolic forms that are more or less adequate to express some religious intentionality to point to transcendence.' *Mended Speech*, New York, 1982, pp. 88 and 93.

4

THE DIALOGICAL DIALOGUE

R. Panikkar

INTRODUCTION

Wilfred Cantwell Smith speaks about the encounter of religions as a living dialogue among human beings. It would be, I guess, to misunderstand him – and certainly me – if we were to interpret this statement in a nominalistic or individualistic way. Human beings carry with them the entire weight of their traditions and the very words they use are pregnant with millennia of crystallized wisdom. 'No Man is an island.'

Many years before I knew Professor Smith personally, I had given a series of lectures on 'Dialogue and Dialectics' at the Banaras Hindu University which have never been published, because, as the Spanish dictum says: 'no se puede repicar e ir en la procesion' (you cannot ring the bells and march in the procession). I have the honor and pleasure now to dedicate to my friend one of those lectures which I have been revising and reworking for many years, since its topic is central to my methodology and I think a contribution to the overall endeavor in which Wilfred Smith is engaged in such an effective way. Says Smith:

> The question as to whether there should be a religious department in the Liberal Arts faculty was interpreted as asking essentially, does the study of religion have its own methodology.

If I am not altogether wrong, the dialogical dialogue could be the 'missing link' between what Professor Smith is espousing and the method of those others who would prefer a more strictly doctrinal approach to the Encounter of Religions.

Tat tvam asi
That are you.

Chāndogya Upaniṣad
VI, 8, 7 (etc.)

I. BACKGROUND

The overall background of these pages is constituted by the awareness of the *pluralistic* and *cross-cultural* nature of our present-day human situation. *Pluralistic*, because no single culture, model, ideology, religion or whatnot can any longer raise a convincing claim to be *the* one, unique or even best system in an absolute sense. *Cross-cultural*, because human communities no longer live in isolation, and consequently any human problem today that is not seen in pluri-cultural parameters is already methodologically wrongly put.

The *philosophical* background of this paper can be seen in the urge to overcome the unconvincing monistic and dualistic answers to the fundamental problem of the 'One and the Many.' Ultimately I am pleading for an advaitic or non-dualistic approach. Its *theological* horizon is the same philosophical dilemma which takes the form of a God which cannot be totally different from or totally identical with Man and/or World without disappearing. Ultimately, it is a challenge to monotheism and to polytheism alike. At this level atheism belongs morphologically to monotheism. I am here making the plea that God is neither the Other nor the Same but the One: the one pole in a cosmotheandric insight. The cosmotheandric vision sees the entire reality as the interaction of a threefold polarity: cosmic, divine and human.

The *epistemological* formulation of the same problematic voices the inadequacy of the subject-object paradigm of knowledge. My contention here is that no knower can be known as knower – it would then become the known – and yet *is*. Being is more than consciousness, although the latter is the manifestation of the former. Both are 'coextensive' from the point of view of consciousness, but not necessarily identical.

Its *sociological* aspect is evident in the apparent aporias that any serious study of comparative civilizations encounters. No religion, system or tradition is totally self-sufficient. We need each other, and yet find our ideas and attitudes mutually incompatible, and ourselves often incapable of bridging the gulf between different world views and different basic human attitudes to reality.

The *anthropological* assumption is that Man is not an individual but a person, i.e. a set of relationships of which the I-Thou-It, in all the genders and numbers, is the most fundamental.

With all the qualifications that the foregoing affirmations need, I submit that one of the causes of this present state of affairs lies in the fact that we need a fundamental reflection on *method* as well as on the nature of *pluralism*. This study concerns the first issue, although it is intimately bound up with the second.

The immensity of the problem would require a whole treatise. I shall limit myself to describing a possible method to deal with the particular problem of the cross-cultural encounter, on an ultimate level obviously, and to unveil some of its assumptions. Let us begin *in medias res*.

I have taken as motto the most important of the Upanishadic *mahāvākyaś* or Great Utterances: *tat tvam asi*. This mantra is not just a repetition of the other Great Utterances affirming that *brahman* is the *ātman*, consciousness and the I. It means properly the discovery of the thou: *brahman* is The Thou. 'That (subject) art thou (predicate)'. *Brahman* cannot be the predicate of anything. So the text does not say you are that, i.e. *brahman*, but *that* (i.e. *brahman*) *are you*. The text does not speak in the third person. It is a dialogue; and thus it does not affirm *brahman* is you, but it reveals to Śvetaketu '*brahman* art you.' Transposing it in the third person, it says that (*brahman*) is a you in you – because *that* (is what) *you are*. But I am not indulging here in Vedic hermeneutics. I am only underscoring the fact that besides the *it*, the objective world, and eventually the *I*, the subjective realm, there is also the *thou*, which is neither the objective world of the *it*, nor the subjective realm of the ego.

In other words, I am trying to overcome both the Cartesian dualism of the *res cogitans* and the *res extensa*, and the idealistic dichotomy of the *Ich* and the *Nicht-Ich*. In the last instance, I am criticizing any type of dualism without, for that matter, subscribing to any kind of monism. I am submitting that we have also the sphere of the *thou* which presents an *ontonomy* irreducible to the spheres of the *I*, and that of the *it*. The *thou* is neither autonomous vis-a-vis the I, nor depends heteronomically on it. It presents a proper *ontonomical* relation, i.e. an internal relation constitutive of its own being. The thou is therefore neither independent of nor dependent on the I, but inter-related. Consciousness is not only I consciousness, it entails also a thou-consciousness, i.e. not my consciousness of you, but 'your' consciousness, you as knower, irreducible to what you (and I) know. Because thou-consciousness for you takes the form of I-conciousness, the '*It*-Philosophy' has tried to lump all consciousness together and forged the concept of a *Bewusstsein überhaupt*, a general consciousness. Then it has hypostasized it on an absolute subject. Whatever this supreme consciousness may be it cannot be the sum-total of all I-consciousness because many of those I-consciousnesses are contradictory and irreducible. If at all it would have to be a supreme *coincidentia oppositorum* or a purely formal consciousness without any content. This conception, be it called God or Brahman or whatever, is what I have designed as monotheism.

Now, coming back to the sublunary world, as the ancients loved to say, in the realm of our human experiences, this implies that in order to have an undistorted vision of reality, we cannot rely exclusively on 'our' consciousness but have somehow to incorporate the consciousness of other people about themselves and the world as well. In order to do this a thematically new method is suggested: the dialogical dialogue. I say 'thematically,' meaning a conscious reflection on the topic, because the method has been spontaneously employed as many times as the dialogue among people is more than 'academic' – and even contemporary anthropology tends to it by stressing participatory approaches and the like.

The perceptive reader will of course discover that the background of the following reflections is also constituted by the contemporary insights of the Sociology of Knowledge (M. Scheler *et al.*), of Hermeneutical Criticism (Gadamer *et al.*), Existential Phenomenology (Strasser *et al.*), Personalism of all sorts (Ebner *et al.*), and Social Theory (Habermas *et al.*), plus the age-old philosophical self-consciousness which goes from Parmenides to

Heidegger and from the Upaniṣads to K. C. Bhattacharya, passing through Husserl, Śaṅkara *et al.*

The relevance of the dialogical dialogue for the Encounter of religious traditions and the so-called Comparative Religion is obvious. I cannot really know – and thus compare – another ultimate system of beliefs unless somehow I share those beliefs, and I cannot do this until I know the holder of those beliefs, the you – not as other (i.e. non-ego), but as a you. Please note that I speak of beliefs and not just objectified opinions about things.

This much for an overcondensed introduction to the problematic.

II. THESIS

The foundation for the thesis of this paper rests on the assumption that the ultimate nature of reality does not have to be dialectical. If we postulate it to be so, we do it by the already dialectical axiom that affirms reality to be solely or ultimately dialectical. Reality has no foundation other than itself, and if we assume it to be dialectical we are already postulating what reality has to be, and imprisoning it in the dialectical frame, large and flexible as one may conceive this latter to be. The postulate of the dialectical nature of reality is an extrapolation of the conviction about the dialectical nature of the mind; it subordinates reality to mind.

My thesis is that the dialogical dialogue is not a modification of the dialectical method or a substitution for it. It is a method which both limits the field of dialectics and complements it. It *limits* dialectics, insofar as it prevents dialectics from becoming logical monism, by putting forward another method which does not assume the exclusively dialectical nature of reality. It *complements* dialectics by the same token. It is not a direct critique of dialectics, but only a guard against dialectical totalitarianism.

The thesis says, further, that the dialogical dialogue is the proper, although not exclusive, method for what I have called *diatopical* hermeneutics. By diatopical hermeneutics I understand a hermeneutic which is more than the purely morphological (drawing from the already known deposit of a particular tradition) and the merely diachronical one (when we have to bridge a temporal gap in order to arrive at a legitimate interpretation). It is a hermeneutic dealing with understanding the contents of diverse cultures which do not have cultural or direct historical links with one another. They belong to different loci, *topoi*, so that before anything else we have to forge the tools of understanding in the encounter itself, for we cannot – should not – assume a priori a common language. The privileged place of this hermeneutic is obviously the encounter of religious traditions. A Christian cannot assume at the outset that he knows what a Buddhist means when speaking about *nirvāṇa* and *anātman*, just as a Buddhist cannot immediately be expected to understand what a Christian means by God and Christ before they have encountered not just the concepts but their living contexts which include different ways at looking at reality: they have to encounter each other before any meeting of doctrines. This is what the dialogical dialogue purports to be: the method for the encounter of persons and not just individuals, on the one hand, or mere doctrines on the other.

III. DIALOGUE AND DIALECTICS

Let me emphatically assert that this essay is neither an attack on dialectics, nor a critique of rationality. Dialectics, in spite of its many meanings, stands for the dignity of the human logos endowed with the extraordinary prerogative of discriminating between truth and error by means of thinking: *ars iudicandi*, said the Scholastics, condensing Cicero's definition of dialectics as *veri et falsi iudicandi scientia*. It is of course a matter of philosophical dispute where to locate this human power, its name and nature; at any rate we may accept the well-known Hegelian description of dialectics as: *die wissenschaftliche Anwendung der in der Natur des Denkens liegenden Gesetzmässigkeit* (the scientific application of the inner structure [the internal law, the law-governedness] inherent in the nature of thinking).

We could, of course, try to harmonize most of the thinkers who have in the past used this word (in the present, the inflation makes any overview almost impossible) and define it as διαλεκτικὴ τεχνή or as *ars scientiaque disputandi*, i.e., the craft of human verbal intercourse. In this definition we would embrace Plato's 'conversation' in questions and answers, as well as Aristotle's conception of reasoning on probable opinions, Kant's logic of appearances and, through Hegel's dictum that *das Selbstbewusstsein wesentliches Moment des Wahren ist* ('self-consciousness is an essential moment of truth'), the Marxist's interpretation of dialectics as the method of true thinking because it constitutes the expression of the dynamic coherence of otherwise contradictory historical reality. In this wider sense the dialogical dialogue is still dialogue and thus dialectical or conversational. But we may legitimately assume that when nowadays people use the word 'dialectic' they imply that tight relationship between thinking and being about which I shall later express my critical doubts. They mean also a technique which empowers one to pass judgements on other people's opinions and not a mere art of conversation. In this sense the dialogical dialogue lies outside the sphere of dialectics. *Dia-logical* here would stand for piercing, going through the logical and overcoming – not denying – it. The dialogical dialogue is in its proper place when dealing with *personal, cross-cultural* and *pluralistic* problems. In all three cases we deal with situations not totally reducible to the logos.

Personal problems are those in which the complexity of the whole human person is at stake and not merely mental quandaries or, for that matter, any other partial queries. A personal problem is not a sheer technical puzzle of how to re-establish the proper functioning of the human organism. The human being is certainly a rational animal and rationality may be its most precious gift, but the realm of reason does not exhaust the human field. It is not by dialectically convincing the patients that the psychotherapist will cure them. It is not by proving one side to be right that a war can be avoided. There is no dialectical proof for love. Not less, but something more is required.

A *cross-cultural* problem arises from the encounter of two cultures, e.g. when somebody defends that the earth is a living being and should be treated as such against a technological view of the planet. It cannot be solved dialectically. We should avoid using the word cross-cultural when we mean only the study of another culture different from our own but still with the categories of the latter. A cross-cultural approach to Asia, for instance, does not mean 'orientalism' in the Victorian sense of the word. Cross-cultural studies deal with the very perspective in which the 'problem' is approached, they reformulate the very problem by using categories derived from the two cultures concerned. Scholastically speaking, we may say that cross-cultural studies are not characterized by their 'material object' (say, India or Hinduism from a western stance), but by their 'formal object' (say, the scale of values, perspectives, views, categories we apply to apprehend the very 'problem'). I am saying here that dialectics are not cross-cultural enough. Dialectics are a knowledge with an 'interest' arising from a particular world view. And the very interest to universalize the dialectical method – especially the historical dialectics (of the ideologies of the two political superpowers) reinforces our affirmation. We need another method for cross-cultural studies – before any discussion in the dialectical arena.

IV. DIALECTICAL DIALOGUE

The dialectical dialogue supposes that we are rational beings and that our knowledge is governed above all by the principle of non-contradiction. You and I admit it as a given, and if you lead me into contradiction I will either have to give up my opinion or attempt to overcome the impasse. We present our respective points of view to the Tribunal of Reason, in spite of the variety of interpretations that we may hold even of the nature of reason. The dialectical dialogue trusts Reason and in a way the reasonableness of the other – or of the whole historical process. It admits, further, that none of us exhausts the knowledge of the data. On this basis we engage in dialogue. If we refuse the dialogue it is because, even without saying it, we assume that someone is motivated by ill will and not ready to abide by the fair play of dialectics, or else is mentally weak, fears defeat or the like. It is obvious that there are fields proper to the dialectical dialogue, and even that it can never be bypassed. If we deny reason or reasonableness, we make impossible any type of dialogue.

As we shall expound later again, the dialectical dialogue is a necessary intermediary in the communication between human beings. Dialectics have an irreplaceable mediating function at the human level. The dialectical dialogue cannot be brushed away in any truly human exchange. We have the need to judge and to discriminate for ourselves – not necessarily for others – between right and wrong. It would amount to falling into sheer irrationalism to ignore this essential role of dialectics.

V. DIALOGICAL DIALOGUE

The dialectical dialogue is a dialogue about objects which, interestingly enough, the English language calls 'subject-matters'. The dialogical dialogue, on the other hand, is a dialogue among subjects aiming at being a dialogue about subjects. They want to dialogue not about something, but about themselves: they dialogue themselves. In short, if all thinking is dialogue, not all dialogue is dialogical. The dialogical dialogue is not so much about opinions (the famous *endoxa*, ἔνδοξα of Aristotle about which dialectics deal) as about those who have such opinions and eventually not about you, but about me to you. To dialogue about opinions, doctrines, views, the dialectical dialogue is indispensable. In the dialogical dialogue the partner is not an object or a subject merely putting forth some objective thoughts to be discussed, but a you, a real you and not an it. I must deal with you, and not merely with your thought. And of course, vice-versa, You yourself are a source of understanding.

Now, two persons cannot talk each other; they have to talk to each other. This means that the talk has to be mediated by something else. The medium is a language, and if there is language there is thought. They cannot dialogue themselves, they need the mediation of language. In any dialogue there is something outside of and in a way superior to the partners which links them together. They have to be speaking about something and this something has an inner structure which the participants have to respect and acknowledge. But this something is only a mediator conveying to each other not just 'thoughts', i.e. objectifiable ideas but thematically a part of themselves. In other words, this something is not made independent, 'objective', but is seen in its peculiar *dialogical intentionality*.

In order to describe the characteristics of this dialogical dialogue we have been contrasting it with the dialectical one. It should be made clear that the relation between the two is not dialectical, they are two intertwined moments of the dialogical character of the human being. There is no pure dialectical dialogue. When two persons enter in dialogue, in spite of all the efforts to keep the 'personal' to a bare minimum, it emerges all along. We never have an encounter of pure ideas. We always have an encounter of two (or more) persons. This aspect of the human being often emerges conspicuously in the actual praxis of the dialectical dialogue, in which the partners, forgetting that they are supposed to be thinking beings, indulge in getting involved in quite different but also real aspects of human life. To discard those aspects as 'sentimental', or as 'passions' obscuring the work of Reason misses the point. Sentiments also belong to the human being. There are, further, cases in which what is at issue are not emotional ingredients but fundamental options stemming from different self-understandings. But there is much more than this. There is no pure *theory*. It is always 'tinged' with interests and connected with the milieu which accepts it as theory.

Similarly, there is no dialogical dialogue alone. Two subjects can only enter in dialogue if they 'talk' about something, even if they are interested in knowing each other and in wanting to know themselves better by means of the mirror-effect on the other. The dialogical dialogue is not a mute act of love. It is a total human encounter and thus it has an important intellectual component. It is precisely the importance of the very subject-matter of the dialogue that unveils the depths of the respective personalities and leads to the dialogical dialogue proper.

This emphasizes a fact which is often only latent in the merely dialectical dialogue: the will to dialogue. This will is here paramount. It is not that if I do not will to enter into dialogue I keep my mouth shut. It is that if I do not have that will even if I speak with my partner I will not enter into any dialogical dialogue. Here no pretense would do. The dialectical dialogue can be an instrument to power and can be a means to the will to power. This is not the case with the dialogical dialogue. It is for this reason that any further intention, like to convert, to dominate or even to know the other for ulterior motives, destroys the dialogical dialogue.

The trusting in the other, considering the other a true source of understanding and knowledge, the listening attitude toward my partner, the common search for truth, (without assuming that we already know what words mean to each of us), the acceptance of the risk of being defeated, converted, or simply upset and left without a north . . . these are not pragmatic devices to enable us to live in peaceful coexistence because the other is already too powerful or vociferous and cannot be silenced. It is not because reason has failed us or that humankind has suddenly experienced a disenchantment with the idea of a possible *pax mundialis* as it is traditionally expressed in the models of One God, One Church, One Empire, One Religion, One Civilization, and now One Technology. The justification of the dialogical dialogue lies much deeper; it is to be found in the very nature of the real, namely in the fact that reality is not wholly objectifiable, ultimately because I myself, a subject, am also a part of it, am *in* it, and cannot extricate myself from it. The dialogical dialogue assumes a radical dynamism of reality, namely that reality is not given once and for all, but is real precisely in the fact that it is continually creating itself – and not just unfolding from already existing premises or starting points.

This is certainly what the modern understanding of dialectics also espouses: reality is in a state of constant flux, everything depends on everything else, and immutability is not a feature of reality. Still more: modern dialectics accept the changing nature of reality in such a way that change is made imperative. Change is not contingent but necessary, and it brings about qualitative leaps in the order of things. The overcoming of internal contradictions belongs to the very nature of reality. All this is dialectics. But there is one thing that dialectics cannot give up: the pliability of reality to the dialectical laws of thinking. It is here that the ultimate character of the dialogical dialogue appears clearly as we shall see in a moment.

From what has been said so far we may gather the impression that the dialogical dialogue is inbuilt in any authentic and deep dialogue. This is certainly so, but the evolution of human culture, especially in the West has given the predominance to the dialectical aspect of the dialogue and the dialogical one has been relegated to playing second fiddle. We would like now to unearth some of the assumptions underlying this dialogue. We will then better see its revolutionary character. It challenges, in point of fact, many of the commonly accepted foundations of modern culture. To restore or install the dialogical dialogue in human relations among individuals, families, groups, societies, nations and cultures, may be one of the most urgent things to do in our times threatened by the dialectical opposition of two monstrous ideologies which menace all life on the planet. In point of fact, one feature of contemporary western culture – mainly subcultures – is the praxis of a certain approach to the dialogical dialogue in the form of social work and psychotherapies. Yet in many cases, the lack of the 'dialogical intentionality' makes such methods ineffective.

VI.   THINKING AND BEING

The dialogical dialogue assumes, we said, that nobody can predict or fathom the dynamism of being because this latter is not mere evolution but also creativity. Even the mind has to recoil and stand back, we could say paraphrasing an Upaniṣad. Science is that astonishing feat made possible because our thinking can foretell how beings are going to behave. This is an incontrovertible fact. But nothing stands in the way of reality expressing itself freely in ways not predictable by thinking of any kind. The spontaneity and creativity of Nature may be hidden in the very recesses of it, perhaps at the origins of time and at the infra-atomic levels, as modern science begins to surmise, but certainly (the human) being possesses a factor of creativity and spontaneity which cannot be encapsulated in any a priori scheme. This creativity constitutes the locus of the dialogical dialogue. To sum up. Dialectics, in one way or another, deals with the power of our mind, but assumes a peculiar relation between thinking and being.

Here comes the great divide. It is one thing to assert that thinking tells us what being is and another thing to make being utterly dependent on thinking. In other words, the justification of dialectics does not depend on the often uncritically accepted hypothesis that the nature of reality is dialectical. Reality certainly has a dialectical aspect, but this aspect does not have to be all of the real. It is in this hiatus between thinking and being that the dialogical dialogue finds its *ultimate* justification. There are human situations that do not necessarily fall under the jurisdiction of the dialectical dialogue because reality does not have to be exhaustively dialectical. The laws of thought are laws of being, and this makes science possible, but not necessarily vice-versa. Or rather, being does not have to have – or always follow – laws, however useful such a hypothesis may be. Being is not exclusively restricted to be what thinking postulates. This makes ontic freedom possible and constitutes the ultimate onto-logical problem: The *logos* of the *on* is only the *on* of the *logos*, but this latter is not identical with the former. The *on* is 'bigger' than the *logos*. The *logos* may be coextensive with the *on*, but still there 'is' the *pneuma* 'between', and 'where Spirit, freedom'. And where there is freedom, thought cannot dictate, foresee or even necessarily follow the 'expansion', 'explosion', life of Being. We may as well recall that Plato believed that ideas had a life of their own.

'Being is said in many ways' τὸ ὄυ πολλαχῶς λέγεται is the famous sentence of Aristotle. But being 'is' also unsaid, at least inasmuch as it has not yet been said. Further, we cannot think how being will speak, i.e. will say itself. And yet this unsaid accompanies being. This silent companion may not be in principle unspeakable, but it is actually unspoken. Real silence is not repression of the word and incapacity to think, but absence of the word and transcending of thought.

The dialogical dialogue makes room for this sovereign freedom of being to speak new languages – or languages unknown to the other.

Be this as it may, for even without this ultimate foundation, there is place for the dialogical dialogue.

VII.   SUBJECT AND OBJECT

The most immediate assumption of the dialogical dialogue is that the other is not just an other (*alius*), and much less an object of my knowledge (*aliud*), but another self (*alter*) who is a source of self-understanding, and also of understanding, not necessarily reducible to my own.

Another way of putting it: reality is not totally objectifiable. The dialectical dialogue takes place in the sphere of the objectifiable reality. We discuss, agree or disagree on objective grounds, following objective rules. Something is objectifiable when it is in principle conceptualizable. It can then be an object of some thought. What is objectifiable is the conceptual aspect of reality apprehended as such by the subject. But this apparently leaves the subject out of it.

Anything we say about an objective state of affairs is an abstraction. It abstracts from the subject and ignores its influence on the object. It is like freezing the flow of the real. This freezing may well be necessary for a moment in order more easily to apprehend something, but it can become a trap we fall into the moment we forget that it is only a device, and a provisional one, a scaffold we use to reach outside ourselves and grasp something. In other words, the trap is to mistake the objective idea for the real, the concept for the thing – eventually identifying the two. In this setting the others are able only somewhat to qualify or correct my assertions, but certainly not to con-vert me radically, i.e. to throw me out of the fortress of my 'own' private world. From here to an ideology of power there is only a short way to go.

The dialogical dialogue, on the other hand, considers the other as another subject, i.e. as another source of (self)-understanding. The others as subjects do not have to be necessarily reduced to an ultimately unique source. This is the question of pluralism (that we said we were leaving aside) and its connection with monotheism: The different subjects participating, each in their own way, from the one single Source of intelligence and intelligibility.

The dialogical dialogue is not concerned so much about opinions as about the different viewpoints from which the respective opinions are arrived at. Now, to deal with a perspective means to deal with very fundamental springs in the knowing subject. A new epistemology is required here. Just as any knowledge of an object requires a certain connaturality and identification with the object to be known, any knowledge of the subject necessitates also a similar identification. This is what has led me to formulate the principle of 'Understanding as Convincement'. We cannot understand a person's ultimate convictions unless we *somehow* share them.

VIII.   I AND THOU

This is not the place to describe the rich evolution of the idea of dialectics. Suffice it to say that it was probably F. H. Jacobi who first saw, in the post-Cartesian age, the implicit solipsism of any idealism (including Kant's) and began to develop the idea of a dialogical thinking transcending the constriction of objective dialectics. But it was Feuerbach criticizing Hegel who tried to develop a dialogical dialectic which is a forerunner of the dialogical thinkers of the beginning of this century, Buber, Rosenzweig and Ebner. Says Feuerbach: 'Die wahre Dialektik ist kein Monolog des einsamen Denkers mit sich selbst, sie ist ein Dialog zwischen Ich und Du.' (The true dialectic is not a monologue of the individual thinker with himself, but a dialogue between I and Thou).

Yet, without now entering into a detailed analysis of those predecessors, I may add that the dialogical dialogue I am espousing claims to transcend the realm of dialectics by realizing that the relation I/Thou is irreducible to any relation I/It or I/Non-I, and thus equally ultimate.

A certain type of philosophy, which could be designated broadly as idealism, has potentiated the knowledge of all potential subjects and called it the ultimate or true I as the bearer of all knowledge, as absolute consciousness. Over against this I there remains only the Non-I, be it called world, matter, extension, evil, illusion, appearance or whatever.

Another type of philosophy, which could broadly be called sociology of knowledge, has stressed the fact of the dependency of the thinking individual on both collectivity and environment. Any individual's thinking, expresses only what is thinkable within the community in which one thinks, and one's personal contribution makes sense only within the larger context of the community. Furthermore, one's thinking is also a part of human thinking and not only a disconnected heap of human thoughts.

In the first case we have the ultimate dialectical opposition between the I and the Non-I. The individual is part of that I and when in dialogue with other egos it has only to deepen its participation in the absolute consciousness. The other as subject is invited to do the same; as object it belongs to the sphere of the Non-I.

In the second case the individual's thinking is situated vis-a-vis the collectivity, of which it is also a part. The others are members of the same or a different community sharing in the same or another *Zeitgeist*, as it were.

In both cases the dialogue with the other is directed toward the source of our understanding of reality by means of a sharing in either an absolute consciousness or a collective consciousness of a group in space and time, or even the entire humanity.

This may be true, but there is still more to it. When the individual thinks, he does not think individualistically, he does not think out of himself alone, nor only in contemplation of God or intercourse with the world, i.e. with the object of his thinking (his thought), but he thinks already in conformity, harmony with and/or reaction to, stimulated by and in dialogue with, other people. Thinking is not an individualistic process, but an act of language.

But language is primarily neither a private activity nor a mystical act in connection with Consciousness or Humanity. It is an exchange with someone in front of us and at our level. It is fundamentally a dialogical activity. What the two just mentioned considerations have overlooked is precisely that our first verbal relationship is not dialectical but dialogical. We begin by listening, learning, assimilating, comparing and the like. We are not confronting a non-ego but a thou with whom we have a common language, or we strive for one.

In order to think, we cannot succeed alone. We need dialogue with the *thou*. In point of fact, the *I* can only express 'itself' in intercourse with the *thou* or with the *it*. We need the living dialogue because the 'I love,' 'I will,' and even 'I think' acquires only its full meaning in confrontation with what a 'you' loves, wills, and thinks. This amounts to saying that thinking is only possible within one – our – world, and thus, one language, our language.

I am not excluding the dialogue with the it, i.e. with things. This is one of the fascinations of Science, and I am even prepared to reinstate animism in the traditional sense of the *anima mundi* and the belief that in one way or another everything is alive, conscious of the fact that this will – would – introduce a revolution in Science: not only physics become biology, but science itself becomes dialogical. But in the human dialogue with things, in spite of the fact that things react, offer resistance, are not pliable to the wishes of the human intellect and in a certain way respond to the human dialogue, they do not have the same interiority and consciousness as human beings have. In brief, for the full development of human thinking, even when thinking about things, human dialogue is imperative.

The dialogical dialogue takes you my partner as seriously as myself, and by this very fact, wakes me up from the slumber of solipsistic speculations, or the dreaming fantasies of a docile partner. We encounter the hard reality of an opposition, another will, another source of opinions, perspectives. The dialogue maintains the constitutive polarity of reality which cannot be split into subject and object without the previous awareness of different subjects speaking. There is not only a subject and an object, but also a subject and another subject, although mediated by an object. This is even inbuilt in language itself. The I and thou statements can never set the speaking subject aside; they cannot be substantives in the sense of being reified, cut off from the I and the thou and made into eternal, immutable 'truths.' In the dialogue we are reminded constantly of our temporality, our contingency, our own constitutive limitations. Humility is not primarily a moral virtue but an ontological one; it is the awareness of the place of my ego, the truthfulness of accepting my real situation, i.e., that I am a situated being, a vision's angle on the real, an existence.

As already indicated, the rationale for the dialogical dialogue is that the *thou* has a proper and inalienable *ontonomy*. The thou is a source of self-understanding which I cannot assimilate from my own perspective alone. It is not as if we all would see 'the same thing' but from a different vantage point. This may be true, but the dialogical dialogue is not just the locus for perspectivism. It does not assume a 'thing in itself', the Elephant in the dark room of the Indian story (one describing 'reality' as a shaft, the other as a pillar, the third as a winnowing fan and so on). Nor does it assume a mere atomistic view as if each human being were an independent monad without windows. It assumes, on the contrary, that we all share in a reality which does not exist independently and outside our own sharing in it and yet without exhausting it. Our participation is always partial and reality is more than just the sum total of its parts.

IX. MYTH AND LOGOS

To be sure, many things happen in the dialectical dialogue: there are winners and losers, some conclusions are arrived at, some new light is shed on the subject matter, new distinctions are made, and so on. Besides and above those things the dialogical dialogue changes the partners themselves in unexpected ways and may open new vistas not logically implied in the premises. The very 'rules' of this dialogue are not fixed 'a priori,' they emerge out of the dialogue itself. The dialogue is not a 'duologue', but a going through the logos, *dia ton logon*, διά τὸν λὸγον, beyond the logos-structure of reality. It pierces the logos and uncovers the respective myths of the partners. In the dialogical dialogue, we are vulnerable because we allow ourselves to be 'seen' by our partner, and vice versa. It is the other who discovers my myth, what I take for granted, my horizon of intelligibility, the convictions of which lie at the source of my expressed beliefs. It is the other who will detect the hidden reasons for my choice of words, metaphors and ways of thinking. It is the other who will interpret my silences and omissions in (for me) unsuspected ways.

Now, in order to allow this to happen we need to unearth our presuppositions. But this we cannot do alone. We need the other. We are more or less conscious of our assumptions, i.e., the axioms or convictions that we put at the starting point and we use as foundation of our views. But those very assumptions themselves rest on underlying 'pre-sub-positions' which for us 'go without saying' and are 'taken for granted.' But this does not need to be the case for our partner and he will point them out to us and bring them to the forum of analysis and discussion. We may then either discard them or convert them into conscious assumptions as bases for further thinking.

The dialogical dialogue challenges us on a much deeper level than the dialectical one. With the dialectical dialogue we are unable to explore realms of human experience, spheres of reality or aspects of being that belong to the first and second persons, i.e. to the *am* and *art* aspects of reality. In other words, with the dialectical dialogue we can only reach the *it is* aspect of the real and cannot be in full communication with other subjects and their most intimate convictions. With the dialectical dialogue, we may discuss religious doctrines once we have clarified the context, but we need the dialogical dialogue to discuss beliefs, as those conscious attitudes we have in face of the ultimate issues of our existence and life.

In the dialogical dialogue, I trust the other not out of an ethical principle (because it is good) or an epistemological one (because I recognize that it is intelligent to do so), but because I have discovered (experience) the *thou* as the counterpart of the I, as belonging *to* the I (and not as not-I). I trust the partner's understanding and self-understanding because I do not start out by putting my ego as the foundation of everything. It is not that I do not examine my partner's credentials (he could be wicked or a fool), not that I fall into irrationalism (or any type of sentimentalism) giving up my stance, but that I find in his actual presence something irreducible to my ego and yet not belonging to a non-ego: I discover the *thou* as part of a Self that is as much mine as his – or to be more precise, that is as little my property as his.

Now, this discovery of the *ātman*, the human nature, a common essence, a divine undercurrent, or whatever, is not, properly speaking, *my* discovery of *it*, but my discovery of *me*, the discovery of myself as *me* – and not as I: *Me-consciousness*.

Further, this dawning of me-consciousness cannot occur without the *thou* spurring it on, and ultimately the real or ultimate I (*aham*) performing it. Leaving aside now the awareness of the transcendent-immanent I, the fact still remains that without a *thou* calling and challenging me, my me-consciousness would not emerge. In the dialogical dialogue my partner is not the *other* (it is not he/she, and much less it), but the *thou*. The thou is neither the other nor the non-ego. The thou is the very thou of the I in the sense of the subjective genitive.

It is the cross-cultural challenge of our times that unless the barbarian, the mleccha, goy, infidel, nigger, kafir, the foreigner and stranger are invited to be my *thou*, beyond those of my own clan, tribe, race, church, or ideology, there is not much hope left for the planet.

This on a world-scale is a *novum*, but an indispensable element for a present-day civilization worthy of Man. We have mentioned already the importance of the dialogical dialogue for the Encounter of Religions. It is, I submit, the neglect of this method and the application of a predominantly dialectical dialogue among religious traditions that is at the root of so many misunderstandings and enmities among the followers of so many religions. The lack of proper understanding among religions is not so much matter of doctrinal differences – these exist also among schools of the same religion – but of existential attitudes – down often to economic, administrative and political reasons.

And so, we close the circle. We began by saying that true dialogue is a dialogue among human beings and have underscored that a person is more than a thinking subject; persons are fields of interaction where the real has been woven or striped by means of all the complexity of reality; they are knots in the continuous weaving of the net of reality.

APPENDIX

Millenia ago, Chuang Tsu said:

> Assume you and I argue. If you win and I lose, are you right and I wrong? If I win and you lose, am I right and you wrong? Are we both partially right and wrong? Are we both right or both wrong? If you and I cannot see the the truth, other people will find it harder.
>
> Whom shall we ask to be the judge? Someone who agrees with you? If he agrees with you how can he be a fair judge? Shall I ask someone who agrees with me? If he does, how can he be a fair judge? Shall I ask someone who agrees with both of us? If he already agrees with both of us, how can he be a fair judge? If you and I and other cannot decide, shall we wait for still another?

Since the standard of judging right or wrong depends on the changing relative phenomena, then there is fundamentally no standard at all.

Seeing everything in relation to the natural cosmic perspective, argument stops, right and wrong cease to be. We are then free and at ease.

What do I mean by 'seeing everything in relation to the natural cosmic perspective, then argument stops'? This is to say that 'right' *can be said* to be 'wrong', 'being', 'non-being'. If something is really right, it naturally has its distinction from wrong. There is no need for argument. Being is naturally distinguished from non-being. There is no need for argument either. Forget all about differentiation between life and death, right and wrong. Be free. Live and play with the infinite.*

---

* On the basis of G-F. Fend and J. English published version, retranslated by Agnes Lee, to whom thanks are expressed.

Note: The synthetic and condensed nature of this chapter would require a footnote after each paragraph. As I have done such footnoting in my courses and other writings, I spare the reader of this burden and refer to my other publications, apologizing here for the conciseness of my presentation.

5

BANGALORE REVISITED: BALANCING UNDERSTANDING AND EVALUATION IN THE COMPARATIVE STUDY OF RELIGION

John B. Carman

In September 1967 a consultation was held at the Shilton Hotel in Bangalore on 'The Study of Religion in Indian Universities'. The background of this meeting was Wilfred Smith's proposal in August 1965 to the Kothari Commission on Education in India. He recommended that strong departments of Comparative Religion be established at a few Indian universities in which faculty members specializing in a number of different religious traditions would collaborate on comparative seminars, one subject for which would be the process of secularization in India. His recommendations were accepted in principle by the Commission, and the following year he gave me the assignment of coming to India in order to keep in touch with developments at Indian universities towards implementing the Commission's recommendations. Dr. Smith came to India and participated in the Bangalore Consultation, contributing a working paper and delivering the final address.

Our recent stay at the Shilton Hotel was a reminder both of that meeting and of the problematic that engaged it. The following reflections are written in awareness of the concern that Dr. Smith and I share for the academic dimensions of the interaction of religious communities in India. Our somewhat different approaches to comparative religion may be clarified by focussing on this particular Indian context.

The inaugural address by Prof. V. K. Gokak, Vice-Chancellor of Bangalore University, was much more than a polite welcome. Not only did he develop a systematic position on a number of issues on our agenda, but he took specific issue with a number of

222

points in my preparatory paper, sent to participants in advance, in which I had said that comparative religion starts neither from *belief*, like Indian philosophy, nor from *disbelief*, like post-Enlightenment Western philosophy. He did not agree that Indian philosophy starts from belief but

> Even assuming it does, I should like to know what is the improvement secured by starting, neither from *belief* nor from *disbelief*, but from non-belief as the scientific study of religion is expected to do. This is a study of social phenomena in the manner of sociology, history or economics. It will have neither spiritual nor utility value. . . . The plea for the introduction of Comparative Religion as a University discipline has been made because such a study is expected to promote moral and spiritual values. A discipline which starts from non-belief cannot promote these values any better than a subject like physics, sociology, literature, linguistics or commerce. . . . The prime need of the time is to remedy our bankruptcy of soul. But the very manner in which the study of this subject has been formulated makes it as mundane a discipline as petrology or zoology. While an unthinking adherence to religion leads to bigotry, the scientific study of religion refines away the essence of religion itself to vanishing point . . . Our original intention was to provide for some course of study in the curriculum by which students might be made aware of spiritual values. We now find ourselves advocating the study of a discipline that has hardly anything to do with Spirit (pp. 27, 28).

Prof. Gokak then proceeded to outline various types of university study that would promote moral and spiritual values among the students, noting in conclusion that the only purpose of 'scientific' Comparative Religion, in India or elsewhere is 'secularity or tolerance, not spirituality . . . primarily useful for training and broadening the minds of ecclesiastical officials serving the people that profess one religion or the other in our country' (p. 32).

Prof. Gokak was in fact drawing a forthright conclusion from a point I had made in my preparatory paper that although the Kothari Commission drew the distinction between 'religious

223

education' and 'education about religion' basic to much modern study of religion, it continued the expectation of earlier Education Commissions that the comparative study of religion would help in 'the inculcation of right values' (cited on p. 4 of my paper). I agreed that one of the indispensable tools of moral education is 'a knowledge of the ethical norms and the classical ethical problems in the various religious traditions, especially those in the family background of the numbers of the class.' I expressed doubt, however, as to 'whether values can be "inculcated" in contemporary Indian students by teaching them some elementary facts about the religious traditions current in India' (p. 7). The viewpoint of the Kothari Commission is related to its interpretation of the Government of India's secularist policy: that ... all citizens, irrespective of their religious faith, will enjoy equality of rights, that no religious community will be favoured or discriminated against, and that instruction in religious dogmas will not be provided in the State schools. But it is *not* an irreligious or anti-religious policy; it does *not* belittle the importance of religion as such. It gives to every citizen the fullest freedom of religious beliefs and worship. It is anxious to ensure good relations amongst different religious groups and to promote not only religious tolerance but also an active reverence for all religions. (*Report of the Education Commission*, 1964–66: Education and National Development. 1.78, p. 20, cited on p. 5 of my paper).

Prof. T. M. P. Mahadevan quoted the first part of the same paragraph, along with the views expressed by earlier Education Commissions, in a paper arguing forcefully that the 'secularist' policy in education, inherited from the British, should be given up despite the apparent prohibition of religious instruction in Article 28 of the Indian Constitution 'in any educational institution wholly maintained out of State funds.'

> It is not the teaching of religion as such that Article 28 prohibits, but the teaching of dogmatic religion. A reverent study of the essentials of all religions would be ... in perfect accord with the spirit of the Constitution; and it would be in conformity with the genius of our culture. ('Problems of Teaching Religion in Indian Universities' p. 51).

Prof. Mahadevan endorsed the recommendation of the earlier Radhakrishnan Commission that 'all educational institutions start work with a few minutes for silent meditation,' that the lives of the great religious leaders of the world be taught in the first year, 'universalist' selections from the Scriptures of the world be studied in the second year, and 'central problems of the philosophy of religion be considered in the third year' (I., p. 303, cited on p. 56). He advised against establishing independent Religion Departments, which would be

> fraught with practical difficulties. Moreover, in our country, Philosophy and Religion have maintained very close kinship. To separate them would neither be easy nor wise . . . what we have to stress in the teaching of religion to the generality of University students is the philosophical approach. Our immediate objective should, therefore, be the institution of one or more chairs for the study of religion, especially the philosophy of religion and Comparative Religion, in our Universities, and attach them to Departments of Philosophy (p. 58).

Dr. Krishna Sivaraman put his reaction to the Western secular approach to the study of religion as follows:

> We have really no concept of approaching religion except as a pursuit in itself. So that we find it somewhat against our grain to distinguish between 'approaching religion' and 'approaching study of religion' . . . To speak or think about the meaning of religion without a sense of implicit commitment to it as real and true is like being asked to think and speak about beauty in a painting detachedly without responding with delight . . . Religious meaning cannot be contemplated without existential involvement in the truth of religion . . . That is why there seems to be a kind of built-in protest in Hinduism, and I suppose in all Eastern religions, against an academic study of religion construed mainly on lines of *Religionswissenschaft* which is descriptive and scholarly . . . objective accuracy and scholarship must go with appreciative understanding and existential involvement

(cited on p. 100, in my 'Survey of the Special Papers Read at the Seminar').

A number of the non-Hindu scholars participating, however, were concerned to separate the comparative study of religion, both conceptually and institutionally, from philosophy of religion, which in the Indian context was considered to involve a Vedantic Hindu understanding of the unity of religions. In addition, there was a widespread feeling, shared even by some of the Hindu philosophers that there are dimensions of religion not adequately considered in most philosophical approaches. Dr. Sivaraman, for example, added that

> We must seek to comprehend religion concretely in relation to culture also. Man and society even in India are the products of historical process just as their ways of thinking are also products of human intelligence even when they are brought to bear on the transcendent (p. 101).

The paper by the sociologist Dr. Hasan Askari, entitled 'Study of Religion in a Multi-Religious Society,' was critical of many recent Western approaches to the study of religion and put forward the notion of double subjectivity (of the person and of the religious group) as a way of avoiding the onesidedness of both 'sociologism and existentialism' (pp. 60–61). In order to have conceptual clarity, the 'study of religion' should be recognized as being different from 'acceptance of religion', yet the distinction is arbitrary, and many Western approaches to the study of religion fall into a 'reductionism' that endangers religion both as a social and a spiritual entity'. Objectivity as understood in the social sciences, moreover, is inappropriate to a realm that arouses man's concern and his involvement. To go beyond the collection of information to understanding 'is to evaluate with a certain conscious or unconscious criterion.' Since norms derived from one religion lead to a misunderstanding of another, we should recognize the norms that 'already exist in the very religions themselves.' We can evaluate the extent to which a given religion's 'institutions embody its essential content, its element of concern, its basic need' (pp. 61–62; 65–68).

For Dr. Askari the foregoing statements set the background for considering the concept of a multi-religious society.

> A multi-religious society becomes an object of study only when each religious tradition within that society is conscious of itself as a separate tradition, and when each tradition as such has freedom to institutionalize its self-consciousness. ... Religions, when they are disengaged from their original and basic content, start to communalize secular phenomena. It is the communal version of religion that destroys the secular and democratic polity and shakes the foundations of the multi-religious society. ... The task of comparative religion in India is not only to study, in abstract and academic terms, the different religions but also to attempt to (1) construct bridges between different religions by means of participation in common programmes of study and research, and (2) institute dialogue between the different sections of the Indian youth. The process of communalism should be reversed; not by pleading an empty rootless secularism, but by restoring the true meaning of religion to the young generation of the country (pp. 69, 71–72).

The major paper of the Consultation was Prof. T. L. Mehta's, 'Problems of Inter-cultural Understanding in University Studies of Religion.' Dr. Mehta noted that the first task of religious studies, the understanding of 'the faith of other men' is by no means so easy as it might appear.

> It must strive to comprehend the other in its otherness, let it speak to us in its difference from us and allow it to lay hold of us in its claim to truth. I make bold to suggest that such an approach to what is other is somewhat alien to the genius of our entire tradition and the task therefore (is) correspondingly difficult and against the grain for us ... In its understanding of both itself and the other, India has followed the way of growth through absorption and assimilation. ... The Indian cultural tradition thus has retained its identity and continuity but it has at no time *defined itself* in relation to the other, nor acknowledged the

227

other in its unassimilable otherness, nor in consequence occupied itself with the problem of relationship as it arises in any concrete encounter with the other ... The Western approach has been markedly different ... The West's relationship to other cultures is determined by its characteristic mode of thinking in concepts ... This negative separative intellect of the West does not leave the world as it is, but works it over, changes it, analyses it into its elements, puts them together again and in this manner makes it its own (pp. 35–37).

Dr. Mehta saw the enterprise of 'understanding' as characteristically Western, but also as recent. Until recently, 'the occident has ... treated the other merely as its own negation, without caring to determine it in itself or seeking to understand it from within.' So far in India, on the other hand,

we have been mostly engaged in exploring other cultures and religious traditions with a view to discovering points of similarity, if not confirmation of basic insights of our own ... It is time that we opened ourselves to the differences now, coming to closer grips with the truth of these other traditions, and turn the monologue of the past into a real dialogue. Perhaps the other may then present itself to us a truer face, come nearer to us and help us in comprehending our own selves, (somewhat differently perhaps but certainly more deeply and truly. True dialogue is less a telling each other than a questioning of each other and it never leaves us where we were before, either in respect of our understanding of the other or of ourselves) (p. 39).

The second task, Dr. Mehta continued, is to understand 'the "other" within the complex fabric which is the heritage of the Hindu student of religion' (p. 39). The third and central task is one of 'understanding our own religious and cultural tradition'. It is in the present context, shaped in part by scientific thinking, by a secular climate, and a 'free encounter with other traditions, religious and cultural', that 'we are required to understand and reappropriate our tradition and make it truly our own' (p. 40). It is our very alienation from our cultural past in the modern world that makes it possible for the question of understanding to arise.

> Understanding seeks to overcome the alienation by letting tradition speak to us once again in all its revelatory power ... we can neither go back to any epoch of our past nor regain the immediacy of a bygone form of consciousness; it is, therefore, all the more incumbent upon us ... to strive to recapture, from the perspective of our own station in time and place, the truth revealed and yet hidden in our religious tradition and express it for our time, for ourselves (p. 43).

This creative reappropriation of one's tradition also requires a new awareness of alternatives in other traditions, and an adventurous exploration that seeks its goal, not through

> any sort of cultural and conceptual conquest, nor merely through a peaceful co-existence of religious traditions, but solely through this reaching out to the other in active understanding and in the service of a truth which will perhaps never shed its mystery but to which each tradition bears witness and is in this united with each other) (pp. 44-45).

He who seeks to understand, his own tradition or that of other cultures, can do so only from his own particular standpoint; his 'prejudices' not only restrict his vision but enable it. In the act of understanding, this vision is both enlarged and corrected, at the same time, making us explicitly aware of these 'prejudices', which are not just peripheral but constitute the very core of our particularity. The critical awareness of these prejudices alters, however slightly, this core itself and all understanding, therefore, changes us and presupposes a readiness for that. But all understanding, in the next place, changes what is understood. ... It is the very essence of the 'hermeneutic experience', i.e. the explicit comprehension of the voice of the past and the other, that in it the horizons, within which both he who seeks to understand and what is understood exist, open out, move towards and fuse with each other, in however small a degree ... The problem of inter-cultural understanding as a movement of living thought is not the problem of discovering a formula for the 'other' culture, or of grasping it in concept, but of a mutual sharing of horizons, however imperfectly, and of a fusion of these horizons, however slightly. ... The two partners in the dialogue of thought that is understanding are not so much the agents of this process as themselves taken up in it and carried by the movement ... Understanding is thus a dynamic and creative process, and what is understood in it is this movement of truth towards novelty. Language is the medium in which this movement is accomplished, leading to the forging of a new and common language, which alone enables participation in a common meaning and a common truth in its actuality. For it is not we but language that speaks. Self-understanding, is thus inseparable from the understanding of the other, and it reaches its fulfilment only with the fashioning of a language which mediates us with the other and our present with our past (pp. 46–47).

Wilfred Smith's concluding paper was entitled, 'University Studies of Religion in a Global Context', and he began with some brief comments on the state of such studies in various parts of the world, ending with the listing of some distinctions made in studies of Religion in the West. These included that between university studies and those in theological seminaries (between one's own and other men's), that between normative and descriptive studies (between ideal and actual), that between studies of religion in the past, and in the present, that between the study of religion and the study of religions, and, finally that between 'the incidental and the deliberate study of religion' (pp. 74–79). He then went on to suggest that the religious/secular polarity of Western life, derived from the two distinct sources of Western civilization, Greece and Palestine, was quite inappropriate to India before the Western impact, 'and is appropriate today only with serious qualification'. Dr. Smith put his most provocative observation as follows:

One of the reasons why religion ... departments are springing up with such power in western ... universities at the present time is ... that a very deep level indeed the Western world is today asking itself a question as to what religion really is ... Now it is my impression that India is asking itself no such question. Hindu society is on the whole convinced that it knows what religion is (am I wrong on this?) Muslim society here is on the whole too frightened to be interested in other men's faith; and too bewildered to ask systematic questions about its own ...

A society that is not asking itself such a question does not have the urge to institute departments of religion. My guess is that a desire to perpetuate traditional values is not in itself an adequate basis for such study. A University is not that kind of a place ... there are a couple of other questions in this realm that an outside observer might suppose to be genuine here, and pressing ... The first ... is the relation of religious considerations to economic planning, to political functioning, and in general to the issue of actively constructing here on earth a flourishing society ... the other question ... that would provide one motivation for a *comparative* religion department, is the question of religious diversity ... it seems to me that no society on earth has yet solved the matter of inter-religious co-existence, not even India; and that it will not be solved without a good deal of new, hard thinking. The West has certainly not begun to solve it or even to identify it. I recognize, however, that Hindu intellectuals generally do not see a problem here, do not feel an urgent question. I have also been rather surprised that the Muslim intellectual community at least has not felt it and launched a vigorous programme at Aligarh (pp. 81–83).

Dr. Smith's final point is a familiar theme:

Each of us belongs to but one community, that of mankind – a community of which the Christian, the Muslim, the Hindu cohesions are subgroups; uncomprehended and alienated but not alien ... the task of the universities in this nascent situation is to intellectualize the process of its becoming, in order that it may in fact become ... Throughout the world, each of the major religious communities of mankind is

231

beginning to be conscious of itself as within the context – the developing context – of the others . . . The philosophers have given their answer to the question of what do the religions of the world have in common; and have affirmed that all are one. I am an historian, and give an historical answer to the question, and affirm that all are not one, but are in the process of becoming so – historically. . . . It is our historical convergence that to a Western mind is the foundation for the intellectual and spiritual unity of mankind; and it is not metaphysically given but has to be constructed by us here on earth. What is metaphysically given is not our unity, but the imperative and the capacity to achieve it (pp. 84–87).

Re-reading these papers after more than fifteen years leaves me with somewhat different impressions than I had at the time, when I was most struck with the difference between the Hindu philosophers' emphasis on the common values in all religions, on the one hand, and the plea from scholars in minority religious communities for the development of separate studies of each religious tradition in India, on the other. Now I am more impressed with the overlap of perspectives, so that there appears in retrospect to have been more a difference in emphasis than a confrontation. Looking back I am also struck at the Western character of the contributions by Wilfred Smith and myself. Part of that 'Westernness' was our deliberate effort to represent a broader range of Western scholarship than we could personally espouse, but there was also an insistence on certain Western distinctions precisely because of our sense of their neglect in the Hindu philosophical approach to religious studies.

Dr. Smith avoided the usual choice between unity and diversity by proposing that the 'essence' of religion was a truth still in process of discovery and that the unity of religion was not a metaphysical truth but the anticipated outcome of an historical process. Here again there was conscious emphasis on a Western notion of historical process and perhaps a less fully self-conscious utilization of what Dr. Smith himself has shown to be the very Western notion of religion.

Still more significant for my own reflection was the widespread rejection or severe qualification of modern Western notions of objectivity, including Dr. Askari's: 'double subjectivity', Dr. Mehta's elucidation of Heidegger's and Gadamer's critique of liberal Western hermeneutics and Dr. Smith's treatment of the comparative study of religion as a single enterprise, historical and theological at the same time. With the exception of my own presentation, Indian reluctance to accept a Western notion of objectivity seemed to meet two Western critiques of objective scholarship in a range of positions that would allow a small but limited place for objectivity or would transform that notion altogether.

The distinction between 'religious education' and 'education about religion' won surprisingly wide acceptance, even from Dr. Mahadevan, but clearly different scholars interpreted this in different ways. At about this same time in North America scholars in religious studies were convincing the courts and university trustees of the validity of the distinction. That made the expansion of religion departments institutionally possible, but the increase in student interest in the middle end late sixties that made such an expansion viable was not overly concerned with this distinction. Some American students explicitly rejected it. They sought some saving wisdom through an academic guru, and they were – and still are – impatient with their teachers' emphasis on scholarly objectivity.

In the years since 1967 my joint teaching with Dr. Mehta and my ongoing collaboration in doctoral programs with Dr. Smith have provided a continuing challenge to my 'methodology', reinforcing both the voices from India and the impatience of some American students with my concern for objectivity. There have, of course, been voices from other directions: demands for a rigorously scientific methodology and objections to the 'intuitionism' or 'covert theology' of my brand of phenomenology of religion. Still it is Dr. Mehta and Dr. Smith from whom I have learned the most during these years, so it is especially to them that I owe a reformulation of my distinctions between understanding and evaluation, between meaning and truth.

Such defense of my approach to the academic study of religion can only in small part be based on general academic consensus as to right procedures. There is some consensus on the canons of rational inquiry that is worldwide. It may never have been only

Western; in any case it is no longer so. The consensus, however, breaks down at the most crucial points. The procedures for acquiring objective knowledge should not apply when objective knowledge is not our aim or when the subject matter is such that objectivity is pointless – or impossible. Teaching at a university where the comparative study of religion has only recently been accepted as an undergraduate major, I am keenly aware of this lack of consensus. My inclination is to justify and define this study within one school of the University, the Divinity School, but I am also aware that many theological schools in the United States do not even recognize comparative religion as a part of their curriculum, and some of those who do, employ one part-time lecturer to 'cover' the religions of the world. My methodological mentor van der Leeuw, working in the Netherlands could much more easily assume an acceptance of 'history and phenomenology of religion' both within the theological faculty and within the university as a whole, but he was aware that such acceptance was both recent and fragile. Without such cultural consensus behind me in either India or North America I would nonetheless agree with van der Leeuw that comparative religion finds its deepest ground in a particular theological vision, a modern Logos theology, but that it should seek to commend itself to all on general hermeneutical principles as an integral part of 'arts' or humane sciences.

Both Dr. Mehta and Dr. Smith, as well as most of the other participants at the Bangalore consultation, regard understanding and evaluation as part of a single mental and indeed spiritual process. I have always been in agreement with them that if one includes the entire life and work of the religiously committed student of religion, understanding and evaluation are and should both be present. It seems to me worthwhile, however, within this total human and scholarly vocation to designate a realm in which understanding is held distinct from evaluation. The meaning that I try to understand must be translated if I am to understand it, translated into terms meaningful for me, with full recognition of the approximation involved in all translation. This translation language cannot help but use value-laden terms, yet the purpose of the translation should be to understand what these values mean to the other, not whether I can affirm them in that other form.

Such explicit evaluation is both legitimate and necessary, but if it is to be more than the expression of personal or cultural prejudices, it also calls for an effort to identify within one's own religious traditions those values that have the universality of Truth. We must listen to the Divine Word where we can best expect to hear it if we want to hear its echoes where we have thus far not expected it.

In a recent article Frank Reynolds has noted four prominent characteristics of 'history of religions'.

> The first of these characteristics is that those working within the history of religions do approach the study of religion in ways that are, or at least intend to be, non-confessional and non-reductive. These approaches are non-confessional in that they do not presuppose the truth or falsity of any particular religion. They are also non-confessional in that they eschew categories of interpretation that are primarily identified with one specific tradition. They are non-reductive in that they reject the primacy of categories of interpretation or modes of explanation that investigate or account for religion simply as an epiphenomenon of a non-religious aspect of human existence. ('History of Religions: Condition and Prospects,' *The Council on the Study of Religion Bulletin* Vol. 13, No. 5, 1982), p. 129.

With the proviso that the historian of religions may at times also need to be a theologian, I would agree that the history of religions is non-confessional, but neither its general notion of religion (on the basis of which one tries to avoid the pitfalls of reductionism) nor its more specific categories can escape identification with one or more particular tradition, indeed very often one or more specific sub-tradition within a larger tradition. One surely is responsible for choosing the most appropriate categories, and one should surely seek as far as possible to interpret a religion through its own categories, yet in two senses the categories of a particular tradition or traditions remain indispensable. The first sense I have noted above, the need for a translation into personally meaningful categories. The second is the importance of Western Christianity, the Western monotheistic religions and the religions of the ancient

Mediterranian world in shaping both our general concept of religion and the specific categories we employ. Certainly both the general concept and the various aspects of religion have been altered and sometimes even transformed as they are applied to a greater and greater range of religious phenomena, but they never entirely 'outgrow' their earlier usage in a particular cultic context. We have no more precise method of understanding than that of analogy, the understanding of the strange with the aid of the familiar. Certainly the use of analogies can lead to misunderstandings, and quite clearly the process of refining our understanding calls for a recognition of both similarities and differences. Yet the language of religious studies not only bears the marks of its past history but continues to be partially determined, even as it seeks comprehension of the entire human religious consciousness, by the religious and intellectual traditions of the West.

It is much clearer to me now than fifteen years ago that 'religion', in the related senses assumed and explored by the comparative study of religion, has a Western character, just as does the process of 'understanding' religion. This does not mean, however, that neither 'religion' nor 'understanding' are meaningful outside the Western university or that the university context need remain merely Western. Japan is best known for its borrowing and creative refashioning of elements of Western culture. The same kind of process has been going on for a much longer time, though often in a less self-conscious way, here in India. Dr. Mehta is 'borrowing' Western hermeneutics to make that process more self-conscious, thereby both altering Hindu self-consciousness and giving the enterprise of understanding an authentically Hindu form.

Later in the same paper (p. 132) Frank Reynolds refers to the comparative study of moral values that Mark Juergensmeyer and I initiated and to which he and his colleagues at the University of Chicago have greatly contributed. That project has deliberately sought to go beyond the circle of historians of religion, involving religious ethicists, anthropologists, and policy makers. Perhaps precisely because of this inter-disciplinary conversation, the fundamental problematic of the relation of understanding to evaluation has been evident in striking ways. There has been the same kind of debate as to whether comparison should be limited to the descriptive level and the same kind of question as to whether Western ethical categories are appropriate even for the description of non-Western moral systems. There have been familiar complaints from the ethicists about the vagueness and looseness of the categories employed by historians of religion, and there have been impatient voices urging us to climb down from the ivory tower and take a stand against injustice and oppression, even if enshrined in some venerable system of moral values. There have also been exciting moments of discovery and periods of dialogue in which each partner internalized the questions and even the insights of the other. While we may seem very far indeed from a 'global ethic', we have caught some glimpses of the universal human community that for Dr. Smith is an incipient reality.

These recent discussions have confirmed my conviction that understanding and evaluation need to be distinguished but they cannot in a larger human context be entirely separated. A healthy dose of cultural relativism challenges our parochialism and enlarges our vision of human possibilities, but a complete moral relativism belies not only our own instincts but also such accumulated knowledge as we have of the norm-filled and goal-directed character of human cultural activity. I am increasingly doubtful, however, that we shall reach consensus, even among Western historians of religion, as to how understanding and evaluation either are or should be both distinguished and related.

When put in this way, it may seem that my differences with Dr. Smith and Dr. Mehta, and indeed with the other scholars cited, are little more than a scholarly quibble. I do believe that we are engaged in a scholarly enterprise, Western in origin but increasingly international in scope and intercultural in spirit, in which the task we share is vastly more important than the differences we articulate concerning our respective 'methodologies'. Yet the discussion of those differences is part of our continuing reflection on *how* we do what we do (method in the strict sense) and *why* we do it, which brings us to reflect on *who* we are. For this reason I venture some final observations on the tasks of the historian and the theologian.

If we wish to make the history of religion (and religions) a

237

common human enterprise, we need to develop a common language with common terms and ways of speaking. Some provisional agreement on the scope and nature of the subject matter is clearly requisite, but the more theological or philosophical or social-scientific definition is insisted upon, the more are potential participants excluded. A certain acceptance of conventions is necessary in learning any human craft, but in a new craft in which we have to learn together, the entrance requirement to the guild should be as flexible as possible. Some sense of historical process may be needed, for example, but to make belief in the onward flow of history to a higher goal a prerequisite for historians of religion seems to me self-defeating, especially if it is assumed that such direction in history becomes clear from historical study itself.

Dr. Mehta voices the sentiments of many Hindu scholars in finding openness to truth a necessary aspect of true understanding. I can understand his impatience with a postponement to some theological realm beyond understanding of the grappling with truth, but the very definiteness of the Western concept of truth may make the direct encounter of different 'truths' a fruitless clash unless it is first prepared through an effort at understanding in which we attempt to comprehend both similarities and differences without assessment. It seems to me that a Christian theologian's notion of truth makes it impossible to recognize radically new truth but quite possible to discover new forms of truth already known. This may be differently expressed: new truths are recognized as truth by reference to the Truth, not that one possesses but by whom one is possessed.

The quest for a non-reductionist understanding is an effort to grasp the intentions of a religious community, and one takes note in such an effort of the internal judgments made about failures to conform to the norms acknowledged by the community. Theological evaluation, on the other hand, seeks to discern a Divine judgment that first of all is a critique of one's own religion. It is only in a rather approximate and very cautious way that one can discern the Divine judgment on some other religious community. The most familiar Christian critique of Hinduism concerns its 'idolatry', yet this judgment was originally directed to those within the community of Israel who broke their exclusive covenant with the God of Israel. It is a critique that Christians must seriously apply to themselves before they can decide what relevance such Divine judgment has to the 'idols' of the Hindu community. The same applies to other Divine judgments voiced by the prophets against God's own people. Only after the personal and institutional involvement of Christians in the grinding down of the poor is taken to heart is it possible to consider theologically the injustice of the caste system. At the same time the Christian must take to heart the judgments of outside prophets on the Christian community, for there too we may recognize, perhaps in the midst of much misunderstanding and prejudice, the voice of Truth.

Those engaged in the comparative study of religion will each have to decide how they should try to relate understanding and evaluation. It is easy for others to see how far such efforts fail. The task remains for all of us in the contemporary world to explore our common human subjectivity in the sphere we call religion but also to discern the Presence beyond our human community, a Presence expressed in both order and upheaval, in imperative and invitation.

Note. The Report of the Consultation held in Bangalore in September, 1967, under the title, *Study of Religion in Indian Universities.* It was distributed by the Christian Institute for the Study of Religion and Society in• Bangalore. Some copies are still available, at the Centre for the Study of World Religions, Harvard University, 42 Francis Ave., Cambridge, MA 02138.

6

THEMATIC COMPARISON

Geoffrey Parrinder

'There are those who would disdain comparative or empirical study' of religion, wrote Wilfred Cantwell Smith in *The Meaning and End of Religion*.[1] The title 'comparative religion' has been criticized or rejected in favour of 'history of religion' or 'study of religion' although, in Great Britain at least, there is a tendency to revert to Comparative Religion as a popular description which is sufficiently wide to allow of various interpretations. It is not competitive religion, or of merely historical or antiquarian interest, and Comparative Religion may reveal something of the varieties of religion in the multi-religious societies in which we live nowadays.

There was a great expansion of comparative studies of religion in the 1960s, and many schools and colleges developed courses in general and specialist religious studies. But in the later seventies and the present decade there have come restrictions and hardening of attitudes. Partly this is due to financial pressures, and where economies have been forced by central government the victims of cuts have often been those small but adventurous developments which could not compete with older and larger traditional interests. At the same time there has been growing resistance from those who suspect Comparative Religion itself, and who claim that the knowledge of what religion involves can only be obtained from within one's own religious tradition, usually Christianity. Comparative Religion is made to appear as unbelief, or treason, and even without such overt condemnation it is astonishing how many theological institutions send their clergy out into the world with no knowledge of other religions.

This is shortsighted, since the laity are often more aware of the problems of the plurality of religions than their spiritual leaders, and may ask them questions the latter are not qualified to answer. Wilfred Smith's words are as relevant today as they were twenty years ago when he wrote that 'the future of one's own cherished faith even within one's own community, depends more largely than most of us have realized upon the ability to solve the question of comparative religion'.[2]

Whether an individual, a community or even a generation can resolve all the problems of Comparative Religion may be doubted, but the neglect by many church and educational authorities of any attempt at tackling the questions is blatant. If the problems of the encounter of religions are not easily answered at least they should be tackled. In the past Christians had to work out their faith in a Christian environment untroubled by challenges from other faiths, whereas Muslims, Hindus, Sikhs and Buddhists were more accustomed generally to religious plurality. Like it or not, the situation has changed.

How then can studies of Comparative Religion proceed? This volume suggests approaches from various angles and disciplines. My own assignment, or task, is to look at some thematic comparisons that may be or are being made at present, and consider the advantages and the problems of such comparisons. This approach may commend itself to theologians and teachers of religion in general, and the different ways in which themes have been considered and presented may be instructive of the gains and perils of thematic comparison.

The Gifford Lectures in Scotland have produced contributions from many distinguished philosophers, theologians and scientists for nearly a hundred years. They have ranged from James and Frazer, to Bergson and Whitehead, and to Schweitzer and Barth. Some of the lectures were important or interesting, others were duller or ephemeral. But that the importance of Comparative Religion is now apparent to the academic world is shown in a galaxy of recent Giffords: Seyyed Hossein Nasr on *Knowledge and the Sacred*, Frederick Copleston on *Religion and the One*, and Ninian Smart on *Beyond Ideology*.[3] Ake Hultkrantz's 1982 Giffords in Aberdeen have not yet been published, and we have not all been able to travel so far north, so I must restrict comments to the three books named above, while noting that the last is well spoken of and to be awaited. But what a lively time they are having in Ultima Thule, giving an example to Sassenachs and others beyond the Pale of the need not only to study and lecture but also to write!

Of these three books Hossein Nasr's is the longest, most lavishly annotated, and the most ambitious. His comparison is the wide one of the nature and appreciation of sacred knowledge in the cultures of East and West. He was the first Muslim, and 'in fact the first Oriental', to deliver Gifford lectures in Edinburgh and he aimed at fulfilling Adam Gifford's purpose, in expounding 'the *knowledge* of God.' Seyyed Nasr plunges into a sustained attack on the intellectual and spiritual impoverishment of the West, a rebuttal of the claims of modern Christianity, which he attributes to total secularization and the eclipse of the sacred content of knowledge. This is traced back through the nineteenth century to Descartes and ultimately to the Greeks. Christianity itself, he claims, has lost it way through the 'so-called higher criticism' by which its 'sapiential dimension' has been veiled or destroyed, and a purely ethical teaching has been substituted for the way of knowledge or sapience. The only way in which the West can revive its mystical knowledge of the Sacred is by 'authentic contact with the Oriental traditions.'[4]

Study of eastern religions is not enough in itself, however, indeed it may be positively misleading or blinding, for Western studies even of Oriental religions have helped towards the 'secularization of the East'. Not only society and culture, but religion and sacred traditions have been misinterpreted by 'historicism, evolutionism, scientism, and the many other ways whereby the sacred is reduced to the profane.'[5] There have been a few honourable exceptions among orientalists, admits Dr. Nasr, but the general trend has been towards secular interpretations which have but led to misinterpretation, hindering instead of helping the task of Comparative Religion. The few Western writers who are acceptable, indeed as masters of sapience, are such as Frithjof Schuon with his synthesis of 'the transcendent unity of religions' or René Guénon who in expounding the Orient to the West was 'chosen for this task by Tradition itself.'[6]

Seyyed Hossein Nasr's long concern with mysticism is well known, but he illustrates the danger of expounding varied teachings in the light of one dominant tradition. The claim, made by R. C. Zaehner and others, that Sufism derived its monistic or pantheistic elements from Hinduism would be supported by Dr. Nasr's own adoption of monistic Hindu philosophy and mysticism. The very first sentence of these lectures affirms that 'In the beginning Reality was at once being, knowledge, and bliss (the *sat, chit*, and *ānanda* of the Hindu tradition)', and these are said to be among the names of Allah in Islam. After this start it is hardly surprising that the non-dualist Śaṅkara is hailed as 'the master of Hindu gnosis.' Divergent streams of Hindu thought or religion are ignored, and Rāmānuja is not mentioned. Hinduism is called 'that oldest of religions', a claim that might be queried by Jews or Parsis, and age alone does not guarantee validity. But the purpose here is to emphasize the virtues of the agelong Oriental, and largely Indian, cherishing of the Sacred, the perennial Tradition, the Scientia Sacra.

Seyyed Nasr expounds the theme of Sacred or Principial Knowledge at great length and with many references to writers from both East and West, though he claims that it now flourishes only in the East. His lush style produces remarkable alliterations, such as 'the multiple refractions and reflections of Reality upon the myriad mirrors of both macrocosmic and microcosmic manifestation.' His many comparisons are all in favour of the Orient, 'the source of light', and against western rationalism.[7]

This is where criticism might hold, with some justice, that comparison becomes competition, now of East against West, reversing previous trends. Pointed questions might be asked: Is the Orient really the source of light? Which Orient? Palestine, Arabia, Iran, India, China, Japan? Do they all teach 'sapiential knowledge'? Is there indeed 'but one Tradition'? Does the Bhagavad-Gītā truly teach freewill as a 'central concern'? Is Christian mysticism 'nearly completely emptied of intellectual and metaphysical content'? And so on.

It is difficult to define Dr. Nasr's meaning of 'sapience' or 'the sapiential dimension.' It seems to be mystical or mysterious, and in particular the monistic philosophy of Śaṅkara. For it is affirmed that while sacred knowledge is 'ultimately related to the Divine Intellect', it has a monistic interpretation as 'the primordial soul of man yearning for the Absolute.' Seyyed

Hossein Nasr was doubtless right to protest against that
secularism which blinds people to the claims of religion and
philosophy but, rather than affirming the sole virtues of a
mysterious Orient, the aims of Comparative Religion might be
better served by combining critical discipline with religious
apprehensions, east and west. A satisfactory thematic comparison
needs to look at the virtues of both sides, or of different methods
of seeking to understand the spiritual world and the material.

There could hardly be a greater contrast to Hossein Nasr's
Giffords with those delivered the year before in Aberdeen by the
Jesuit philosopher Frederick Copleston. The latter's book is
shorter, with few notes, and business-like. Nasr may have
bemused his hearers with romantic mysticism, Copleston perhaps
risked wearying them with dry tack. But to some readers,
'westerners', Copleston may be more straightforward, logical and
convincing. Professor Copleston is a distinguished philosopher,
and I remember Hossein Nasr at a dinner in London
congratulating him on the completion of the Persian translation
of the nine volumes of *A History of Philosophy*. In return Dr.
Copleston justifies Schuon's exposition of Ibn 'Arabī by saying
that 'his books on Islam won high praise from the distinguished
Iranian scholar, himself a Muslim, Dr. S. H. Nasr.'[8]

Dr. Copleston's classic *History of Philosophy* was all on
European philosophy, and it is noteworthy that he now confesses
that 'in advanced years' he has taken an interest in 'the
philosophical thought of non-western cultures.' The full title
given to these Gifford lectures was 'Religion and the Metaphysics
of the One', and the author suggests that something like 'Religious
Aspects of the Metaphysics of the One' might have been more
suitable, as indicating that he was not concerned with religion in
general but with religious philosophy in its search for unity. The
book is a careful thematic comparison, the concept of the One
being traced in different traditions, as the ultimate source of the
Many.

Clearly, almost clinically, Professor Copleston first sketches the
idea of the One in Taoism, Buddhism, Hinduism, Islamic
mysticism and western philosophy. Then he turns to general
questions of the world and the self in relation to the One,

mysticism and knowledge (vastly different from Seyyed Nasr's treatment of knowledge), ethics and society, systems and truth. It is interesting that China is selected as starting point, with the Taoist concept of the indefinable One, the nameless, transcendent and immanent, the One which is the mother and source of the Many. That seminal and beguiling work, the *Tao Te Ching* or the *Lao Tzu*, exerts its fascination on our philosopher, followed by the *Chuang Tzu*. Some affinity with the Buddhist concept of the Void or Emptiness is recognized, though Dr. Copleston notes that students of practised religion, like Melford Spiro in *Buddhism and Society*,[9] have shown that such abstract concepts may play little part in Buddhist daily life. And the theories of no-self, or a mere succession of states, are explained as having 'a purely pragmatic function', to help towards detachment.[10]

Frederick Copleston gives great attention to Upaniṣadic and Śaṅkarite *advaita*, and confesses that for him it has 'an abiding interest.' It asserts the existence of the One, though the status of the Many is not easy to define. He pays proper attention to critics of Śaṅkara, Rāmānuja and Madhva, but despite all the objections they raised against full monism, he notes that *advaita* arose within Hinduism, it claims scriptural support, it recognizes popular cults while seeing one reality behind them, and it has given rise to mystical experiences.

Turning to Islam, Copleston remarks that 'emphasis on the divine transcendence has been a prominent feature', which is putting it mildly. Muhammad's own faith was clearly in a personal God distinct from all other beings and the theology was as different from *advaita* as possible. There was no association with any creature, no identity of God with the world, and no question of regarding the soul as a mode of the divine substance. Yet paradoxically mysticism came to flourish in Islam, to the scandal of some orthodox theologians. The Sufis for their part were not averse to making provocative statements which might suggest their identity with the One: 'glory to me' of Bistāmī, or 'I am the Truth' of Hallāj. The teachings of Ghazālī, Suhrawardī and Mullā Sadrā, in particular, are sketched, bringing Copleston to interesting interpretations that affect his whole thesis.

While some Sufis used exaggerated or near-blasphemous expressions they were poets rather than philosophers, and it is remarked that poetic language may be 'a much better medium of expression for mystical visions than the conceptual, abstract thought of the philosopher which desiccates what it endeavours to express'. Copleston may be reproaching himself here, for while he is attracted to the non-dualism of Śaṅkara and similar philosophers, and might appreciate the blurring of distinctions between divine and human in claims to mystical union, yet when the mystics write of love he is fair enough to comment that 'a distinction between lover and beloved is required, if the idea of love is to make any sense.'[11] He had previously noted that Hindu *bhakti*, in the Bhagavad-Gītā and elsewhere, was a prime reason for the attacks on Śaṅkara's monism by those who felt that personal religion was threatened in theories of a suprapersonal Absolute with its identity of *ātman* and Brahman.

This is an important recognition of the qualifications demanded by the mysticism of love to the understanding of transcendent reality. Yet Dr. Copleston's chapter on Mysticism in general is less forceful. He properly agrees that the statements of mystics may be accepted as genuine expressions of their experience, though they are interpretations. But he considers that mystical experiences are 'relatively rare', and does not claim to have had any himself, and he does not connect mysticism with ordinary religious experience. His philosophical reserve finds difficulty in discovering 'a really convincing argument' from mystical experiences for the existence of a transcendent reality, the One. A major difficulty is that claims are made for some experiences which may be mystical but have little to do with religion. Copleston refers to R. C. Zaehner's description of Richard Jeffries as a nature mystic and Ibn 'Arabī as a heretical monist, though he finds the latter's position 'not clear' and, rightly or wrongly, he does not pursue Zaehner's interesting distinctions of kinds of mysticism.

At the end of a discussion of Mysticism and Knowledge Professor Copleston simply admits that mystical experiences figure 'as one strand among others' in a cumulative argument on the nature of reality. He finds 'a sort of awareness of the divine presence' in both religious mysticism and in philosophical reflection. The latter, for him, is 'a movement towards the ultimate reality, the One', and it may converge in this respect, and 'up to a certain point', with mysticism. Mystics, like theistic philosophers, may recognize that the divine transcends our conceptions, but in addition they stress 'intuitive apprehension of the divine presence'.[12]

Ninian Smart's Gifford lectures, which were delivered in the University of Edinburgh in 1979–80, are entitled *Beyond Ideology*. But since they are very much about ideologies one may wonder how much the title owes to the publishers. For such gentlemen are notorious for choosing titles which they think will help to sell the book, they should be easy to grasp and if possible topical. It has been noted above that Dr. Copleston's lecture titles were longer than that of the published book.

Sub-titles are sometimes more informative of the contents of a book. Copleston's was 'Philosophies East and West', and Ninian Smart's is 'Religion and the Future of Western Civilization.' This seems one-sided for a teacher of world religions who has been very much concerned with eastern civilizations, until one finds at the end of the book an emphasis upon 'the Pacific Mind', which seems to link it up with Hossein Nasr's call to return to the sapience of the Orient.

Cover pictures also often indicate the way in which the publisher has understood or misunderstood the book, or more simply has instructed his designer to produce something likely to catch the public eye. Dr. Copleston's cover has two photographs, of Sarvepalli Radhakrishnan and Karl Jaspers. The former is only once mentioned briefly in the text and the latter is considered in some four pages. Would not a picture of the author have been more appropriate and interesting? Dr. Smart's dust cover has imaginary pictures of Christ and Buddha and a photograph of Albert Einstein who is mentioned once in the book. Marx would have been more suitable, since his ideas and influence are discussed at length. Seyyed Nasr's book cover merely pictures an apple. Why? Is it the apple of knowledge from Genesis? But there was no apple in Genesis, and the fruit of either the tree of life or the tree of the knowledge of good and evil would more likely have been a peach in the mind of the author.

Professor Smart has had much longer experience of the study of world religions, most of a lifetime, than Frederick Copleston who only came to it in later years. He is more clear and discriminating than Hossein Nasr, and he is too careful a scholar to confuse religious notions in an attempt to show the oneness of everything or maintain the sole virtues of Asia. Amid the confusing and competing ideologies of the modern world he offers as solution 'a certain outlook, based on the complementarity of Buddhism and Christianity.'[13] This is comparative religion, recognizing differences as well as similarities, and to suggest complementarity is to recognize that there are truths in other traditions while not renouncing the truths of one's own religion.

Buddhism is one of Dr. Smart's special interests, chiefly Theravāda and the philosophical concerns of Mahāyāna, and much less attention has been given to popular cults, which constitute much of the religion, whether Theravāda or Mahāyāna. Basic Buddhist doctrines are expounded with professional competence, indicating that they balance realism and idealism in an analytic temper. Philosophical Buddhist criticisms of personal deities and an apprehensible (not 'apprehensive' as one review printed it!) self, are given fair consideration. The Buddhist sense of the undefined numinous is called 'pure mysticism.'

Suggested Buddhist views of Christianity, 'as seen from Adam's Peak', allow Professor Smart to continue the consideration of this complex religion, which he summarized more successfully in some modern variations in *The Phenomenon of Christianity*. Here discussion is too short to do justice to some elements of the religion, notably Protestantism and, surprisingly, Christian mysticism. But Smart suggests something of 'the Buddhist Meaning of Christianity' and 'the Christian Meaning of Buddhism', in his overriding purpose of showing that these two religions which have deceptive similarities can be regarded as complementary to each other. Here and later he admits that these religions are 'much at variance' and both need to 'undergo some radical restructuring', but he finds valuable insights in the Christian affirmation of personal identity in history and sacrament, and in Buddhist analysis of 'the emptiness of the atoms of consciousness.'[14]

Buddhism has admittedly suffered greatly under modern strains, from Korea to Kampuchea, and may seem to be in full decline. But Ninian Smart is encouraged by western studies and practices of forms of Buddhism, from California to Kent, or in his own academic peregrination from California to Lancaster. Yet is it strange that Islam, which has had notable revivals and advances in recent times, receives little mention and is dismissed with the phrase 'the tragedy of Islam is its very clarity.'

Professor Smart gives much more place than the other two Giffords to the challenges of modern secularism and especially Marxism. For although Hossein Nasr constantly attacks western secularism, he does not discuss Marxism in any detail, despite its world following. But Ninian Smart sees the religious appeal of Marxism, and after analysing secular ideologies, both scientific and political, he criticizes the Marxist states though in a popular and qualified manner. Thus Communist societies are 'for the most part totalitarian', and China is 'relatively ruthless.' In contrast, he offers the world-views of both Buddhism and Christianity as superior to collectivism and 'flat secularism.' The appeals of nationalism or social restructuring are too limited to answer the greatest human needs.

Dr. Smart's book is much more popular, in the broadest sense, than the other two Giffords and according to reports his lectures aroused considerable interest. Perhaps it will sell the best. That we now live in a 'global city' is a constant refrain, with a persistent attempt to shake us out of the limited or parochial views of past times into truly international views of society and religion. This is indeed Smart's main theme, a thematic comparison which does not just juxtapose Christianity and Buddhism but present them together as part of the universal search for spiritual truth. While avoiding suggestions that all religions are the same, or that the Orient is virtuous and the West wicked, Ninian Smart provides a hopeful contribution towards that aim of being a Christian intelligently and spiritually in a world society of Christians, Buddhists, Muslims, Marxists and the rest, which Cantwell Smith has claimed to be essential.

The three examples of recent Gifford lectures attempt different comparisons: of kinds of knowledge, of the search for the One, and of religious ideologies. But they may be open to the criticism that they are all about theories or doctrines. That Greek inheritance which has been 'a massive influence in Christian history' and which is 'intellectualist *par excellence*',[15] makes it only too easy for the comparative study of religions to be predominantly a comparison of doctrines, of God or the absolute, of the soul or non-self. 'Words, words,' says a Jewish joke, 'you only talk words.' It is difficult to blame philosophers or theologians for exercising their special skills and concentrating upon the interests which they are most competent to judge. Nevertheless, religion, in all its variety, does not receive an adequate comparison merely by discussing themes like monotheism or monism. Perhaps Shakespeare's words are appropriate: 'Words, words, mere words, no matter from the heart.'

Ninian Smart's earlier book on *The Religious Experience of Mankind* is widely used, and his 'six dimensions' of religion give a wider outlook than the doctrinal. Religious experience itself is considered, followed by myth, ritual, ethics, and social development and organization. This is a brave effort, though religious experience is exceedingly difficult to describe without lapsing into the doctrinal or the biographical.

An interesting recent example of the approach through religious experience concentrates usefully upon one country, Nigeria, and on Christian sanctity there. Edited by Elizabeth Isichei, professor of history in the university of Jos, *Varieties of Christian Experience in Nigeria* begins well by the editor insisting that beyond 'the anatomy of religion', doctrine and organization of which many believers know little, there is the inner experience and attempts to live by its light. The chapters that follow, however, are mostly simple stories of African saints and martyrs in various churches during the last hundred years. Their faith and fervour were undoubted, and they demonstrated fasting and chastity, poverty and generosity, but their inner life remains hidden. Further, a desirable comparison with the older African faith, or with Islam, is virtually missing. The editor claims that 'many Nigerian Christians carried over an indigenous tradition of mystical experience', but hardly any effort is made in the ensuing chapters to compare or contrast Christian with other quests for the divine.[16]

Since I have been engaged in a good deal of writing on comparative themes, and it may be for that reason I was chosen to write this chapter, it may not be immodest to refer to some of my own efforts. In *Mysticism in the World's Religions* I attempted to discuss various classifications of mysticism, going rather more widely than R. C. Zaehner to include nature mysticism as a valid category of religious experience.[17] I tried also to suggest a continuity between the religious experience of the ordinary believer and the heightened experiences claimed by specialists. In other words, it seemed that mysticism was different in degree rather than in kind, it was continuous with normal spiritual experience, and therefore it was much more widely practised than might be thought. Contrary to Professor Copleston's opinion, it was common rather than 'relatively rare.' Nevertheless the difficulty remained of describing experience, any experience. It is one's own possession and difficult to communicate. Mystics often claim to have heard 'unspeakable words, which it is not lawful for a man to utter.' Asked in India whether I had had mystical experiences, I took refuge in this Pauline statement. Yet, as J. N. Findlay has caustically remarked, mystics have uttered a great deal.[18]

To return to Africa for a moment, since this was my first and has remained one of my principal interests. How can mysticism or religious experience be described or discussed in cultures which are illiterate, or non-literate, or preliterate as modern fashion prefers to describe them? I avoid the word 'primal', since it seems to have the same unfortunate implications as 'primitive.' But our dependence upon written sources of information and expositions of schemes of doctrine, becomes a handicap when looking at religions that have no scriptures. Perhaps even more unfortunately, they have no written spiritual autobiographies. Thus there is no available explanation from inside the religion, no statement of what it is like to hold a particular faith, and description can only be external, of rites or artefacts.

Anthropologists, who have had much to say about African and similar religions, accuse theologians of imposing their own schemes of thought upon the subjects of their study, such as magic or fetishism, polytheism or monotheism. In return theologians retort that the anthropological picture reduces religion to a mere function of society, following Durkheim's still popular view that religion, while not a hallucination, was the worship of society: 'the god of the clan, the totemic principle, can therefore be nothing else

251

than the clan itself.'[19] No religious person, African or other, would agree with that dogma, which is still an intellectualist explanation, imposed from the outside.

Yet if there is no literature to reveal the secret thoughts of many religious people, there are means of expression, notably in art. This is indeed where Wilfred Cantwell Smith suggests we should begin in considering the expressions of religious faith: 'not to begin with what to many in Western Europe has come to seem the prime area of such expression; namely, ideas – the expression of faith in the form of belief.' Rather he indicates that 'the gentlest introduction to our subject may be gained by considering first men's expression of their faith in art.'[20]

In *African Mythology* I wrote of 'the language of art' through which Africans themselves gave expression to their feelings and beliefs, providing a sacred literature, basically human, with man and woman together. Every stage of human existence is revealed, with constant belief in life after death revealed in countless death masks and societies to represent the living ancestors.[21] Paintings, sculptures, masks, and even clay buildings give truly native representations of outlook upon this world and the next. Many kinds of material have been and are being used: wood, stone, gold, ivory, pottery, leather, cloth, and so on. The vitality of African art has been recognized in our day, and its powerful influence has been accepted by western, or northern artists such as Jacob Epstein and Henry Moore.

The major difficulty lies in understanding the art of other peoples, often without anyone to interpret the meaning. Probably many folk still regard Picasso's paintings as a con-trick, or the emperor without any clothes, which they may be, but extra efforts are required to appreciate the unfamiliar from other continents and cultures. African, Maya or Japanese arts are different, to say the least, from Greek sculptures or Renaissance paintings or Constable's landscapes. Arab or Indian music may sound discordant to lovers of Beethoven or Sullivan. It is often difficult therefore to make comparison between the arts of different nations. They do reveal the infinite diversity of mankind, and they may teach us to study and contemplate, to make extra efforts in appreciation rather than to judge or categorize. Contemplation may be an important part of the comparative study of religions.

Whether art can be transferred from one ideological scheme to another is much debated. There are those who have persuaded African carvers to illustrate Christian themes, even when the artists themselves were not Christian. Thus Kevin Carroll maintains that 'even a pagan carver can soon learn to know and reverence Christ and the saints and can vividly carve the stories and anecdotes concerning them.' Kevin Carroll is a Roman Catholic priest who has persuaded African workmen to carve Christian figures for his churches. But he has been strongly criticized by Ulli Beier, a lecturer on art, who maintains that 'the Church has been able to provide the carver with new work but not with new inspiration . . . Their figures are dull and puppet-like . . . It is only the christian carvings that give a profane impression.' It is interesting that Father Carroll justifies his practice by claiming that African art is humanistic, but the agnostic Beier retorts that in African life 'it is impossible to divide the sacred from the profane.'[22] If there is a solution to this problem it will come when Arfican artists become or are born Christians and produce new art from within the new faith.

A similar point has been made on the changing morality of the African scene. A sociologist, C. K. Meek, years ago criticized the assumptions that traditional morality was ideal and that change necessarily brings degeneration. There was often bribery in the past to obtain favourable or unfavourable decisions from priests and other guardians of morality. 'Some of the old ethics will disappear with the old gods, but new gods will create new ethical values' and 'new sanctions will be found for such social regulations as continue to be serviceable'.[23]

After art and morality, ritual may be a useful field of study and comparison though, as already indicated, if there is no explanation from the inside, it may only allow of a superficial description. A handy thematic comparison on *Sacrifice*, edited by the anthropologist Meyer Fortes and the theologian M. F. C. Bourdillon, illustrates different approaches and means of interpretation.[24] This book is useful in that it is restricted to a limited theme, bringing together diverse contributors, who seem to have learnt to appreciate each other's disciplines.

But prejudices appear in various articles. For example, there is a coldly external description of 'the Mass in a convent setting', where the observer concludes that the Mass has 'a totemic significance in communion with the gods.' Then the Day of Atonement is discussed as a 'rite of passage', though a Biblical commentator objects that 'it is not clear to me who or what is supposed to be changing its status.' And against an anthropological characterization of the death of Christ as a ritual, again a theologian points out that it was 'a judicial execution, not a ritual in the usual anthropological sense', though he has to explain Paul's atonement theories as due to 'the chronically unsystematisable character' of his thought.

On the whole in this comparative study of sacrifice the Biblical papers are the most workmanlike and the anthropological the most speculative. Which is strange, if anthropologists are supposed to study facts and theologians to propound theories. But when it comes to one's own faith, only the insider can explain what it means to be a believer. Michael Bourdillon who is described as 'priest and sociologist', noted the 'embarrassed silence' of anthropologists on 'the relationship between the effects of rituals and what participants expect to achieve through them.' They study religions, usually of 'primitives', but they do not believe them. As Evans-Pritchard wrote of the pioneers of anthropology, 'the persons whose writings have been most influential have been at the time they wrote agnostics or atheists ... Religious belief was to these anthropologists absurd, and it is so to most anthropologists of yesterday and today.'[25] They considered that by demonstrating the fallacy or absurdity of primitive beliefs the whole foundation of religion would be undermined, with fatal effects upon the higher religions, notably Judaism and Christianity.

In *Sacrifice* the theologians take a more sympathetic attitude even to alien religious practices, because of the direct link with their own religion. They are 'part of the tradition they study' and so can speak from the inside. Evans-Pritchard again has maintained that this attitude is not only more sympathetic but more scholarly than that of the outside observer. 'The non-believer seeks for some theory – biological, psychological, or sociological – which will explain the illusion [of religion]; the believer seeks rather to understand the manner in which a people conceives of a reality and their relations to it.'[26]

The most useful thematic comparisons are probably in limited fields and between related subjects, rather than taking the whole gamut of religion for comparative study, except where they are largely descriptive as in comparisons of worship or theories of sex, and provided they are undertaken with sympathy and as much from the inside as possible. In my own work I have found such limitations salutary, comparing beliefs in Jesus in the Qur'ān and the New Testament, or the Indian ideas of Avatars with Christian faith in the Incarnation.

If 'the end of religion is God' then that end is unutterable, but every channel of religious expression needs to be explored to find what light it can shed. Comparisons can be made that are neither 'odious' nor 'odorous.' Copleston may be right in suggesting that poetic language is a better medium for expression of the inner vision than philosophical argument, and a poetical comparison may give light on the eternal:

> The One who, himself without colour, by the manifold
>   application of his power
> Distributes many colours in his hidden purpose ...

says the Upaniṣad, paralleled by Shelley,

> The One remains, the many change and pass ...
> Life, like a dome of many-coloured glass,
> Stains the white radiance of Eternity.[27]

NOTES

1. *The Meaning and End of Religion*, Mentor Books, 1964, p. 10 f.
2. ibid., p. 15.
3. S. H. Nasr, *Knowledge and the Sacred*, 1981; F. Copleston, *Religion and the One*, 1982; N. Smart, *Beyond Ideology*, 1981.
4. *Knowledge and the Sacred*, pp. vii, 13.
5. ibid., p. viii.
6. ibid., p. 100 ff.
7. ibid., p. 1.

 8. *Religion and the One*, p. 105.
 9. ibid., p. 13n.
10. ibid., p. 57.
11. ibid., pp. 112, 115.
12. ibid., pp. 221, 272.
13. *Beyond Ideology*, pp. 309, 35.
14. ibid., pp. 69 ff., 302, 309 ff.
15. *The Meaning and End of Religion*, p. 163.
16. *Varieties of Christian Experience in Nigeria*, 1982, pp. 1, 8.
17. *Mysticism in the World's Religions*, 1976, p. 23 ff.
18. *Ascent to the Absolute*, 1970, pp. 164, 182.
19. *The Elementary Forms of the Religious Life*, Eng. trs. 1915, p. 206.
20. *The Meaning and End of Religion*, p. 156.
21. *African Mythology*, 2nd. edn. 1982, p. 8.
22. *Yoruba Religious Carving*, 1967, p. 70; U. Beier, *Art in Nigeria*, 1960, p. 14 f.
23. *Law and Authority in a Nigerian Tribe*, 1950, p. 341.
24. *Sacrifice*, 1980.
25. *Theories of Primitive Religion*, 1965, p. 15.
26. ibid., p. 121.
27. Śvetāśvatara Upaniṣad, 4, 1, trs. R. E. Hume; Adonais, lii.

7

SCIENTIFIC PHENOMENOLOGY AND WILFRED CANTWELL SMITH'S MISGIVINGS

Ninian Smart

One of Wilfred Cantwell Smith's most interesting contributions is the essay which he published in a collection edited by Robert Baird, *Methodological Issues in Religious Studies*, in 1975. The essay was called 'Methodology and the Study of Religion: Some Misgivings.' His criticism of certain ideas about methodology are illuminating and I think right. Anyone who takes phenomenology of religion seriously must be able to answer these criticisms. I want here therefore to build upon the foundation of Cantwell Smith's misgivings. But before I get on to that, a word about the other part of my title is in order. For the notion of phenomenology may be obscure, and to call it 'scientific' adds a possible further cloud of mystification.

Briefly, the concept of phenomenology has at least two main uses in the field of the history of religions. In one usage, it is the attempt to describe religious phenomena 'as they are', and without obtruding our own presuppositions upon them. It involves what I prefer to call structured empathy. Here in a sense the religious believer is monarch: it is her or his attitudes and feelings and beliefs that we attempt to delineate. In a second sense, the phenomenology of religion, dealing in essences, is a kind of typology. It is what often used to be called the comparative study of religion. It involves, as in Gerardus van der Leeuw's great work, a systematic typology of forms of religious belief and practice. Eliade's work uncovering the symbolic forms of archaic religion can be seen, too, as typological phenomenology. Should such attempts to delineate religious phenomena and to classify them be deemed scientific? To that I shall return, in the course of treating Wilfred Cantwell Smith's misgivings.

The first and major misgiving arises from a perceived shift from subject to method, from matter to discipline. Largely, his objection lies in the way this shift means a concern with abstraction and theory rather than concrete actuality. Moreover there is the danger that when a discipline is thus methodologically defined whole regions of human feeling and behavior may be neglected because they cannot be dealt with by the relevant method. He cites the case of a social scientist studying Muslim political behavior in India who could not deal properly with elements of the religious factor, because his methods were unable to handle matters of that kind (p. 7).

The objection is well taken if it be aimed at forms of positivism: that is, doctrines which identify the whole of a realm of meaning with a particular method of getting at it. And I think it is reasonable to hold that this becomes a problem wherever fields become defined by method. Later on Smith criticizes the attempt to find a 'peculiar method' to correspond to and justify the study of religion. Nor is he impressed with attempts to defend against this criticism of definition-by-method by stating that a field, for instance religion, is interdisciplinary.

In order to come to grips with such misgivings, it is useful first to make a few distinctions. Some subjects are roughly speaking defined by cultural or historical-cultural area: French studies, Indology, Judaica, Latin American studies and so on. Others are roughly defined by reference to some aspect of human behavior and experience: economics deal with economic behavior and institutions, politics with political ones, linguistics with human use of language. These can be called 'aspectual studies'. It is of course an elementary truth, though one which is often overlooked that in speaking of an aspect we are artificially abstracting from the total being and behavior of individuals and groups. My decision to buy a record is an economic one, but it is also involved in social relations, aesthetic experience, perhaps religious feelings and so forth. It becomes necessary for economic historians to study much beyond immediate economic arrangements: deep value structures in Japanese society are relevant to the Japanese economic miracle, and so on.

Sometimes cultural-area studies, such as French, are very selective as to aspects of French culture to explore – often it is language and literature, but not so much economics, politics and gastronomy, or even art history or music. Such selectivities go back to the histories of the development of various subjects in Western universities – the model of Classics sometimes came to dominate the early history of then new subjects like English and French.

Generally, one would say that what Religious Studies explores is, of course, religion. It is in this sense an aspectual field – dealing with an aspect of human life – religious behavior, feelings, creations, institutions, symbols. But it does have to be concrete – directed not to something which is religion-in-general, but the religious traditions of humanity. Here Smith's famous critique of the concept of religion is rightly relevant. We start with religious traditions, and within those sub-traditions, right down to the basic unit: the individual human being.

It is here that something important can be said about phenomenology taken as the descriptive exploration of the life and experience of human beings, in so far as they are religious. Here the study of religion does not differ from much that goes on elsewhere – in history and political science for instance. It is necessary to use structured empathy to 'enter into' the experience of others. Part of this entering may be by a kind of dialogue. In getting to know a Buddhist I get to know what it is like to be a Buddhist of that kind. The empathetic understanding of human beings is necessary in all kinds of history. There is then nothing here peculiar to the study of religion. But two important comments need to be made.

First, Religious Studies has had to fight a bit of a battle to get away from institutionalized theology, because of its quest for pluralism and crosscultural studies. It has also often had to struggle to clarify how it is that we can explore religion without imposing our own categories on the cultures and feelings of others. In both connections phenomenology has served as a rallying cry for a particular reason: that the doctrine of *epochē* (used often, by the way, in a manner wholly different from that envisaged by Husserl) helped to show that we should suspend our own beliefs and try to be 'objective' about the beliefs of others. It is for this that there has been a concern for 'value-free' explorations. Religious Studies' sensitivity on this score has an important lesson often neglected in the social sciences and humanities. Often scholars impose their own slants onto the material in these areas, without pausing to take the 'value-free' program seriously. Its importance lies in the fact that the follower of Khomeini or of Pope John Paul believes what she or he does with whatever vigor and intensity quite independently of what we think about the matter. It is the power of ideas and symbols which constitutes the dynamics of the real human world, not what we think of their truth (whoever 'we' are). So Religion as a subject, with its sensitivity about *epochē*, can help to remind the other human sciences about the importance of self-analysis and self-awareness as a method of trying to avoid the projection of our ideas and feelings onto those of others. This aspect of the field is truly *scientific*, because it tries to get at the deep human facts – the behavior and feelings and beliefs of human beings. Cantwell Smith also wishes to argue for a truly human science, thinking that aping the natural sciences is destructive of the genuinely scientific aspects of our humane explorations.

Much more needs to be said about how *epochē* and empathetic explorations are possible. I shall return to this 'much more' in a little while. The second main comment about the fact that such exploration is not peculiar to Religion as a subject concerns the famous question of definition. Really the demand for informed or structured empathy is a slogan, a program. If it is a valid slogan then it can be applied to all kinds of beliefs and values and not just traditionally religious ones (the cumulative traditions of which Smith speaks). The question which ought to exercise us pragmatically is this – How far can the insights and theories which arise out of religious material be used to illuminate secular beliefs and values? Is the study of traditional religion a good jumping off point for understanding other worldviews? I personally think it is, because there are sensitivities to symbolism and ritual for example that the Religion scholar has which can help to illuminate such phenomena as nationalism and other forms of secular ideology. The traffic however can often go the other way: some of Weber's ideas have influenced Religion, and more recently there has been an importation of ideas from anthropology – from writers such as Lévi-Strauss, Mary Douglas and Victor Turner.

However, the fact that we are first of all concerned with the data, that is the living human facts, does not mean that theories are to be eschewed. Sometimes Smith writes in a way that might be interpreted as being hostile to theory. This is because of his correct reaction against mere abstraction and inhumane forms of positivism. But it does seem to me that out of the particularities we can form typological accounts (now moving to the second meaning of the phrase 'phenomenology of religion') which are both mini-theories in themselves – for every classification is a primitive theory – and suggestive of questions which ask for explanations, and so further theorising. Thus is it right to classify the mysticism of differing religions together? The debate on the possible unity of all mysticism in recent writings from Stace and Zaehner onwards is an interesting and important one from various angles: it raises acute questions about the relationship between experience and its interpretation; it affects the way we explain the rise of the various movements and groups (Rhineland mystics, Persian Sufis, Theravāda Buddhism and so on); it relates to apologetic and other debates about the relationship of the religions; and so on.

Such theories belong to the scientific study of religion in that they have a descriptive or explanatory intent. This differs from theological or philosophical attempts to delineate or evaluate the ultimate. A theology properly speaking is meant to express the mind of a community or of an individual who feels identified with a certain tradition. Thus W. Cantwell Smith's recent *Towards A World Theology* looks forward to a kind of global faith, and tries to give it some preliminary articulation. A theology may have to take account of theories concerning religion; but it is not in main intent a theory of religion; it may be a theory about the ultimate, but that is a different matter. It is true that some reductionist theories of religion, such as Freud's in *The Future of an Illusion*, imply the falseness of traditional Christian and Jewish theology, and other forms of theism. Conversely a theology may wish to affirm the validity of religious experience. So there is an important interface between theory and theology. But theories can themselves treat the ultimate simply phenomenologically – that is, they can affirm the power of religious experience of the ultimate without affirming or denying the truth of the theologies of religions which affirm the ultimate. It seems to me that such

261

phenomenological theories represent the main substance of 'the science of religion', together with the data of the various traditions that form the basis upon which those theories are built.

But do such theories fall under Smith's category of the inhumane abstraction? Do they merely ape real science while distorting the nature of what it is we deal with? I think not. It is of deep personal significance for a Christian to discover (as Thomas Merton attempted) whether his spiritual life converges with that of Buddhist friends. This is both a personal and a theoretical question. It is clear that some of the deepest questions of method arise over the problem of whether we can clearly distinguish experience from interpretation (discussions which have had one expression in the writings assembled by Steven Katz in *Mysticism and Philosophical Analysis*). Again, the various theses and classifications which scholars ranging from Vittorio Lanternari to Bryan Wilson have advanced concerning new religious movements in the Third World and particularly among smaller scale societies are sketches of alternative living responses to the forces of White domination, economic change and social dislocation. The scholar can help to bring out the living options of peoples faced with these crises. Indeed the new religious movements are among other things exercises in the conservation and re-creation of meaning in lives where older meanings have been eroded and undermined. So there is no incompatibility between theory and humaneness.

But Smith's warnings are much to the point. He reminds us that there is an ethic of human research. The anthropologist who has no real interest in the villagers he studies, but only in the theory which they test, as walking data, is already in danger of so dehumanizing them that he could be accused of a heartless selfishness. But what lesson does this hold for us methodologically? It must surely tell us two things: that we are dealing not with moons and atoms, which have no feelings or wills, but with human beings, whose 'insides' are of crucial importance if we are to understand anything of what is *going on*; and that we as explorers of an aspect of the human condition have to cherish, in some sense, that which we explore – or rather, those whom we explore.

There is a paradox in this that needs to be brought into the open. For is there not a tension between this requirement of love of those whom we engage with as objects of our exploration and the scientific need for *epochē*? Our field, and many others in the humanities and social sciences, have been distorted enough by the biases of believers in describing their own and others' traditions. The demand of love may throw open the floodgates of subjectivity and propaganda. Does the Hitler-lover make the best historian of the Nazi period? The paradox is that the historian needs *epochē* and a degree of detachment, and yet also enthusiasm for his 'subject'. How do these things go together?

It is insufficiently appreciated that certain *human* qualities are needed for the exercise of phenomenology. It also turns out that those who are engaged in crosscultural explorations differ as to the traditions which they deal best with. I sometimes put this by saying: What you are good at in the study of religion depends on what you were in a previous life. I use this thought merely figuratively, for it is not for me to pre-judge whether the doctrine of reincarnation is true. It may turn out that one person is more drawn towards Buddhism and another towards Islam, and each will probably explore his or her 'own' religion better than the other. So there are human qualities which enter into the procedures of structured empathy.

Because religions are often so gripping, so dynamizing, so intense, there can of course be a tension between the demands of faith and the relative detachment needed for imaginative *epochē*. Conversely, atheistic and antireligious scholars can find it hard to enter into religion's point of view. So whereas the private convictions of the geologist do not affect, save indirectly, the quality of his work, there is a much tighter bond between capacity to deal empathetically with a faith and personal qualities. In saying this I am not trying to subjectivize the study of religion – except in so far as subjectivity is needed to explore subjectivity; I am not that is saying that the true picture of a given set of human and religious facts depends upon the 'observer's' subjective or existential choice or reaction. But I am saying that to get at something approximating a true picture of the other the Religion scientist needs to use his own powers of feeling and of entering imaginatively into the thought and action world of other human beings (again this is not something *peculiar* to religion as a field). It

263

is part of what we mean in the social sciences by 'participant observation'; it is part of the procedures of the humanist. And such capacities depend in part on wider attitudes and – to be blunt – on character.

The question of Hitler, to which I referred earlier, remains obscure. Does it mean that I need to be a Hitler-lover to understand him? In a sense yes, and in a sense no. It is important for us to take him as a person seriously, and doubtless we might find this impossible if bitterness at the enormity of his crimes affects us with special closeness. But if we are indeed to get into his soul we have to drop our preconceptions, and treat Hitler as a human being who had his own thought world: we can follow him through his Austrian childhood and relationship to his father and dear mother; through his scholastic failures and outcast status in Vienna; through his years in the trenches fighting in France . . . and so on. To do this is, as I say, to take him seriously as a human being. And what we are trying to do in all this after all is to uncover the facts – concerning the ideas and feelings that fueled his amazing meteoric and catastrophic career. But all this is strictly *empathy*, 'getting the feel of '. The facts when uncovered, the deep, human facts, do not entail in any way the rightness of his creed or program. Of course not: so we can still deplore his deeds once we have understood them.

There is here a largely unexplored area of enquiry about the way we use and convey feelings. For an empathetic description of another person and her values will have in some degree to be *evocative*. This implies some correspondence of feelings between people: and sometimes analogy. I cannot except by some analogy of imagination know what it feels like to give birth to a child or to fall in love with another man or to know what it feels like to actually kill someone. It is part of the function of fiction and drama and movies to help us with such imaginative leaps. Anyway, there is a lot to be done in exploring the geography of empathy. We may call this the human side of the methodology.

It is complicated by the fact that religious persons enter into relationship with various Foci of faith, such as Christ, Krishna, the goal of liberation, and so on. In so far as we practise *epochē* and attempt fairness of presentation we are methodologically agnostic about these Foci – neither affirming nor denying them. So we need a phenomenology which allows such Foci power, whether they exist or not. They can be *real*, even when they do not exist 'out there' (but how do we know whether God exists? – I think that when Jung gave that famous answer about whether he believed in God or not, namely that he *knew* it, he was referring to the reality of religious experience, not necessarily its validity, however that might be decided).

The fact that we must, to practice a phenomenological approach towards others, adopt a kind of 'neutralist' stance does often in the religiously committed induce a certain impatience, and it can in ourselves create tensions; but of course more judgmental, argumentative, evaluative, theological, committed stances in regard to our own or others' traditions is entirely compatible with it. How can you judge indeed if you do not know, and knowing here precedes judgment?

All this supposes that we have to understand our own feelings and presuppositions. So it seems to be part of the procedures for one who approaches a religion crossculturally that he or she should stimulate some degree of self-awareness. It is as though we should undergo axioanalysis – a kind of evaluational equivalent to psycho-analysis: what has also been called more broadly 'values clarification'. Or perhaps we might call it 'own-worldview analysis'. This incidentally represents a side benefit of the phenomenological approach – by looking at ourselves in the mirror of other cultures and points of view we come to a better knowledge of ourselves. And we may hope thereby also to get a better knowledge of the other by making ourselves transparent too – both a mirror and a window.

Thus it may turn out that when we are thinking about method we are or should be at least in part thinking about the personal qualities and attitudes which are needed in the religious researcher. One desirable quality is self-knowledge, as we have just indicated. Cantwell Smith is correct when he writes:

> It would seem to me relatively easy to argue, and indeed to demonstrate, that the attitude, the philosophy, and the general orientation of an author are of major consequence for any scholarly study; are at least equally important, and

> usually more important, than the method employed ...
> (pp. 15–16).

One may go further and emphasize too the intentions, and so indirectly the character of the scholar. But this is not a matter of moralizing: it is recognizing that sensitivity is important in the exploration of religion, and that so far as we are talking about the empirical study the intention to be descriptive (and not judgmental or untrue to the feelings and the beliefs of those with whom we may be concerned) is important.

The question of intention is important in part because the study of religion in the modern way has had to struggle with contending institutional forces on either side. On the one hand it has been hard sometimes to break away from both the assumptions and the institutional grip of the Divinity School; while on the other side the secular university, in which a kind of antireligious rationalism is strongly entrenched, suspects the study of religion as being crypto-Christian – not always without reason. It is sometimes hard to put across the idea that a substantial part of Religious Studies is concerned with trying to describe religions 'as they are', as human facts. But of course this is not the only area where the descriptive approach is foreign to people's initial thinking, for notoriously the task of understanding other values than our own has not been inculcated in most cultures, and schools are conceived as transmitters of home values and often look upon crosscultural empathy with some suspicion. So we are to some extent involved in an institutional struggle, to convey the message that the understanding of worldviews and of the people and social collectivities in which they are embodied is an important part of the humanities and the social sciences, and can be done with objectivity, that is to say with a fair degree of descriptive success. But this requires integrity of intentions, and this in turn needs a degree of self-analysis about our own individual assumptions which some people find hard to achieve. We have to steer between religious and anti-religious enthusiasm of a degree which precludes any significant amount of distancing on the one hand and a cold and often pseudoscientific limitation of enquiry to externals on the other.

But though the qualities of the individual who researches and explores is important, as I have argued, it does not follow that we have to be individualistic in regard to the object of enquiry. That is, though a certain personalism has to be incorporated into our thinking about methodology, we scarcely need to confine ourselves, as Cantwell Smith rather suggests, to interpersonal relationships in our investigations. That is, we do not need to ignore an important insight of, and indeed the central justification for, the social sciences. We do not need to ignore the social dimension of religion: ritual and religious organization, religious creeds – there is much in typical religion which can only be understood as arising out of and through collectivities. It is not possible to analyse most religion on a purely individual basis, even if conversely it is quite wrong to forget that ultimately collectivities are composed of individuals who have their own private experiences and acts of will. Naturally, religions and worldviews differ markedly as to the degree of emphasis placed upon the individual. Modern Protestantism in particular has moved very far in an individualistic and experience-oriented direction. It is unwise to use this as the sole or even main model for understanding historic religions, and this is a danger in Cantwell Smith's emphasis upon faith, which is a concept (and a reality) characteristic of only one main motif in religious history. In brief, the fact that we may emphasize personal qualities and intentions in the investigator of religions and worldviews does not entail a personalistic analysis of religions, but only of those which indeed are genuinely individualistic.

We may sum up this part of my argument by stating three conclusions arising from Cantwell Smith's misgivings:

(1) The intentions of the religious researcher are important, and it is important that she or he clearly and honestly intends (among other things) to strive for descriptive success in writing or speaking about religious 'phenomena', i.e. about people in so far as they are thinking, feeling or acting religiously.

(2) Personal qualities are a qualification, for certain sorts or characteristics are necessary for good descriptive success, such as warmth, empathy, some degree of detachment, integrity in pursuing descriptive exploration, imaginative skill and treating other human beings as indeed human beings.

(3) The personalism here of method does not entail however

that we should ignore collectivities in the phenomena – typically the object of the social sciences.

In any case, it is worth learning from the discussion also that disputes about method are often in the last resort not really about method but about intentions and *programme*. The divisions which exist in our field are really more about differing programmes and value emphases. Those who argue for the importance of the 'insider', or for the necessity for a certain subjectivity, are concerned to validate the practise of theology of one kind or another: they think that religious truth is the primary quest. On the other hand the objectivists are often really arguing that it is more important to find out the facts of religion, the way religions and worldviews actually exist and function as phenomena, the modes in which they have power, or lack it. Neither the quest for truth nor the search to discover the realities of human religion can be cut out: they can feed one another.

But the concern for understanding how religion actually works is a relatively new one. It is an important one, and on the whole has less institutional expression that the theological-philosophical search for truth. The history of religions and the science of religion are still relatively weak in the academic scene. Practically every campus has a philosophy department, but many do not have any pluralistic, empirical enquiry into religions. Consequently, the preoccupation with method in the enquiry into religion is itself in part an expression of a desire for a stronger institutionalization of the history of religions and its empirical partners.

Moreover, I think we could argue on solid grounds that a good basis of knowledge about religion and religions as having such human power as they have (and divine power no doubt so long as this is humanly registered and expressed) is a necessary condition of a sensitive exploration of truth. The real problem with traditional theology is not that the latter goes in for judgments and constructs worldviews, but that on the empirical and descriptive, historical side it so restricts enquiry through the modes of its institutionalization. It is naturally enough so very selective as to what historically it treats in depth, and often thus blocks the wider flourishing, even within Christianity and its penumbra, of descriptive studies.

Now one of the reasons why I myself have devoted a lot of my energies to Religion as a field is that I believe passionately that a wider knowledge of the human world is good for us, not just from a technical point of view – though that is important enough, when we consider the phenomenological ignorance and incompetence of many of our nuclear-wielding leaders and their advisers – but because we become more sensitive and informed human beings. Wilfred Cantwell Smith refers to the way our field makes us 'more human', and I guess that he means that we deepen our experience through knowledge of what other men have thought and felt and done.

Because this is so, the science of religion is not simply a matter of technique, though we can do with more help on this; it is a matter of knowledge and sensitivity too. These are important methodological points. In this essay I have stressed the human qualities which we in Religion need: moderation, openness, warmth, imagination, concern with other cultures than our own, learning – above all the desire for descriptive and evocative success. In the human sciences human qualities are highly relevant. Cantwell Smith is right to draw attention to this side of the matter: it is methodology with a human face.

All this may suggest that we underrate the importance of literature, film, television and so forth as tools, beyond the written word, for giving expression to crosscultural knowledge. But that itself raises a nest of questions which cannot be dealt with here: namely the state of mind and culture of those to whom we communicate our findings and the fruits of exploration. That is another human dimension of Religion as a science.

To sum up: Cantwell Smith's misgivings remind us that human qualities are a vital part of the tools of our trade. Above all we need right intentions.

Section D

BIBLIOGRAPHY OF THE WORKS OF WILFRED CANTWELL SMITH

BIBLIOGRAPHY

BOOKS

Modern Islām in India: A Social Analysis. Lahore, Minerva, 1943.
Revised edition: London, V. Gollancz, '1946' (*sc.* 1947).
Reissued: Lahore, Sh. M. Ashraf, 1963, 1969; New York, Russell & Russell, 1972; and pirated edition, Lahore, Ripon, 1947 (with a spurious chapter 'Towards Pakistan' by an unknown other hand).
New edition: New Delhi, Usha, 1979.
Pakistan as an Islamic State. Lahore, Sh. M. Ashraf, '1951' (*sc.* 1954).
Islam in Modern History. Princeton, Princeton University Press, 1957.
Reissued: London, Oxford University Press, 1958; New York, New American Library (Mentor Books), 1959; London, New English Library (Mentor Books), 1965; Princeton and London, Princeton University Press (Princeton Paperback), 1977.
Taped for Recording for the Blind, Inc., Washington, 1973.
Translated into: Arabic (pirated, 1960; authorized, 1975), Swedish (1961), French (1962), Indonesian (1962–1964), German (1963), and Japanese (1974). Portions translated into: Urdu (1958–1959, 1960) and Arabic (1960).
The Faith of Other Men. Toronto, Canadian Broadcasting Corporation, 1962.
Enlarged edition: New York, New American Library, 1963.
Reissued: New York, New American Library, (Mentor Books), 1965; London, New English Library (Mentor Books), 1965; New York and London, Harper & Row (Torchbook), 1972.
Translated into: Swedish (1965).
Part II ('The Christian in a Religiously Plural World') reprinted in *Religious Diversity* (infra) in slightly abridged form; also in

273

John Hick and Brian Hebblethwaite, edd., *Christianity and Other Religions*, [London:] Collins (Fount Paperbacks), 1980, pp. 87–107.

The Meaning and End of Religion: A New Approach to the Religious Traditions of Mankind. New York, Macmillan, 1963. Reissued: New York, New American Library (Mentor Books), 1964; London, New English Library (Mentor Books), 1965; San Francisco, Harper & Row, and London: S.P.C.K., 1978.

Modernisation of a Traditional Society. Bombay, Calcutta, etc., Asia Publishing House, 1965.

Chapter 1, reprinted in slightly abridged form in *Religious Diversity* (infra).

Questions of Religious Truth. New York, Charles Scribner's Sons; and London, V. Gollancz Ltd., 1967.

Translated into: Japanese (1971).

Second chapter ('Is the Qur'an the Word of God?') reprinted in slightly abridged form in *Religious Diversity* (infra).

Religious Diversity. Willard G. Oxtoby, ed. New York and London, Harper & Row, 1976.

New edition: New York, Crossroad, 1982.

Belief and History. Charlottesville: University Press of Virginia, 1977.

Faith and Belief. Princeton: Princeton University Press, 1979.

Towards a World Theology. London, Macmillan, and Philadelphia, Westminster, 1981.

On Understanding Islam. Selected Studies. The Hague, Paris, New York: Mouton. 1981. 351 pp. (Religion and Reason: method and theory in the study and interpretation of religion. Jacques Waardenburg, gen. ed.; #19.)

ARTICLES ON RELIGION GENERALLY

'The Comparative Study of Religion: Reflections on the Possibility and Purpose of a Religious Science', *McGill University, Faculty of Divinity, Inaugural Lectures* (Montreal, McGill University, 1950), pp. 39–60.

'The Christian and the Religions of Asia', *Changing Asia: Report of the Twenty-Eighth Annual Couchiching Conference: A Joint*

Project of the Canadian Institute on Public Affairs and the Canadian Broadcasting Corporation (Toronto, Canadian Institute on Public Affairs, 1959), pp. 9–16.

Reprinted: *Occasional Papers.* Department of Missionary Studies, International Missionary Council (World Council of Churches), London, no. 5 (April, 1960); also as 'Christianity's Third Great Challenge', *The Christian Century* 77:17 (April 27, 1960) 505–08; also, abridged, *The Beacon*, London, 39 (1962), 337–40.

'Comparative Religion: Whither – and Why?', Mircea Eliade and Joseph M. Kitagawa, eds., *The History of Religions: Essays in Methodology* (Chicago, The University of Chicago Press, 1959), pp. 31–58.

Reprinted in abridged form in *Religious Diversity* (supra).

Translated into: Urdu (1962), Japanese (1962), and German (1963).

'Mankind's Religiously Divided History Approaches Self Consciousness', *Harvard Divinity Bulletin* 29:1 (1964), pp. 1–17.

Reprinted in slightly abridged form in *Religious Diversity* (supra).

Translated into: German (1967).

'Secularism: The Problem Posed', *Seminar*, New Delhi, 67 (1965), pp. 10–12.

'Religious Atheism? Early Buddhist and Recent American', *Milla wa-Milla*, Melbourne, 6 (1966), pp. 5–30.

Reprinted: John Bowman, ed., *Comparative Religion: The Charles Strong Trust Lectures 1961–70* (Leiden, E. J. Brill, 1972), pp. 53–81.

'The Mission of the Church and the Future of Missions', George Johnston and Wolfgang Roth, eds., *The Church in the Modern World: Essays in Honour of James Sutherland Thomson* (Toronto, The Ryerson Press, 1967), pp. 154–170.

' "Traditional Religions and Modern Culture" ', *Proceedings of the XIth International Congress of the International Association for the History of Religions*, I, The Impact of Modern Culture on Traditional Religions (Leiden, E. J. Brill, 1968), pp. 55–72.

Reprinted in slightly abridged form in *Religious Diversity* (supra).

'Secularity and the History of Religion', Albert Schlitzer, ed., *The Spirit and Power of Christian Secularity* (Notre Dame and London, University of Notre Dame Press, 1969), pp. 33–58. Discussion follows, pp. 59–70.

'University Studies of Religion in a Global Context', *Study of Religion in Indian Universities: A Report of the Consultation held in Bangalore in September, 1967* ([Bangalore], Bangalore Press, n.d. [1970]), pp. 74–87.

'Participation: The Changing Christian Role in Other Cultures,' *Occasional Bulletin*, Missionary Research Library, New York, 20:4 (1969) 1–13.

Reprinted: *Religion and Society*, Bangalore, 17:1 (1970) 56–74; in abridged form in Gerald H. Anderson and Thomas F. Stransky, eds., *Mission Trends No. 2* (New York, Paulist Press, and Grand Rapids, Eerdmans, 1975), pp. 218–29; and in *Religious Diversity* (supra).

'The Study of Religion and the Study of the Bible,' *Journal of the American Academy of Religion* 39 (1971) 131–40.

Reprinted with minor alterations in *Religious Diversity* (supra).

'A Human View of Truth,' *SR: Studies in Religion/Sciences religieuses,* I (1971) 6–24.

Reprinted: John Hick, ed., *Truth and Dialogue: The Relationship between World Religions* (London, Sheldon Press, 1974); *Truth and Dialogue in World Religions: Conflicting Truth-Claims* (Philadelphia, Westminster Press, 1974), pp. 20–44, with a new addendum, 'Conflicting Truth-Claims: A Rejoinder,' ibid., pp. 156–62.

'Programme Notes for a Mitigated Cacophony' (a review article on R. C. Zaehner, *Concordant Discord*, 1970), *The Journal of Religion* 53 (1973) 377–81.

'On "Dialogue and Faith": A Rejoinder' [to Eric J. Sharpe, 'Dialogue and Faith,' in the same issue], *Religion* 3 (1973) 106–14.

' "The Finger That Points to the Moon": Reply to Per Kværne' [Kværne, ' "Comparative Religion: Whither – and Why?" A Reply to Wilfred Cantwell Smith,' in the same issue], *Temenos*, Helsinki, 9 (1973) 169–72.

'World Religions' (in the section, 'What's in Store for '74? Looking Ahead in Various Areas of Contemporary Life'), *The Christian Century*, 91:1 (1974) 16.

'Religion as Symbolism,' introduction to Propædia, part 8, 'Religion,' *Encyclopædia Britannica*, 15th ed. (Chicago, Encyclopædia Britannica, 1974), I, pp. 498–500.

'Methodology and the Study of Religion: Some Misgivings', Robert D. Baird, ed., *Methodological Issues in Religious Studies* (Chico, Calif., New Horizons Press, 1975), pp. 1–25 ('Discussion,' pp. 25–30). 'Is the Comparative Study of Religion Possible? Panel Discussion,' with Jacob Neusner, Hans H. Penner, ibid., pp. 95–109. 'Rejoinder,' pp. 123–24.

'An Historian of Faith Reflects on What We are Doing Here'. Donald G. Dawe and John B. Carman, edd., *Christian Faith in a Religiously Plural World* (Maryknoll, New York: Orbis, 1978), pp. 139–48.

Divisiveness and Unity', Gremillion, Joseph, ed., *Food/Energy and the Major Faiths* (Maryknoll, New York: Orbis, 1978), pp. 71–85.

'Belief: a reply to a response', *Numen*, 27 (1980): [247]–55.

'An Attempt at Summation', Gerald H. Anderson and Thomas F. Stransky, edd., *Christ's Lordship and Pluralism*. Maryknoll, New York: Orbis. 1981. pp. 196–203.

'Traditions in Contact and Change: towards a history of religion in the singular', Slater, Peter, and Donald Wiebe, with Maurice Boutin and Harold Coward, edd., *Traditions in Contact and Change: Proceedings of the XIVth Congress of the International Association for the History of Religions*. Waterloo: Wilfrid Laurier University Press, 1983. pp. [1]–23.

ARTICLES ON EDUCATION, WEST/EAST STUDIES, AND CULTURE CONCERN GENERALLY

'Achievement Tests in History,' *Education*, Lucknow, 24:1 (1945) 57–62.

'Objective Tests in History,' *Education*, Lucknow, 24:2 (1945) 53–60.
Reprinted: *The Punjab Educational Journal*, Lahore, 29 (1944) 309–13, 336–45.

'The Place of Oriental Studies in a Western University,' *Diogenes* no. 16 (1956) 104–11.

Translated into: French (1956), German (1957), and Spanish (1958).

'The YMCA and the Present,' *Bulletin*, National Council of Young Men's Christian Associations of Canada, Toronto, 34:4 (June, 1960) 3–5.

'Non-Western Studies: The Religious Approach', *A Report on an Invitational Conference on the Study of Religion in the State University. Held October 23–25, 1964 at Indiana University Medical Center* (New Haven, The Society for Religion in Higher Education, [1965]), pp. 50–62. Comments and discussion follow, pp. 62–67.

'Objectivity and the Humane Sciences: A New Proposal', *Transactions of the Royal Society of Canada* (Ottawa, Royal Society of Canada, 1975), 4/12 (1974), pp. 81–102.
Reprinted in abridged form in *Religious Diversity* (supra).
Reprinted in: Claude Fortier et al., *Symposium on the Frontiers and Limitations of Knowledge/Colloque sur les frontières et limites du savoir* (Ottawa, Royal Society of Canada, 1975), pp. 81–102.

The Role of Asian Studies in the American University. The plenary address of the New York State Conference for Asian Studies, Colgate University, October 10–12, 1975. [Hamilton, N.Y.]: Colgate University, [1976]. (Pamphlet.)

'The University,' Review article of: Murray Ross, *The University: The Anatomy of Academe*, New York, 1976, in *Dalhousie Review*, 57 (1977–78): 540–49.

'Thinking about Persons', *Humanitas*, 15 (1979): 147–52.

'History in Relation to both Science and Religion', *Scottish Journal of Religious Studies*, 2 (1981): [3]–10.

ARTICLES ON ISLAMIC SUBJECTS

'The Mughal Empire and the Middle Class: A Hypothesis', *Islamic Culture*, Hyderabad, 18 (1944), pp. 349–63.

'Lower-Class Uprisings in the Mughal Empire', *Islamic Culture*, Hyderabad, 20 (1946), pp. 21–40.

'The Muslim World', *One Family* (Toronto, Missionary Society of the Church of England in Canada, 2 volumes 1947–48), II, pp. 27–32.

'Hyderabad: Muslim Tragedy', *Middle East Journal*, 4 (1950), pp. 27–51.

'The Muslims and the West', *Foreign Policy Bulletin*, New York, 31:2 (October, 1951), pp. 5–7.

'Islam Confronted by Western Secularism, (A): Revolutionary Reaction', Dorothea Seelye Franck, ed., *Islam in the Modern World: A Series of Addresses Presented at the Fifth Annual Conference on Middle East Affairs, Sponsored by the Middle East Institute* (Washington, Middle East Institute, 1951), pp. 19–30.
Translated into: Arabic (1953).

'Modern Turkey – Islamic Reformation?' *Islamic Culture*, Hyderabad, 25:1 (1952), pp. 155–86.
Reprinted in abridged form, with comments: *Die Welt des Islams*, n.F. 3 (1954) pp. 269–73.
Translated into: Turkish (1953).

'Pakistan', *Collier's Encyclopædia*, 1953.

'The Institute of Islamic Studies [McGill University],' *The Islamic Literature*, Lahore, 5 (1953), pp. 173–76.

'The Importance of Muhammad' (review article), *The Canadian Forum* (September, 1954), pp. 135–36.

'The Intellectuals in the Modern Development of the Islamic World', Sydney Nettleton Fisher, ed., *Social Forces in the Middle East* (Ithaca, Cornell University Press, 1955), pp. 190–204.

'Propaganda (Muslim)', *Twentieth Century Encyclopædia of Religious Knowledge* (Grand Rapids, Baker, 2 volumes, 1955), II, pp. 767–68.

'Ahmadiyyah', *Encyclopædia of Islam*, new edition (Leiden and London, E. J. Brill, 1956).
Translated into: French (1956).

'Amir Ali, Sayyid', *Encyclopædia of Islam*, new edition (Leiden and London, E. J. Brill, 1956).
Translated into: French (1956).

'The Christian and the Near East Crisis,' *The British Weekly*, London, 138, no. 3658 (December 20, 1956), p. 5.
Also published in: *The Presbyterian Record*, Toronto, 82:1 (January, 1957), pp. 16–17.

The Muslim World (pamphlet, Current Affairs for the Canadian Forces series, X, no. 4). Ottawa, Bureau of Current Affairs, Department of National Defense, 1956), 26 pp.
Translated into: French (1956).
'Islam in the Modern World', *Current History*, 32 (1957), pp. 321–25.
Reprinted: *Enterprise*, Karachi, January 4, 1958; *Morning News*, Karachi, April 12, 1959.
'Independence Day in Indonesia', *The McGill News*, Montreal, Winter, 1957, pp. 23–24.
'Aga Khan III', *Encyclopædia Americana* (1958).
'Law and Ijtihad in Islam: Some Considerations on Their Relation to Each Other and to Ultimate and Immediate Problems', *Dawn*, Karachi, January 5, 1958. Reprinted: *Pakistan Quarterly*, Karachi, 8 (1958), pp. 29–31, 63; also in *International Islamic Colloquium Papers: December 29, 1957 – January 8, 1958* (Lahore, Panjab University Press, 1960), pp. 111–14.
Translated into: Urdu (1958), Arabic (1960).
'Some Similarities and Differences between Christianity and Islam: An Essay in Comparative Religon', James Kritzeck and R. Bayly Winder, eds., *The World of Islam: Studies in Honour of Philip K. Hitti* (London, Macmillan; and New York, St. Martin's Press, 1959), pp. 47–59.
Translated into: Urdu (1964).
'India, Religion and Philosophy: Islam', *Encyclopædia Americana* (1960).
Reprinted: W. Norman Brown, ed., *India, Pakistan, Ceylon*, revised edition (Philadelphia, University of Pennsylvania Press; London, Oxford University Press [1964]), pp. 104–07.
'Modern Muslim Historical Writing in English', C. H. Philips, ed., *Historians of India, Pakistan and Ceylon* (Historical Writing on the Peoples of Asia, 1) (London, Oxford University Press, 1961), pp. 319–31.
'The Comparative Study of Religion in General and the Study of Islam as a Religion in Particular', *Colloque sur la sociologie musulmane: Actes, 11–14 septembre 1961* (Correspondance d'Orient, 5) (Bruxelles, publications du Centre pour l'étude des problèmes du monde musulman contemporain [1962]), pp. 217–31.

'Iblis', *Encyclopædia Britannica* (1962).

'The Historical Development in Islam of the Concept of Islam as an Historical Development', Bernard Lewis and P. M. Holt, eds., *Historians of the Middle East* (Historical Writing on the Peoples of Asia, 4) (London, Oxford University Press, 1962), pp. 484–502.

'The "Ulamā" in Indian Politics', C. H. Philips, ed., *Politics and Society in India* (London, George Allen & Unwin Ltd., 1963), pp. 39–51.

'Druze', *Encyclopædia Britannica* (1963).

'Koran (Qur'ān)', *Encyclopædia Britannica* (1964).

'The Concept of Shari'a among Some Mutakallimun', George Makdisi, ed., *Arabic and Islamic Studies in Honor of Hamilton A. R. Gibb* (Leiden, E. J. Brill, 1965), pp. 581–602.

'The Islamic near East: Intellectual Role of Librarianship,' *Library Quarterly 35* (1965) 283–94. Discussion follows, pp. 294–97.
  Reprinted: Tsuen-Hsuin Tsien and Howard W. Winger, edd., *Area Studies and the Library* (Chicago & London, The University of Chicago Press, 1966), pp. 81–92 (92–95).

'The Crystallization of Religious Communities in Mughul India', Mojtaba Minovi and Iraj Afshar, eds., *Yād-Nāme-ye-Irāini* [sic]*-ye Minorsky* (Ganjine-ye Taḥqiqāt-e Irāni, no. 57; Publications of Tehran university, no. 1241) (Tehran, Intishārāt Dāneshgāh, 1969), pp. 197–220.

'The End is Near' [annotated translation from Urdū of Ṣiddiq Ḥasan Khān, reputed author, *Iqtirāb al-Sā'ah*]. Published anonymously in: Aziz Ahmad and G. E. von Grunebaum, eds., *Muslim Self-Statement in India and pakistan 1857–1968* (Wiesbaden, Otto Harrassowitz, 1970), pp. 85–89.

Orientalism and Truth: A Public Lecture in Honor of T. Cuyler Young, Horatio Whitridge Garrett Professor of Persian Language and History, Chairman of the Department of Oriental Studies. Princeton, Program in Near Eastern Studies, Princeton University, 1969, 16 pp. (Pamphlet.)

'Arkān', David P. Little, ed., *Essays on Islamic Civilization Presented to Niyazi Berkes*, Leiden: E. J. Brill, 1976. pp. [303]–16.
  Translated into: Turkish (1977).

'Faith and Belief (some considerations from the Islamic instance)' and 'Faith and Belief (some considerations from the Christian instance)'. *Al-Hikmat: A Research Journal of the Department of Philosophy*, University of the Punjab, Lahore, 6: 1–20, 21–43, '1975' [sc. 1976].

'Interpreting religious interrelations: An Historian's View of Christian and Muslim', *SR: Studies in Religion/Sciences religieuses*, 6 (1976–77); 515–26.

'Tauḥid and the Integration of Personality.' *Studies in Islam*: Quarterly Journal of the Indian Institute of Islamic Studies, New Delhi, 16 (1979): 127–28. (Discussion, pp. 128–29.)

'Aziz Ahmad, 1913–78.' (obituary), *Proceedings of the Royal Society of Canada*, 18 (1980): [44]–46.

'The True Meaning of Scripture: an empirical historian's non-reductionist interpretation of the Qur'an', *International Journal of Middle East Studies*, 11 (1980): [487]–505.

'Understanding Islam', *Funk & Wagnalls New Encyclopædia 1981 Yearbook*. n.p. [sc. New York]: Funk & Wagnalls, 1981. pp. 22–35.

'Faith as Tasdīq', Parviz Morewedge, ed., *Islamic Philosophical Theology*. (Albany: State University of New York Press, n.d. [sc. 1981]), pp. 96–119.

'Islamic Studies and the History of Religions', Isma'īl Raji al Fārūqī, ed., *Essays in Islamic and Comparative Studies: papers presented to the 1979 meeting of the American Academy of Religion*. n.p.: International Institute of Islamic Thought, 1402/1982. pp. 2–7.

PUBLICATIONS IN TRANSLATION

Arabic

('Islam Confronted by Western Secularism: Revolutionary Reaction', 1951) 'Al-Islām yuwājih al-'ilmāniyah al-gharbiyah', trans. Isḥāq Mūsá al-Ḥusayni with notes by 'Ali 'Abd al-Wāḥid Wāfi, Philip K. Hitti, et al., *Al-Islām fi naẓar al-Gharb* (Bayrūt, Dār Bayrūt, 1953), pp. 38–59.

(*Islam in Modern History*, 1957, partial translation) 'Al-Islām wa al-taṭawwur', 'Al-Islām fi al-ta'rikh al-ḥadith', Niqūlā Ziyādah, ed., *Dirāsāt Islāmiyah* (Bayrūt, Dār al-Andalus, 1960), pp. 295–402.

(*Islam in Modern History*, 1957, pirated edition, abridged) *Al-Islām fi al-ta'rikh al-ḥadith* (Kutub siyāsiyah, 163). Cairo, n.d. [1960].

(*Islam in Modern History*, 1957, authorized translation) *Al-Islām fi al-ta'rikh al-ḥadith*, trans. and with a foreword by Dr. M. Kāmil Ḥusayn. Bayrūt, al-Mu'assasah al-'Arabiyah li-al-baḥth wa-al-nashr, 1975.

French

('The Place of Oriental Studies in a Western University,' 1956) 'Le Rôle de l'université dans un monde à civilisations multiples,' *Diogène*, Paris, 16 (1956) 3–13. Traduit par Nicole Laming.

('Ahmadiyyah,' 1956) 'Ahmadiyyah', *Encyclopédie de l'Islam*, nouvelle édition, Leiden and Paris, E. J. Brill, 1956.

('Amir Ali, Sayyid,' 1956) 'Amir Ali, Sayyid,' *Encyclopédie de l'Islam*, nouvelle édition, Leiden and Paris, E. J. Brill, 1956.

(*The Muslim World*, 1956) *Le monde musulman* (brochure, in the series Actualités, revue destinée aux forces canadiennes, X, no. 4). Ottawa, Bureau des actualités, Ministère de la Défense nationale, 1956, 26 pp.

(*Islam in Modern History*, 1957) *L'Islam dans le monde moderne*, préface et traduction de A. Guimbretière. Paris, Payot, 1962.

German

('The Place of Oriental Studies in a Western University,' 1956) 'Die Orientwissenschaft an einer Universität des Westens.' *Diogenes*, Köln-Marienburg, 16 (1957) 522–30.

(*Islam in Modern History*, 1957) *Der Islam in der Gegenwart*, übertragen von Hermann Stiehl. Frankfurt und Hamburg, Fischer Bücherei, 1963.

('Comparative Religion: Whither – and Why?' 1959) 'Vergleichende Religionswissenschaft: wohin – warum?' übersetzt von Dr. Elizabeth Schmitz-Mayr-Harting. Mircea Eliade und Joseph M. Kitagawa, hrsg., *Grundfragen der Religionswissenschaft: Acht Studien* (Salzburg, Otto Müller Verlag, 1963), pp. 75–105, 239–56.

('Mankind's Religiously Divided History Approaches Self-Consciousness,' 1964) 'Das erwachende Selbstbewusstsein von der geschichtlichen Vielfalt der Religionen,' von Hans-Joachim Klimkeit ins Deutsche übertragen, Rudolf Thomas, hrsg., *Religion und Religionen: Festschrift für Gustav Mensching zu seinem 65. Geburtstag* (Bonn, Ludwig Rohrscheid Verlag, 1967), pp. 190–208.

Indonesian

(*Islam in Modern History*, 1957) *Islam dalam sedjarah modern*, diter-djemahkan oleh Abusalamah. Djakarta, Bhratara, 2 volumes, 1962–64.

Japanese

('Comparative Religion: Whither – and Why?' 1959) 'Korekara no hikaku-shūkyōgaku no arikata', M. Eliade, J. M. Kitagawa, hen., *Shūkyōgaku nyumon*, Kishimoto Hideo, kanyaku (Tokyo, Tōkyō daigaku-shuppankai, 1962), pp. 47–84. Reprinted 1966.

'Shoshūkyō no kyōryoku wa kanōka – Jinrui kyōdōtai e rekishi-teki shimei-kan o' ['Is inter-religious co-operation possible? The problem of world community in historical perspective'], *Yomiuri Shimbun*, Tokyo, January 9, 1966, p. 11. (Published only in Japanese.)

(*Questions of Religious Truth*, 1967) *Shūkyō no shinri*, Kasai Minoru, yaku. Tokyo, Riso Sha, 1971. (Shūkyō shisōsen sho, 10).

(*Islam in Modern History*, 1957) *Gendai ni okeru isuramu*, Nakamura Kojiro, yaku. Tokyo, Kinokuniya, 1974.

Spanish

('The Place of Oriental Studies in a Western University,' 1956) 'La Función de la universidad en el complejo cultural de nuestro mundo,' *Diógenes*, Buenos Aires, 3 (1958) 3–12.

Swedish

(*Islam in Modern History*, 1957) *Islam i modern tid*, förord av H. S. Nyberg, till svenska av Ulla Carlsted. Stockholm, Natur och Kultur, 1961.
(*The Faith of Other Men*, 1963) *Människor av annan tro*, till svenska av Axel Ljungberg och Alf Ahlberg. Stockholm, Natur och Kultur, 1965.

Turkish

('Modern Turkey – Islamic Reformation?' 1952) 'Modern Türkiye dini bir reforma mï gidiyor?' *Ilâhiyat Fakültesi Dergisi*, Ankara, 2 (1953) 7–20.
('Arkān,' 1976) *'Erkân,'* cev. Mehmet Dağ. *Islâm Ilimleri Enstitüsü Dergisi*, Ankara, 3 (1977): 301–14.

Urdu

'Ek Sawāl' ['A Question'], Aligarh Maygazin, Aligarh, 1955, pp. 81–83. (Published only in Urdu.)
(*Islam in Modern History*, 1957, partial translation) 'Islām in māḍarn hisṭari: Ek bāb kā tarjamah,' Mutarjim: Ziyā'u-l-Ḥasan Fārūqi, *Burhān*, Delhi, 14 (1958) 285–300, 349–64; 15 (1959) 45–58.
(*Islam in Modern History*, 1957, partial paraphrase) 'Pākistān ki Islāmi riyāsat, parofaysar Ismith ki naẓar men,' paraphrase by 'Abdu-r-Raḥmān 'Abd, *Chirāgh-i-Rāh* (Naẓariyah'-i Pākistān nambar), Karachi, 12:12 (December, 1960) 277–90. 'Istidrāk,' (Khurshid Aḥmad), pp. 290–94. 'Muzākirah: Pākistān awr

Islāmi naẓariyah – Ḍākṭar Wilfarayḍ Kaynṭwal Ismith' ['Discussion: Pakistan and Islamic theory']. (Response to, and elaboration of, pp. 277–94; published only in Urdu.) pp. 363–66.

('Comparative Religion: Whither – and Why?' 1959) 'Mazhab kā taqābuli muṭāli'ah: Kiyūṇ awr kis ṭaraḥ,' mutarjamah'-i jināb Sayyid Mubārizu-d-Din Ṣāḥib Raf'at awr Ḍākṭar Abū Naṣr Muḥammad Ṣāḥib Khālidi, *Burhān*, Delhi, 49 (1962) 197–216, 262–81, 348–55.

('Some Similarities and Differences between Christianity and Islam,' 1959) 'Islām awr Masiḥiyat – Kuchh farq, kuchh yaksāniyān: Ek taqābuli muṭāli'ah'-i mazāhib'. *Dunyā-e Islām*, tarjamah'-i Sayyid Hāshimi Faridābādī (Lahore, Maqbūl Akayḍami, 1964), pp. 73–94.

Section E

NOTES ON CONTRIBUTORS

NOTES ON CONTRIBUTORS

John B. Carman was born in India in 1930. After an early education in India, he received a B.A. from Haverford College, and a B.D., M.A., and Ph.D. from Yale. From 1957–63 he taught in India at Bangalore and Ramapatnam. Since then he has taught at Harvard where he is presently Professor of Comparative Religion, Chairman of the History of Religion Department, and Director of the Center for the Study of World Religions. His articles have ranged widely over Hindu Life and Thought, Relations between Christians and Hindus, Comparative Religion, and Christian Theological Interpretations of Religion. He has been involved in the writing of five books: the translation of W. Brede Kristensen's *The Meaning of Religion*, 1960; *Study of Religion in Indian Universities*, 1967; *Village Christians and Hindu Culture*, 1968; *The Theology of Rāmānuja*, 1974; *Christian Faith in a Religiously Plural World*, 1978.

John Hick was born in England in 1922 and educated at Edinburgh and Oxford Universities and Westminster College Cambridge. He has taught in the Philosophy Department at Cornell University, at Princeton Theological Seminary (where he was Stuart Professor of Christian Philosophy), at Cambridge University, and as H. G. Wood Professor of Theology at Birmingham University, and is now Danforth Professor of Religion at Claremont Graduate School, Claremont, California. He has been president of the Society for the Study of Theology, U.K., and is general editor of Macmillan's Library of Philosophy and Religion, and serves on the editorial boards of *Religious Studies* and *The Journal of Religion*. He is the author of *Faith and Knowledge, Philosophy of Religion, Evil and the God of Love, The Center of Christianity, Arguments for the Existence of God, God and the Universe of Faiths, Death and Eternal Life, God has many names, The Second Christianity*, and (with Michael Goulder) *Why Believe in God?* and is editor of *The Existence of God, Faith and the*

Philosophers, Classical and Contemporary Readings in the Philosophy of Religion, The Many-faced Argument (with A. C. McGill), *Truth and Dialogue, The Myth of God Incarnate,* and *Christianity and other Religions* (with Brian Hebblethwaite). He has lectured in numerous universities in India, Sri Lanka, Holland and Sweden as well as the U.S.A., Canada, and U.K. He holds doctorates of the universities of Oxford (D.Phil.), Cambridge (Ph.D.), Edinburgh (D.Litt.), and Uppsala (Hon.Teol.Dr.).

Louis Jacobs was born in 1920 in Manchester, England. He was educated at Manchester Central High School and University College London. He holds B.A. and Ph.D. degrees from London University. He is presently Rabbi of the New London Synagogue, Lecturer in Talmud and Jewish Mysticism at Leo Baeck College London, and President of the London Society for the Study of Religion. His many books include: *Studies in Talmudic Logic and Methodology; Principles of the Jewish Faith; A Jewish Theology; Jewish Theological Testimonies: Hasidic Prayer; Theology in the Responsa; Teyku: The Unsolved Problem in the Babylonian Talmud.*

J. L. Mehta holds the degrees of M.A. and Ph.D. from Banaras Hindu University. He taught at Mathura and Jaipur until 1947, and then at Banaras Hindu University from 1947 to 1972 where he became Professor of Philosophy. From 1971–73 he was Professor of Philosophy at the University of Hawaii, and from 1968–69 and 1970–78 he was Visiting Professor at the Harvard Center for the Study of World Religions. He was also a Humboldt Fellow at the Universities of Cologne and Freiburg from 1957–58, and a Whitney-Fulbright Lecturer in the U.S.A. 1964–65. He has written widely in Indian and Western philosophical and religious topics in various Indian and American Journals, and his books include *The Philosophy of Martin Heidegger* (1967, 71, 76) and the English translation of Walter Biemel's *Martin Heidegger* (1976).

Seyyed Hossein Nasr was born in Teheran where he received his early education. He later read Physics at the Massachusetts Institute of Technology, and received an M.A. and Ph.D. from Harvard in the History of Science and Learning with special concentration on Islamic science and philosophy. From 1958 he taught at Teheran University where he became Professor of the History of Science and Philosophy. During 1964–65 he was the first holder of the Chair of Islamic Studies at Beirut, and he has lectured widely throughout America, Europe, the Middle East, Pakistan, India, Japan, and Australia. He has now moved from the Chair of Islamic Studies at Temple University Philadelphia to the same Chair at George Washington University. His books in European languages include: *Three Muslim Sages, Ideals and Realities of Islam, An Introduction to Islamic Cosmological Doctrines, Science and Civilisation in Islam, Jalal al-Din Rumi Supreme Persian Poet and Sage, Sufi Essays, An Annotated Bibliography of Islamic Science, Man and Nature: The Spiritual Crisis of Modern Man, Islam and the Plight of Modern Man, Islamic Science: An Illustrated Study, Sacred Art in Persian Culture, Western Science and Asian Cultures, The Transcendent Theosophy of Sadr al-Din Shirazi, Islamic Life and Thought, Histoire de la Philosophie Islamique* (with H. Corbin), and *Knowledge and the Sacred.*

Raimundo Panikkar was born in Barcelona, Spain, in 1918 and is a citizen of India. Born in two major religious traditions, the Catholic-Christian and the Hindu, he has been striving since his early years towards the harmony of a pluralistic world. He studied Science at Bonn and Barcelona, eventually earning a Chemistry Doctorate at Madrid in 1958; his Doctorate in Philosophy from Madrid dates back to 1946; his Doctorate in Theology was conferred by Rome in 1961. He has lived half his life in Europe, a quarter in India and the last quarter in the United States, although he keeps in close contact with Europe and spends a few months every year in India. He is presently Professor of Religious Studies (Comparative Philosophy of Religion and History of Religions) at the University of California, Santa Barbara. He has published around three hundred articles on topics ranging from the Philosophy of Science to Metaphysics, and from Comparative Religion to Indology. His 28 books include: *The Unknown Christ of Hinduism, Worship and Secular Man, The Trinity and the Religious Experience of Man, The Vedic Experience: Mantramanjari: An Anthology of the Vedas for Modern Man, The*

Intrareligious Dialogue, Myth Faith and Hermeneutics, and *Blessed Simplicity: The Monk as Universal Archetype*. He has been Guest Lecturer in more than a hundred universities around the world, is a member of the Boards of several Journals and Associations, and has held special Appointments and Lectureships in places as far apart as Barcelona, Madrid, Buenos Aires, Cambridge, Harvard, McGill, Columbia, Pittsburg, Rome and Minnesota.

Geoffrey Parrinder was born in 1910, and holds the degrees of M.A., Ph.D., and D.D. from London University. He lived in West Africa from 1933 and pioneered the teaching of Religious Studies at the University College of Ibadan in Nigeria. He moved to London University in 1958 and eventually became Professor of the Comparative Study of Religions at London. Since 1977 he has been Professor Emeritus. His 31 books include: eleven books on African Religion, *Introduction to Asian Religions*, *Worship in the World's Religions*, *Comparative Religion*, *Upanishads*, *Gita and Bible*, *What World Religions Teach*, *The Christian Debate*, *The World's Living Religions*, *A Book of World Religions*, *Jesus in the Qur'an*, *Avatar and Incarnation*, *Dictionary of Non-Christian Religions*, *Man and His Gods*, *The Indestructable Soul*, *Themes for Living*, *The Bhagavad Gita: A Verse Translation*, *Something After Death?*, *The Wisdom of the Forest*, *Mysticism in the World's Religions*, *The Wisdom of the Early Buddhists*, *Sex in the World's Religions*. He is a member of the Boards of various Journals and Associations; has given special sets of lectures in Australia, Oxford, Delhi, Madras, Tokyo; has an Honorary Doctorate from Lancaster; and has contributed numerous articles to various Journals.

George Erik Rupp was born in 1943 and was educated during his youth at Springfield New Jersey. He read German and English Literature at Munich and Princeton where he received his B.A.; his B.D. was from Yale in 1967 and his Ph.D. from Harvard in 1971. He also received the Danforth, Dwight, Tew, Mersick, and Daggett Awards during his graduate studies. After being appointed Vice-Chancellor of Johnston College, Redlands, California, and Dean for Academic Affairs at the University of

Wisconsin Green Bay, he became John Lord O'Brian Professor of Divinity and Dean of Harvard Divinity School in 1979. He is the author of numerous articles in professional Journals, and has written three books: *Christologies and Cultures: Toward a Typology of Religious Worldviews*, *Culture-Protestantism: German Liberal Theology at the Turn of the Twentieth Century*, and *Beyond Existentialism and Zen: Religion in a Pluralistic World*.

Annemarie Schimmel was born in Germany in 1922. She gained a Doctorate in Islamic Studies from the University of Berlin in 1941, and a Doctorate in History of Religion from the University of Marburg in 1951. She taught at Marburg from 1946, became Professor of the History of Religions at Ankara in 1954, Professor of Islamics at Bonn in 1961, and Professor of Indo- Muslim Culture at Harvard in 1970. Her numerous Awards include the Friedrich-Rückert Medal for outstanding translations, the Golden Hammer-Purgstall Medal from Graz Austria, the Johann-Heinrich-Voss Prize for translation from the Deutsche Akademie für Sprache und Dichtung, the Sitara-i Quaid-i Azam and Hilal-i Imtiaz from Pakistan, and the Order of Merit First Class from Germany in 1981. She has Honorary Doctorates from Hyderabad, Islamabad and Peshawar, and she is the present President of the International Association for the History of Religions. Her publications are too numerous to summarise; they include works in Arabic, Turkish, German and English; prominent among them are translations into German from Arabic, Persian, Turkish, Urdu, and Sindhi (and English), especially from the works of Rūmī and Iqbāl. Among her books are: *Gabriel's Wing: A Study in the Religious Ideas of Sir Muhammad Iqbal*, *Islamic Calligraphy*, *Mystical Dimensions of Islam*, *Islam in Indo-Pakistan*, and *As Through a Veil: Mystical Poetry in Islam*.

Ninian Smart was born in 1927, and was educated at Glasgow Academy and Oxford University, where he read Classics, Philosophy and Ancient History and did his graduate work in the Philosophy of Religion. He has taught Philosophy, Theology and Religious Studies at various Universities: Wales 1952–55, London

1956–61, Birmingham 1961–67, Lancaster 1967 ff., and University of California Santa Barbara 1976 ff., where he has held a joint appointment with Lancaster. He founded Britain's first Department of Religious Studies at Lancaster; was Director of a Schools Council Project on Religious Education in Schools 1969–78; helped to plan and execute the BBC television series on World Religions *The Long Search*; and was Pro-Vice-Chancellor for a period at Lancaster University. His numerous books include: *Reasons and Faiths, The Religious Experience of Mankind, Doctrine and Argument in Indian Philosophy, The Science of Religion and the Sociology of Knowledge, Beyond Ideology, Worldviews*; and he has recently brought out *Sacred Texts of the World* with Richard Hecht, and *Religion and Nationalism in the Contemporary World* with Peter Merkl. He is a founder member of the Journal *Religion*, President of the British Association for the History of Religions, President and Founder of the SHAP Working Party, and was founder and President of the Institute of Religion and Theology of Great Britain and Ireland. He has been visiting Professor for a term or more at Banaras Hindu University, Wisconsin-Madison, Princeton, Otago, Queensland, Capetown, and Harvard.

Tu Wei-ming was born in Kunming, China, in 1940. He received a B.A. in Chinese Studies from Tunghai University Taiwan in 1961, an M.A. in East Asian Regional Studies from Harvard in 1963, and a Ph.D. in History and Far Eastern Languages from Harvard in 1968. He taught at Tunghai, Princeton, and Berkeley before taking up his present post as Professor of Chinese History and Philosophy at Harvard in 1981. His research areas are those of Confucian Thought, Chinese Intellectual History, and the Religious Philosophy of East Asia, and he has written widely on these topics. In addition to his work in Chinese, he has written in English: *Traditional China* (with J. T. C. Liu), *Neo-Confucian Thought in Action: Wang Yang-Ming's Youth, Centrality and Commonality: An Essay on Chung-Yung, Humanity and Self-Cultivation: Essays in Confucian Thought.*

Frank Whaling was born at Pontefract, Yorkshire, England in 1934. He was educated at Pontefract, Christ's College Cambridge where he read History, and Wesley House Cambridge where he read Theology. After living in India for four years he took his Doctorate in Comparative Religion at Harvard from 1969–73. He presently co-ordinates the Religious Studies courses, degrees, programmes, and unit at Edinburgh University. He is Chairman of the Scottish Working Party on Religions of the World in Education. In addition to directing the Edinburgh-Farmington and Edinburgh-Cook Projects in Religious Studies, he has received other research awards from Carnegie, Fulbright, the British Academy and the British Council, and prizes including the Peregrine Maitland Fellowship in Comparative Religion from Cambridge and the John E. Theyer Honor Award from Harvard. He was the British Academy Exchange Fellow at the Chinese Academy of Social Sciences in Beijing, and Visiting Professor at Dartmouth, Calcutta and Witwatersrand. He has written or edited: *An Approach to Dialogue: Hinduism and Christianity*, *The Rise of the Religious Significance of Rāma*, *John and Charles Wesley* in the *Classics of Western Spirituality*, *Religions of the World*, *Contemporary Approaches to the Study of Religion: The Humanities*, *Contemporary Approaches to the Study of Religion: The Social Sciences*.

George Huntston Williams was born in Ohio in 1914. He received a B.A. from St. Lawrence University in 1936, a B.D from Meadville Theological Seminary and the University of Chicago in 1939, and a Th.D. from Union Theological Seminary New York in 1946. He has Honorary Doctorates from St. Lawrence, Meadville/ Lombard, Loyola, King's College University and Dalhousie University. He taught at the Pacific School of Religion Berkeley from 1941–47 and thereafter at Harvard where he became the ninth Hollis Professor of Divinity until he became Emeritus in 1980. He is an officer or member of 23 societies; his Awards include Lilley, Fulbright, Gugenheim, and National Endowment for the Humanities Honours; he has been Visiting Professor or Honoured Guest at Strasburg, Jerusalem, Moscow, Leningrad, Jarvenpää (Finland), St. Louis, Union, Lublin, Cambridge, Budapest, and Warsaw, as well as an Observer at the Vatican II Council; he is on the editorial board of eight Journals; he has given named lectures or special papers at over fifty universities or congresses; and he has taken an active part in wider Massachusetts or national affairs. He has contributed to fifteen Festschriften; a Festschrift, *Continuity and Discontinuity in Church History*, was published in his honour in 1979; in 1982 the American Academy of Religion honoured him with a symposium on his writings 'An Historian for all Seasons'. His own writings include: *The Norman Anonymous of ca. 1100, Frederic Henry Hedge, Anabaptist and Spiritual Writers, Anselm and Atonement, Wilderness and Paradise in Christian Thought, The Radical Reformation, Georges Florovsky, American Universalism, The Writings of Thomas Hooker, The Polish Brethren 1601–1685, The Mind of John Paul II, Church State and Society in John Paul II, La Reforma Radical.*

INDEX